THE ANXIOUS SELF

THE ANXIOUS SELF
Diagnosis and Treatment of Fears and Phobias

Ronald A. Kleinknecht, Ph.D.

Western Washington University
Bellingham, Washington

 **HUMAN SCIENCES PRESS, INC.**
72 FIFTH AVENUE
NEW YORK, N.Y. 10011

Copyright © 1986 by Human Sciences Press, Inc.
72 Fifth Avenue, New York, New York 10011

All rights reserved. No part of this work may be reproduced or utilized
in any form or by any means, electronic or mechanical, including
photocopying, microfilm and recording, or by any information storage
and retrieval system without permission in writing from the publisher.

Printed in the United States of America
987654321

Library of Congress Cataloging-in-Publication Data

Kleinknecht, Ronald A.
  The anxious self.

  Includes index.
  1. Anxiety.   2. Fear.   3. Phobias.   I. Title.
RC531.K54   1986   616.85′223   85-14279
ISBN 0-89885-264-1
ISBN 0-89885-266-8 (pbk.)

To Sharon, Lisa, Hans, Erich, and Erica

CONTENTS

PREFACE

Anxiety, fears, and phobias are the most prevalent psychological disturbances in our society today. Greater than 10 percent of the U.S. adult population are so adversely affected by these emotions as to qualify for the psychiatric diagnoses of Anxiety Disorder (Robins, et al., 1984). Further, an additional 10 percent experience distressingly high levels of anxiety that interfere with their daily lives, although not severe enough to qualify for diagnosis (Uhlenhuth, et al., 1983). The vast majority of the remaining population, adult and child alike, frequently experience some form of fear or anxiety, if only on a milder or more transient basis. This topic clearly has personal meaning for all.

Although the conditions of anxiety and phobias have been observed and described for thousands of years, detailed analysis and scientific understanding of these conditions is of relatively recent origin. To a large extent, it was Sigmund Freud's writing and theorizing at the turn of the century that stimulated the current interest in the causes and treatment of anxiety. From these beginnings and particularly over the past 25 years, our understanding of fears, phobias, and anxiety has increased dramatically. Although we have made significant advances in under-

11

standing and treating these anxiety-related disorders, much remains to be learned.

It is the purpose of this book to provide an overview of this now vast area. My goal is to introduce the reader to the concepts, terminology, and current research findings associated with anxiety and phobias. With this introduction, the reader will be better able to understand the characteristics and nature of these distressing emotions. Also, with the background provided here, the reader will be prepared to comprehend the popular literature on this subject as well as the more technical accounts found in the professional and scientific journals.

The first chapter provides an overview of the concepts of anxiety, fear, and phobia and defines a number of terms used throughout the book. Also included is an outline of the elements of the research methods used to gather knowledge in this area.

Chapter 2 presents information concerning the prevalence of fears and phobia among the general population and how the prevalence varies across age and sex distributions. The second part of this chapter describes the various theories that attempt to account for the development of phobias and anxiety. These theories include biological factors, conditioning, cognitive processes, Freud's psychoanalytic position, and existential theories.

The topic of Chapter 3 is the assessment of fear and anxiety. The question addressed in this chapter is: How do psychologists identify and measure the presence of fears and anxiety? Characteristics of psychological measurement are described along with specific procedures used to quantify levels of anxiety. The methods described include the interview, self-report tests and questionnaires, psychophysiological measures and methods of behavioral observations.

Chapter 4 describes the anxiety disorders: those conditions that are of sufficient intensity and duration to disrupt one's daily life. Definitional criteria and case examples are provided to illustrate the range and diversity of these conditions. The specific disorders described include: the simple phobias, social phobia, agoraphobia, generalized anxiety disorder, panic disorder, obsessive-compulsive disorder, and childhood anxiety disorders.

The variety of psychological techniques found most effective in the treatment of anxiety disorders are described in Chapter 5. The first section describes the techniques themselves. Then, specific case examples are used to illustrate the application of these procedures to various anxiety and phobic disorders.

The final chapter addresses two basic areas in which psychological and biological factors interact. First is an overview of the various psychotropic drugs often used to treat anxiety disorders. Next is a summary of the relationship between anxiety and the perception and tolerance of pain and how anxiety treatment can also be used to reduce pain.

The final section of this chapter provides an overview of the area and identifies some areas in which more knowledge is needed and where current and future research is directed.

All names and other identifying information have been fictionalized throughout the text. Resemblance to any persons, living or dead, is not intended.

Chapter 1

INTRODUCTION

Imagine a person so overcome with fear and anxiety at the mere thought of venturing beyond his doorstep that he is virtually a prisoner in his own home. Fear and anxiety of such proportions is clearly one of the most restrictive and limiting human emotional experiences. Yet the capacity to experience this same emotion is present in virtually all of us. It can be useful and perhaps even essential to our survival. Indeed, the person incapable of experiencing anxiety is abnormal. Although the survival function of fear may be less necessary today than it was in our evolutionary past, it still serves to protect us from many dangers. It is not difficult to imagine what might happen to a young child incapable of experiencing fear.

This emotion, as we all know, is not limited to such extreme cases in either its restrictiveness or survival functions. Within its more normal ranges in everyday life, fear and anxiety can serve as important sources of motivation. For example, the student who fears getting a poor grade on an exam may, because of this fear, be motivated to study. Conversely, the athlete who is too calm and relaxed is unlikely to be sufficiently aroused to excel. In situations such as these, which are not directly involved in our physical survival, fear or anxiety can be useful, adaptive, and can facilitate achievement. On the other hand, if our fears are too strong they can interfere with our performance. Anxiety levels that are too high can interfere during an exam with our ability to recall material already learned or can make an athlete so jittery that he is unable to concentrate on the game.

It is obvious that for normal and effective functioning, some balance must be achieved. We must be able to move freely in our environment, function effectively, and enjoy the pleasures of life, while maintaining the capability to respond with fear to motivate us when our physical or psychological well being is threatened.

At the risk of stretching an analogy, one might compare the various effects of fear to those of radiation. While useful in the diagnosis and treatment of cancers, radiation also has the capability of causing illness and death. Fear and anxiety, like radiation, can serve or enslave us. The key to living with both is to achieve control over them and to limit their effects to the more positive while minimizing the negative. Such control can only come from a thorough understanding of the phenomena involved.

The purpose of this book in presenting an overview of what is known about fear and anxiety is to facilitate that understanding. I will discuss what fear and anxiety are and are not, where they come from, how they affect us, how they are expressed and measured, their normal and abnormal manifestations, and some methods by which many of their debilitating aspects can be reduced. Since there are virtually thousands of published research reports on this topic, the coverage will of necessity be selective. I will choose those studies that most clearly demonstrate major findings and concepts and focus on human behavior associated with fear and anxiety.

The purpose of this introductory chapter is to set the stage for the remaining chapters by defining and describing some of the basic terms and concepts used in reference to fear and anxiety. It begins with a discussion of some similarities and differences between the terms fear, anxiety, and phobia. Next, the three response components used to define these emotional states are described, and finally an overview of some of the research methods used to investigate them is presented.

Fear and Anxiety: The Same or Different?

Before delving into a discussion of what fear and anxiety are and what they are not, it is important to clarify the usage of these two terms to be sure we are speaking the same language. For many psychologists, students, and laypeople alike, these two terms are used synonymously. For others they denote somewhat different phenomena. However, most would agree that they refer to an unpleasant feeling state accompanied by various physiological changes in our bodies. Because some authors use these terms differently, a brief review of some of the points of similarity and difference is presented below and is outlined in Table 1.1. These points can be separated into two general categories: 1) *Stimulus properties* associated with the elicitation of the response, and 2) the *Response properties* themselves.

Stimulus Properties

Among those who choose to differentiate these two concepts in terms of stimulus properties, the most widely cited difference concerns the *identifiability* and the *specificity* of the source that triggers the emotional response. Focusing on these stimulus differences, fear is said to be a response to a clearly identifiable and circumscribed stimulus. On the other hand, anxiety is seen as a similar response but the stimulus to which the person is responding is unclear, ambiguous, and/or pervasive (Marks, 1969).

Following this line of differentiation, another characteristic often cited is that if a response is made to a stimulus that is a *realistic* threat and therefore is seen as rational and functional, it is said to be fear. If a response is made to a stimulus that is not seen as a realistic threat and therefore is irrational and dysfunctional, it is called anxiety.

Martin Seligman, a prominent researcher in this area, encompasses some of the above differences into the concept of *predictability*. He states (1975) that the central factor that differentiates fear from anxiety is the predictability of the source of threat to which one responds. That is, when an object or situation provides a clear signal of threat or danger and is therefore predictable, the acute emotional state experienced is called fear.

Table 1.1
Dimensions of Similarity and Difference
Between Fear and Anxiety

Dimension	*Fear*	*Anxiety*
Stimulus Properties		
Identifiability[1,3]	Clear	Unclear/Ambiguous
Specificity[2]	Discrete/Circumscribed	Pervasive
Predictability[2]	Predictable	Unpredictable
Rationality of Threat[3]	Rational	Irrational
Response Properties		
Response Components[1,3,5]	Cognitive, Physiological Behavioral	Cognitive Physiological Behavioral
Duration[1,2]	Acute/Stimulus bound	Chronic/Enduring
Intensity[4]	More intense	less intense

1. Marks, 1969
2. Seligman, 1975
3. Rachman, 1974/1978
4. Kleinknecht and Boucher, 1981
5. Levitt, 1980

However, anxiety is seen as ". . . the chronic fear that occurs when a threatening event is in the offing but is unpredictable" (Seligman, p. 112). This formulation then would seem to encompass the concepts of clarity, rationality, and specificity of the source. Without predictability or clarity of the stimulus a more chronic and pervasive state of anxiety would exist since the person would be unable to determine exactly what the threat was or when it might occur.

Given these differences in stimulus properties for differentiating fear from anxiety, a person in the middle of a violent thunderstorm who is concerned about being struck by a lightning bolt could be said to be fearful. The stimulus is clearly identifiable, predictable, and the threat realistic. However, a person concerned about being injured when and if the sky falls, might be considered anxious.

Response Properties

Most authors who choose *not* to differentiate between the terms fear and anxiety tend to focus on the response properties. They note that despite the possible stimulus differences presented in the previous section, the response or what the person experiences is essentially the same in both cases. A person experiencing fear or anxiety will typically respond with certain thoughts, physical changes, and behavioral responses, no matter what the characteristics of the source. Therefore they see no need to differentiate the terms (Rachman, 1978; Levitt, 1980).

However, there are some possible response differences as well. One such difference is that of *duration* of the response. As noted under stimulus properties, if a source of threat is not predictable and/or not clearly definable, the response might be of longer duration and more pervasive, keeping the person in a state of chronic arousal, apprehension, or anxiety. On the other side, fear was seen as a response to a more discrete, predictable source and would be of a more circumscribed and acute nature.

One final point which can be taken as a response difference between these two terms concerns the *intensity* of reaction. To investigate this possible difference we asked a group of 67 college students to indicate the intensity implied by each of these two terms by making a mark along a line 5 inches long, which they felt corresponded to the intensity of each word. The average length of the mark to indicate fear intensity was 3.30 inches. This was significantly greater than the length of 1.83 inches given to indicate the intensity of anxiety (Kleinknecht & Boucher, 1981). These differences imply, at least among these students, that the two terms connote different degrees of intensity of reaction, with fear being the more intense of the two.

Which to Use?

Although there appears to be some basis on which to justify differentiation of these terms, it is also evident that in many cases there is no clear line of demarcation between them. For example, when is a snake a realistic and predictable threat and therefore a fear stimulus and when is it unrealistic and unpredictable and therefore an anxiety stimulus? Is apprehension and trembling when going to the dentist a realistic or an unrealistic response? Is the outcome predictable or unpredictable? Certainly it can be either depending upon the condition of one's teeth, the particular dentist, the patient's past experiences with dentists and one's sensitivity to pain and discomfort. Ultimately, the term one chooses to use is largely a matter of personal or theoretical preference.

Recognizing the difficulties inherent in differentiating fear from anxiety as labels for similar emotional states, I shall use both terms throughout this book in the more or less conventional way. Fear will generally be used in reference to a response or pattern of responses resulting from an identifiable stimulus situation. I will attempt to make no judgment as to the rationality of the response made by the person. Anxiety will be used to indicate a response pattern when the stimulus is more ambiguous and where this response is more chronic and pervasive. Anxiety will also be used in describing certain concepts conventionally described in the literature as anxiety, such as state and trait anxiety, discussed in a later section. Several areas will be encountered in which these guidelines are of little help. In such cases I will follow the usage of the authors whose work I am describing; where this is not clear, I will use my own preference.

Phobia: A Related Concept

To complicate further this matter of terminology, another similar term needs mention here which will be the topic of some discussion in later chapters: *phobia*. In general, a phobia is typically defined as an exaggerated, irrational fear in response to a specific object or situation, which is out of proportion to the actual threat or danger. In defining this term, Marks (1969) notes that phobia is ". . . a special form of fear which 1) is out of proportion to demands of the situation, 2) cannot be explained or reasoned away, 3) is beyond voluntary control and 4) leads to the avoidance of the feared situation" (Marks, p. 3). These defining characteristics of phobia are generally consistent with the definition given by the American Psychiatric Association. However, they add the additional element that the individual recognizes the excessive or unreasonable proportions of the reaction (APA, 1980).

For the purposes of this book, the combined elements of Marks' and the APA's definition will be used when identifying a response as phobic. As with the terms fear and anxiety, there is no clear line of demarcation between fears and phobias, perhaps with the exception of extreme cases. The person who begins sweating and trembling at the sight of a caged rabbit may qualify for the label of phobia, given the above definition. However, a similar reaction to a loose tiger will obviously qualify as a realistic fear reaction. The cases between these extremes, however, may present some difficulty in defining what is and is not rational and what is and is not out of proportion to actual threat.

Freud's Conception of Anxiety

Before leaving this discussion of terminology, I will note some variations of these concepts proposed by Sigmund Freud. It was Freud who to a large extent made us aware of the powerful role of anxiety in affecting our daily lives. He popularized the very term, anxiety or *angst*, in the psychological and the popular literature (Bromberg, 1954; Jones, 1961). Anxiety played a central role in Freud's theory of personality in general and psychopathology in particular. He saw anxiety very much as it was described above, that is, as a "danger signal" alerting the ego of impending threat or harm. Depending upon the locus of the source of threat, he proposed three types of anxiety: reality anxiety, neurotic anxiety, and moral anxiety. Anxiety resulting from the perception of threat from the external environment was called *Reality Anxiety*, or fear as we have defined it. When the source of threat to the ego was internally generated from unconscious, id impulses (desires), it was termed *neurotic anxiety*. This corresponds to our general definition of anxiety in that no apparent or externally identifiable source is evident and is not tied to specific objects. Further, neurotic anxiety could take on different forms or intensities resulting in phobias, or panic reactions. Freud proposed yet a third type of anxiety which resulted from unconscious conflicts between the id impulses and the superego or the "moral" portion of one's personality. This type, referred to as *Moral Anxiety*, is generally interpreted as shame or guilt. (See Price, 1978, for a brief but clear discussion of Freud's concepts of anxiety.)

In this section I have reviewed several definitions and differentiations of the terms anxiety and fear. There are yet other usages and definitions, some of which will be introduced in Chapter 2 where origins of fears and anxiety are discussed. For our present purposes, fear will be used to indicate an unpleasant emotional reaction in response to an identifiable external stimulus or situation perceived as posing a threat. Anxiety is seen as a similar reaction, but with the source of threat not readily apparent. Although the choice of terms is largely an arbitrary preference, it is important to remember that the response, or what the individual experiences, is essentially the same. These responses will be discussed in greater detail shortly.

State and Trait Anxiety

Continuing the discussion of terminology and conceptions of anxiety and fear, let us look at another way of differentiating types of anxiety. The concepts of *State Anxiety* and *Trait Anxiety* were first explicated by Cattell and Schierer (1961) and subsequently extensively researched by Spielberger and his colleagues (1970). (The term anxiety is used here since that is how these concepts have been traditionally used.) *State Anxiety*, also called A-state, is conceptualized as a transitory or fluctuating emotional state involving feelings of tension and apprehension and heightened autonomic nervous system activity. It is a response to a specific situation that the person perceives as threatening, but changes as the situation changes. In this sense it is similar to what we earlier called fear. The unpleasant feelings we have all experienced in the face of some threat or potential threat, such as taking an exam or entering a new and strange situation, are examples of state anxiety. Once the situation is past or we have become accustomed to it, the anxiety is gone.

Trait Anxiety, on the other hand, is defined as a relatively stable personality characteristic of individuals. Persons high in A-trait are said to be generally anxiety prone. They have a tendency to respond to many situations with increases in A-state. That is, they tend to perceive more situations as threatening than a person who is low in A-trait, and therefore more frequently experience A-states.

Everyone at some time or another has been in situations which were perceived as threatening and have responded with state anxiety. However, the high A-trait person does so more frequently than the low A-trait person. To facilitate the differentiation of these two aspects of anxiety for research purposes, Spielberger and his colleagues have developed inventories to assess A-trait and A-state (Spielberger, Gorsuch, & Lushene, 1970). Use of these inventories called the State-Trait Anxiety Inventory (STAI) has led to significant advances in our understanding of anxiety and many of the studies to be described in this book have relied on them. To illustrate the utility and differences of these concepts, let's look at a study by Auerbach (1973) in which he investigated the effects of surgery-induced stress on measures of state and trait anxiety and the relationship of these anxiety measures to the patients' hospital adjustments. Fifty-six patients were administered the State and Trait anxiety scales 24 hours before they were scheduled to undergo major surgery. Two days following surgery they were again given the A-state measure. About 4 days later, they were again given both A-State and A-Trait Scales along with a measure of emotional adjustment to being hospitalized on which they could express their opinions and feelings about the hospital and indicate their present worries and concerns.

The results were consistent with the state-trait theoretical expectation in that A-trait scores did not change from pre- to postsurgery since they are seen as general, enduring characteristics of people. On the other hand, A-state scores were highest during presurgery, dropped somewhat 2 days after surgery, and were lowest at the final testing. The A-state scores reflected the patients' anxiety state, decreasing as the threat decreased.

Consistent with the characterization of high trait anxious persons as being more reactive to stresses than persons low in trait anxiety, was an additional finding. Patients high in A-trait also had higher preoperative A-state scores. Following surgery, the high and low A-trait patients decreased their A-state scores by approximately equal amounts. However, since high A-trait patients started higher, their final scores were still well above the low group. Finally, it was obseved that higher scores on both anxiety measures were associated with more worrying and more dissatisfaction with the total hospital experience.

Studies such as this make clear the importance of separating these two characterizations of anxiety. Had only a general trait anxiety measure been used, it would have appeared that these patients had little reactivity to the threat of surgery since before and after measures were essentially identical. The state anxiety measure, however, was able to identify the response to threat. These measures themselves will be described in somewhat more detail in Chapter 3 in discussing the various means by which anxiety and fear are measured.

RESPONSE COMPONENTS OF FEAR AND ANXIETY

Thus far the terms fear and anxiety have been used as though they were things or conditions that people possess to varying degrees. Sometimes they were seen as reactions to specific threat situations (fear or state anxiety) and at other times a person was unable to identify the source (anxiety). Although use of these terms as though they were things or entities serves to facilitate discussion, such usage is a gross oversimplification of very complex and not fully understood phenomena. Fear is *not* a thing or an entity. Or, as more colorfully stated by Rachman (1974), "Fear is not a lump" (p.15). Rather, it is viewed by those who study it as a convenient *construct* or concept, used to summarize a series of observations. We do not *directly* see anxiety or fear, nor can we touch it. We infer the presence of this emotional state when we observe certain events taking place, either within ourselves or in others. When we experience certain physical sensations, such as our heart racing, queasy feelings in our stomach, perspiration breaking out on our hands and face, muscular tension increasing, and the like, we then label these feelings anxiety or fear. Or when we see someone else behaving in certain ways, such as stammering when giving a speech, running from a mugger, or trembling at the sight of a tarantula, we infer from these observations that the person is experiencing fear. In each of these examples we have observed certain signs or responses that are typically seen together to make up the construct of anxiety or fear. No one of these elements themselves is fear. Rather it is the presence of the various elements, when brought together, that we label fear or anxiety.

The several sources of information on which we base our inference are often grouped into three categories: 1) the *cognitive experience* (what we think), 2) the *physiological responses* (activation of the autonomic nervous system), and 3) *overt* or *motoric behavior* (what we do). Each of these three response systems will be discussed separately. Then we will see how they go together.

The Cognitive Component

The cognitive component, also referred to as phenomenological or subjective, involves what we experience mentally, or our thoughts about what is happening to us or how we feel. Examples of the cognitive component of anxiety would include thoughts such as: "What was that noise?" "What is going to happen to me now?" "What if I mess up and make a fool of myself?" or "I hope I don't fall off the stage."

When one receives information that a potentially threatening event will or might occur, one of the first responses is that a *cognitive appraisal* process begins in which the person attempts to evaluate the potential consequences of the impending event (Lazarus, 1966). It is at this point often that initial or anticipatory components of anxiety or fear might begin. To the extent that the person is either unsure of the outcome or expects it to be aversive, the anxiety or fear process begins. Often this initial appraisal associated with anticipation of the event is referred to as *anticipatory anxiety*. For example, when a person makes a dental appointment, perhaps for the first time in several years, a common response is that thoughts occur concerning what might happen, such as: "Will I have cavities?" "Will the dentist want to fill them?" "Will it hurt?" or "Will the dentist give me a bad time for not brushing and flossing enough?" When thoughts such as these are experienced in anticipation of an event, we may begin labeling our emotional state at that time as anxious or fearful.

However, there is often more than just these cognitions to our overall response to the threatening event. We might also experience certain bodily changes.

The Physiological Component

Accompanying anticipatory thoughts about what might occur are physiological responses. These responses might include the increases in our heart rate, perspiration on our palms and face, muscle tensions, dry mouth, and queasy feelings in our stomachs that have been noted. These bodily changes result from activation of our *autonomic nervous system* (ANS). The ANS is that portion of the nervous system responsible for the essentially automatic regulation of our internal bodily functions. The ANS is divided into two components which for the most part act antagonistically to one another. That is, when one portion is active, the other is relatively quiescent. Overall, these two systems serve to maintain a balance among our internal physical systems; and among many other critical functions, the ANS is intimately involved in fear and anxiety responses.

The Sympathetic Branch.   The portion of the ANS most often involved in fear or anxiety is the Sympathetic branch, or the *Sympathetic Nervous System (SNS)*. A major function of the SNS is to prepare our bodies for meeting emergencies or physically to deal with threats to our well-being. This preparation helps us to cope with emergencies by mobilizing energy resources and is referred to as the *fight or flight* response (Cannon, 1929). When an event is judged (appraised) as threatening, neural impulses are sent to the adrenal gland (actually, the adrenal medulla), which in turn releases the hormones *epinephrine* (*adrenalin*) and *norepinephrine* (*noradrenaline*) into the bloodstream where they are circulated to various organ systems which they stimulate. The physical changes we perceive when anxious or frightened are partially a result of these hormones stimulating organs innervated by the SNS. As shown in Table 1.2, the result of the SNS stimulation typically involves an increase in heart rate, increasing blood circulation; the liver is stimulated to release glycogen as blood sugar to facilitate muscles; bronchioles in the lungs are dilated for more air; and increased sweating occurs which eliminates energy wastes and releases heat; along with many other effects which prepare us to deal physically with threats. These effects are broadly dispersed throughout the body, affecting many organ systems, and tend to persist for some time. You have most likely noticed when startled or frightened that your heart races and your body tenses, and that even after the danger is gone, these feelings persist for a while.

This sudden emergency rush of energy is thought to have been essential to survival of our evolutionary ancestors in preparing them to meet the many physical dangers that beset them. Today these functions can be extremely useful when we are confronted with a physical danger necessitating strength, endurance, or speed. However, such reactions are not always select-

Table 1.2
Autonomic Nervous System Effects on
Bodily Systems[1]

Organ System	Sympathetic Branch	Parasympathetic Branch
Eyes/pupils	Dilates	Constricts
Heart rate	Increases	Decreases
Bronchia/Lungs	Dilates	Constricts
Salivary glands	Reduces saliva (thick)	Increases saliva (watery)
Stomach	Inhibits function	Stimulates function
Adrenal Medulla	Secretes epinephrine and norepinephrine	No effect
Sweat glands (hands and feet)	Increases sweating	No effect
Blood flow	Increases to skeletal muscles	No effect

1. The patterns described here are general responses but there are many individual variations in response to stresses or threats.

ively adaptive. They can interfere with our functioning as well; particularly when we need to use our head rather than our feet.

The Parasympathetic Branch. The branch of the ANS which is seen as reciprocal or oppositional to the SNS is called the *Parasympathetic Nervous System* (PNS). Its function is largely the conservation of energy and it is most active when we are calm, quiet, and relaxed. For example, heart rate is slowed, blood pressure is reduced, and digestion is facilitated (see Table 1.2). You may have noted that at times when you feel upset or anxious, food tends to sit in your stomach undigested. This is because the SNS is most active, and the PNS is essentially shut down.

Although, for the most part, the PNS does not enter into fear responses, there is a notable exception. In occasional cases of extreme fright or shock and for some people fearful of blood, or injury, a strong PNS response is seen, resulting in lowered blood pressure and dizziness or fainting (Connally, Hallam, & Marx, 1976; Öst, Sterner, & Lindahl, 1984).

In our discussion of the components of fear and anxiety, one might get the impression that the cognitive and physiological components act independently. As we will see later, they do operate separately to some extent, but they also interact with one another as parts of a feedback loop. When we perceive some impending threat, we might initiate "anxious thoughts." These thoughts in turn, particularly if they persist, can stimulate activation of the ANS and lead to the physical responses just described. On the other hand, we might perceive our heart rate to increase, which in turn can lead to thoughts such as "I must be anxious," since in our past experience when anxious or fearful, this is what we felt happening. Thus we can monitor both or either our thoughts and physical state, which in turn can lead to labelling ourselves as anxious or fearful.

The Overt Behavioral Component

The third component that goes into defining anxiety or fear responses is more public. It involves observable behavior resulting from skeletal muscle responses. These responses include bodily movements such as physical attempts to avoid or escape from the threatening situation. Examples of overt *avoidance responses* might include the steps a person, fearful of snakes, would take to avoid natural habitats of snakes. For example, one might detour around grassy or weed patches in an open field. Or the person fearful of closed spaces might climb 20 flights of stairs to avoid entering an elevator.

In situations where avoidance is not possible, the fearful person might exhibit *escape behavior*, such as running, which will remove him rapidly from the threat. In each of these cases the escape or avoidance behaviors serve to reduce the person's felt anxiety.

We often find ourselves in threatening situations where for various reasons escape or avoidance responses are either impossible or impractical. In such situations, we might see other behavioral signs of anxiety or fear such as trembling hands, shaky or stammering speech, fidgeting and squirming, and a variety of such mannerisms. It must be emphasized here that even though all these outward signs which are often associated with anxiety are observed, we do not see anxiety. Rather, we see *behaviors*, and from their presence we infer that the person is experiencing a state of anxiety or fear.

Interaction of the Three Components

For many situations in which we are confronted with some form of threat, whether physical or social, we experience some portion of all three of the response components. When we suddenly come upon a precipitous cliff and look over, we may say to ourselves, "I hope I don't fall," feel our heart begin beating rapidly, and physically back away. In cases as this, there is little question about labeling the overall reaction as fear. However, such consistency among the components is not always evident. A variety of situational constraints can override expression of some of the components, leaving the label of fear in some question. For example, giving a speech in front of a class may result in anticipatory anxiety thoughts such as "I hope I don't mess up", "Will the class laugh at me?" or "I wish I could leave." These thoughts may be accompanied by physiological responses of increased heart rate, a dry mouth, and palmar sweating. However, since the speaker's grade is dependent upon giving the speech, and leaving would be a sure way to look foolish, the speaker might give the speech and present the appearance of being calm and controlled. To outside observers the speaker may appear calm since they cannot read his thoughts nor see his heart racing. Nonetheless, the person feels anxious, although privately so. The lack of complete correspondence among the three components is probably most evident for fear in the middle range of intensities where the person is able to exert some control over the responses. At more intense levels of threat, and/or for severely phobic individuals, we are likely to see greater consistency among the response systems. We will explore these consistencies and inconsistencies in greater detail when discussing the measurement of fear in Chapter 3, and will see that our construct of anxiety is not always as clear cut as we would like.

INVESTIGATION OF FEAR AND ANXIETY

At the beginning of this chapter it was noted that in order to achieve control over the debilitating effects of anxiety and fear we must come to understand the phenomena involved. In this section I will present an overview of some of the processes and research methods used to achieve this understanding. The methods presented here are neither unique to the study of fear and anxiety nor are they exhaustive of the many ways in which these phenomena can be studied. Rather, they are some methods used in most scientific investigation of human behavior. Before describing the various methods, let us first review several of the rules that guide systematic scientific inquiry in general and relate these to our study of anxiety and fear.

Guidelines for Investigation

In order for knowledge to accumulate and for the many investigators to be able to communicate their findings to others, a set of rules or guidelines, agreed upon by the investigators, is essential. Several of these guidelines for investigating natural phenomena are described in this section.

Definition of Concepts.   The initial step in any scientific investigation is for the researchers to define their terms and concepts precisely. Precise definitions serve to delineate clearly what is meant and what is not meant by the terms used in any investigation. Often these definitions are called *operational definitions* since the concepts are defined by the operations or procedures that the researcher uses to measure them. Since our subject of interest here was described as a construct, it is itself neither observable nor directly measurable. It must be defined then by tying the concept, anxiety, to some observable forms of measurement that are consistent with the concept. Operationally defining anxiety or fear is no simple task. We saw earlier that it includes three general classes of behavior, (cognitive, physiological, and overt behavior) each with several different manifestations. Shall we define anxiety as an increase in heart rate, as an avoidance response, or as a subjective thought? Ideally one should include measurements of all of these in a research investigation. But as we shall see, this is not always possible. Nonetheless, any component used in any particular study must be clearly defined so that it is consistent within the study itself and so that other investigators will know clearly how it was defined in order to compare it to their own research. For example, if the purpose of a particular investigation was to study trait anxiety and the investigators chose to define it as scores received on the *State-Trait Anxiety Inventory,* whether or not one agreed with that particular definition, it would be clear what was meant and how it was measured.

Objective Observation.   In order to acquire information concerning anxiety, we must take observations of the phenomena of interest. These observations, to be meaningful, consistent, and communicable, must be objectively obtained. By objective, we mean not only that which is being observed is well defined, but that if others were to make the same observation, they would record the same response. If the occurrence of an observation can be agreed upon by two or more independent observers, it can be said to be objective. For example, we could define the presence of anxiety by the number of "ahs" or "hums" while a subject was making a speech. If two independent observers in the audience substantially agreed on when an "ah" or a "hum" occurred and when it did not, the observations would be considered objective.

Measurement.   Closely tied to the requirements of operational definitions and objectivity of observations is that of measurement. Again, to promote consistency and communication, observations taken of the phenomena need to be quantified or assigned some numerical classification. If in the previous example, the observers of the speech were later asked how many "ahs" were observed and one replied "quite a few," while the other replied "a whole bunch," no one would be quite sure what really happened. Nor would they be able to make any objective comparison between this person's level of speech anxiety and that of another speaker. However, if they simply recorded the *number* of "ahs," they would have *a* quantitative measure for comparison.

Replication.   In order for results from any experiment to be accepted as accurately representing some phenomena, the results should be reproducible by other investigators. It is partly for this reason that we insist on using operational definitions of our concepts, together with objectivity, consistency, and quantification of the observations. If an investigator has abided by these guidelines in conducting and describing an experiment, another investigator should be able to reproduce the experiment and find the same result. To the extent that replication is possible, we will be able to accept the results as accurately representing or describing the phenomena. This, however, is not necessarily to say what the results mean or how they can be used. Interpreting the meaning of results, however objective the measurement might be, depends on a number of other issues such as the investigator's theoretical orientation, the relationship of obtained results to other results, and the investigative method used to acquire the information.

Investigative Methods

There are many methods for acquiring information about fear and anxiety, all of which can be considered scientific as long as they abide by the guidelines given in the previous section. The various methods differ in several important ways such as the breadth of their focus, the precision of measurement, and whether or not one can infer cause-effect relationships. Each has different purposes, advantages, and drawbacks. For our purposes they will be divided into *Descriptive* methods and *Experimental* methods.

Descriptive Methods. The several methods classified as descriptive have in common the general purpose of describing, in varying degrees of detail, the occurrence and characteristics of the phenomena of interest. They are typically rather broad in scope and are used as a first exploratory step toward understanding. One of the major uses of the descriptive method is to map out the territory, to get the lay of the land, or a broad, general overview of the phenomena. From the data acquired, hypotheses about relationships are generated that can then be followed up in more focused and precise investigations.

Survey techniques are used to obtain broad samples of descriptive information from large numbers of subjects. Typically, survey information is obtained through questionnaires which subjects complete themselves or they may be administered to the subjects by an interviewer. By the nature of this method, when used in fear or anxiety research, the investigator is limited to information from only the cognitive component.

One major use of surveys is to obtain estimates of the frequency of occurrence of particular phenomena in the general population. When used to obtain information concerning the *prevalence* (number of persons in the population who have a sign or symptom) or *incidence* (the number of new occurrences in a specified time period) of a phenomenon, this approach is referred to as *epidemiology*. Epidemiological investigations are important sources of information concerning the baseline of occurrence in the general population. This information is typically further subclassified to show how theses rates differ depending on persons' gender, age, geographical area, and socioeconomic status. Such baseline information is important to guide investigators concerning where to focus future research efforts, to evaluate possible changes over time and to provide estimates of relative risk of certain types of individuals having the symptoms or disorder under investigation.

An illustrative epidemiologic survey was conducted by Agras, Sylvester, and Oliveau (1969) in which they studied prevalence rates of common fears and phobias. They obtained a random sample of 325 residents from a medium-sized community. All respondents were interviewed individually, using a structured interview schedule with which they obtained information on the intensity and duration of 40 commonly feared situations. For those respondents who appeared phobic on the basis of the interviews, two psychiatrists independently evaluated their responses further. Persons were then diagnosed as phobic only if both psychiatrists agreed on the diagnosis using clearly defined criteria. Using this methodology, they determined that the prevalence rate of phobia was 76.9 per 1000 population. Although the detailed findings of this study will be presented in Chapter 2 when we discuss the prevalence of fears, two of the authors' conclusions are noteworthy here to illustrate the utility of the survey method. First, prior to this study, the only figures available on prevalence and distribution of phobias were based on the number of persons seeking professional treatment. Information based only on the total seeking treatment suggests that the prevalence is considerably lower than the population estimates given here. Secondly, the type of phobia most commonly seen in clinics (agoraphobia) comprises about 50 percent of phobic clinic patients, but accounted for only 8 percent of the phobias identified in the population survey. Clearly, factors other than overall prevalence of this phobia in the population must be investigated to explain why it alone accounts for half of those seen in clinics.

Surveys such as the one described can provide useful information on the rates of occurrence of fears in the general population and thus provide us with baseline information about the distribution of fears. However, such a survey offers nothing about how people become phobic, why they seek or do not seek treatment, nor how to treat phobias. Surveys are useful for general description but are limited in their ability to tell us more. However, they can provide one additional service: they generate hypotheses to be explored in more detail and with more refined methods of study.

Correlation techniques are probably the most frequent methods used in anxiety and fear research. In general, the correlational approach is used to determine relationships between or among variables or person characteristics. They are descriptive in that they are used to describe the extent to which various characteristics of persons tend to co-vary or occur together. Hypotheses suggested by survey research might be investigated in somewhat more detail using a correlational approach. For example, in the survey by Agras et al., previously described, it was found that two of the common fears most frequently observed were fear of dentists and fear of injury. To investigate further the nature of fears that people commonly feel, we might wonder if people who fear dentists also fear being injured. Through the correlational approach this question could be investigated by administering a questionnaire similar to the interview schedule used by Agras. Responses could be statistically analyzed by calculating a *correlation coefficient* which is a numerical index of the extent to which two variables occur together. In this example, we could compute a correlation coefficient between persons' responses to the question concerning fear of injury, and those same persons' responses to the question concerning fear of dentistry. This procedure could then tell us the extent to which the same people fear both situations. Although I have not seen this specific study done, it would seem reasonable to hypothesize that these two fears are related since there are other data available (also from surveys) showing that many persons who fear dentists report that they fear that the dentist will hurt them (Bernstein, Kleinknecht, & Alexander, 1979).

We could extend this idea somewhat to see if there were a larger group of specific fears that tend to cluster together in the same persons. Fear of flying, also having potential for injury, was found by Agras to have the same prevalence as fear of dentistry. Fear of flying could be submitted to correlational analysis along with fear of dentistry and of injury. We could add even more instances of specific fears that appear to be conceptually related to injury until we have a large number. When the number of variables being investigated becomes large, there are several more sophisticated statistical techniques based on correlation by which the interrelationship can be investigated.

Factor analysis and *cluster analysis* are two such statistical techniques by which we can tell how all these different fears relate to one another. Several such factor analytic studies of fears have been conducted that appear partially to substantiate our hypothesis of a general category of fear of injury and death (Rubin, Lawlis, Tasto, & Namenek, 1969; Bernstein & Allen, 1969; Braun & Reynolds, 1969).

Taking our correlational approach a step farther, results such as those just noted might suggest other possibilities to describe more fully persons who report these groups of fears. Our earlier discussion of conceptions of anxiety noted that state anxiety was defined as a person's reaction to specific situations and was thus like our definition of fear. Trait anxiety was defined as the tendency to respond with state anxiety to many specific situations. Therefore, it would seem reasonable to assume that persons reporting fear of all of these situations would also score highly on a questionnaire designed to measure trait anxiety. This hypothesis, of course, could be investigated by administering a scale such as the STAI, along with the questionnaires in which persons report their specific fears. As is so often the case with such research, each study provides some new information and raises new questions to be investigated. This is particularly true of the descriptive methods and, as noted earlier, one of their purposes is to generate new hypotheses.

Even though the correlational approach to studying fear and anxiety is able to provide us with a broad description of the phenomenon and can suggest new hypotheses to be explored, by its nature it is limited in what it can tell us about fears. Correlational data are mute on the issue of cause and effect, for example. We cannot tell which came first, the chicken or the egg. Given that our correlational analysis confirmed that fear of injury and fear of dentistry tend to occur together, we do not know if fear of injury causes fear of dentistry, or vice versa. Similarly, if we found that persons high in trait anxiety tended to receive lower grades in school, we would not know if it was the experience of receiving low grades that caused the anxiety or whether anxiety caused the poor school performance. We would only know that the two events tended to occur together. It is also possible that the two correlated events are not at all causally related. It might be yet some other factor that is responsible for the occurrence of both. An equally plausible hypothesis could be that the child was bullied at school when he was younger, making him anxious when around other people. It is possible that because he was bullied he avoided school and failed to acquire the necessary basic skills to do well later on. In this case, being bullied could be the cause of both his being generally (trait) anxious *and* receiving poor marks in school.

In order more adequately to investigate cause-effect relationships, we need to be able to control all such extraneous (unwanted) variables experimentally, and thereby rule out other explanations for our results.

Experimental Methods. The research methods described in the previous section were able to provide us with some important information concerning the distribution of fears in the population and the relationship among several specific fears. They also helped to generate further hypotheses to be explored. Although valuable, these studies were not experiments in the technical sense. They lacked the important element of *experimental control.* Consequently we could not evaluate cause-effect relationship among the variables since, as we saw, other factors over which we had no control could have been instrumental in causing or contributing to the observed relationships. Experimental methods do allow for such necessary control.

In its most basic form, the experimental method involves an experimenter arranging or presenting to a subject or group of subjects certain conditions or stimuli referred to as *independent variables,* while keeping constant all other factors that might contaminate the results. Under these controlled conditions, the experimenter observes and records (measures) the effects of these conditions on the subjects. The measures of effects are called *dependent variables* since their values are said to be dependent upon (caused by) the conditions created by the experimenter: that is, the independent variables.

There are several methods by which an experimenter can achieve the degree of control over unwanted influences to ensure that it is the independent variables that are responsible for the effects observed. Typically, a *control group* will be used for this purpose. This is a group of subjects like those who receive the experimental conditions and are exposed to all the procedures except those that the experimenter is investigating. This procedure ensures that the only difference between the two groups is their exposure to the independent variable. Thus it is the only factor that can explain differences in the reactions.

An Experimental Example.   To illustrate this experimental procedure, let us assume an experimenter is interested in studying the fear-producing effects of observing a hypodermic syringe used for giving injections. The experimenter would first acquire a group of subjects willing to participate in such an experiment. The next step would be to assign them to one of the two groups, half in the experimental group and half in the control group. The group assignment would be done *randomly* so that any given subject had an equal chance of being in either group. This random assignment ensures that prior characteristics of the subjects that might affect the responses to the syringe are evenly divided between the two groups, except for chance factors. For example, it might be that some of the subjects have a preexisting high level of trait anxiety that might make them highly responsive to any stimuli. If too many trait-anxious subjects were in one group and too few in the other, the results could be attributed to this additional or extraneous factor, rather than specifically to the hypodermic needle.

Once the groups are formed, the experimenter would bring them into the laboratory where the experimental group would be shown slides of hypodermic needles. The experimenter would need to take some measures of reactions to the slides. As noted earlier, fear or anxiety is often defined by the presence of cognitive, physiological, and behavioral reactions. For our present purposes let us assume the experimenter chose to measure the subjects' reported level of state anxiety (cognitive) and their heart rate change (physiological) from before the slides were presented to during the presentation. The control group would also be brought into the same laboratory where all conditions were identical to those for the experimental group except that the slides they were shown were pictures of neutral objects, perhaps work tools. Measurements of their reactions would be recorded as well.

If the state anxiety and heart rate change measures were greater for the experimental group than for the control group, the experimenter could state that slides of hypodermic needles caused more fear or anxiety (as defined here by cognitive and physiological reactions) than did the slides of tools.

To the extent that all other factors are controlled that might give rise to alternative explanations for the observed results, the experiment can be said to be *internally valid*. That is, if we can be assured that preexisting subject differences were equally distributed between the two groups and that both groups were treated identically except for the conditions in which the experimenter was interested, a cause-effect statement is possible.

An Experimental Analogue Using a Factorial Design. Although the preceding experiment may have been internally valid, thus making it possible to distinguish cause from effect, it was really quite simple in design and did not tell us too much about fear and anxiety.

If our ultimate goal in studying fear is to understand how various factors in the natural everyday environment affect us in these terms, the showing of slides in a laboratory seems quite far removed from our everyday experience. Yet studying fear reactions on the street or in a medical clinic does not allow for the kinds of experimental controls required and thus can be at best correlational in nature. One way to approach this problem is to arrange the experimental setting so that it more closely approximates a real-life experience. Experiments which attempt to parallel the real world as closely as possible, within the confines imposed by the need for experimental control, are called *experi-*

mental analogues. Analogue studies, to the extent that they are internally valid, allow us to move one step closer to understanding how people might react in a live setting.

I will briefly describe another version of our hypodermic needle experiment, within a more realistic analogue setting and expanding it into a *factorial design.* A factorial experiment is one in which more than one independent variable is used.

In the previous example we looked at how subjects in general reacted to the two types of stimuli without consideration of possible subject differences. In fact we attempted to distribute any possible subject differences equally between the two groups by our random assignment procedure. By doing so, however, we lost some potentially interesting information. We were unable to evaluate how people with different characteristics might react differentially to the two types of stimuli. For example, it might be of interest to see if persons who report being fearful of injury react differentially to the two sets of stimuli, compared with persons who report not being fearful of injury. We could systematically *select* two groups, one composed of those who report such fear and another which reports no such fear. Then half of the subjects from each of these two groups could be exposed to one of the independent variable conditions and the other half of each exposed to the other control condition. As with the previous example, heart rate and state anxiety would be monitored as measures of the subjects' fear reactions. A design such as this is referred to as a *2 × 2 factorial design,* since there are two levels of fear (high and low) and two levels of the stimulus condition (hypodermic needle shown and no hypodermic shown). This design is displayed schematically in Table 1.3. We have now taken into account possible preexisting characteristics of the subjects which might be expected to relate differentially to reactions to the stimulus conditions.

Earlier it was noted that the purpose of an analogue study was to parallel more closely real life situations. In our expanded example we could try to create an approximation to a common everyday situation where hypodermic needles are often encountered: a dental office. Rather than simply showing slides of the needle in an otherwise sterile lab we could equip the lab with elements of a dental office so the subjects get the feeling that it is

Table 1.3
Schematic Diagram of Investigation of
Response to Viewing Hypodermic Injection or X Rays in
Persons with High and Low Fear of Injury

	High Fear of Injury	Low Fear of Injury
Views Hypodermic Injection	Measures of Reaction: State Anxiety Heart Rate	State Anxiety Heart Rate
Views X-Rays Taken	State Anxiety Heart Rate	State Anxiety Heart Rate

closer to the real thing. We could include a dental chair, lights, instruments, and even the familiar smells common to all dental offices. Rather than show static slides, we could use a videotaped simulation of a dentist injecting a patient with anesthetic. In this setup the subject would see the dental surroundings while viewing at close hand not just a still slide of the needle, but one being injected into a mouth. The other condition might also include videotaped scenes from the same environment, but more neutral in character. For example, the same dentist could be shown (to keep that factor constant) taking X rays of teeth which would not be expected to produce as much threat. Both conditions would be identical except that one would show a hypodermic needle being injected while the other would show X rays being taken. Differences in the reactions of the subjects viewing these two conditions could then be attributed to the stimulus differences.

This factorial design allows the experimenter to observe several things simultaneously: 1) the effects of the hypodermic needle, 2) the effects of being fearful of injury or not, and 3) whether or not there is a differential effect depending on both the fear level *and* the stimulus condition. This latter effect, when two or more independent variables are present in the same study, is called an *interaction* effect and is frequently found in fear and anxiety research. This interaction effect can be more clearly seen in the hypothetical results of the heart rate measure

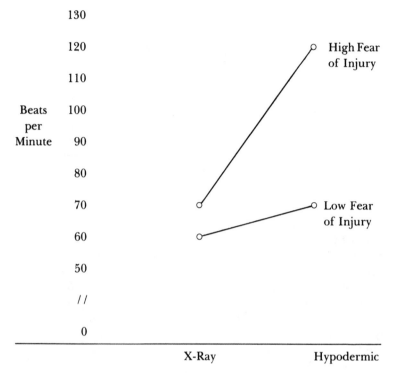

Figure 1. **Heart rate response of subjects with low and high fear of injury while viewing simulated dental stimuli.**

shown in Figure 1. Here we can see that both groups of subjects shown the injection responded with greater heart rate (beats per minute, BPM) than did those subjects shown the X rays. Also, we can see that those subjects reporting high fear of injury responded more to both stimulus conditions. Additionally, we can see that although both fear groups respond more to the injection, the high fear group responded considerably more than did the low fear group. Therefore, in interpreting these results we could say that one's fear reactions (heart rate) to a hypodermic needle is a result of both seeing the injection on videotape *and* the person's reported preexisting level of fear of injury in general. That is, fear of injury and the stimulus conditions interact with one another.

In further interpreting results such as these in terms of cause and effect there is a possible limitation even though we have been careful to control for other influences. Since the experimenter did not create the fear levels, as he did the different scenes, one cannot say in a strict experimental sense that fear of injury caused the reactions observed. However, we are on fairly safe ground in saying that heart rate reaction (as one measure of fear) is partially dependent upon preexisting levels of fear of injury. Although this may appear to be a rather fine distinction, recognizing such caution in interpretation is important in our experimental efforts to understand cause-effects relationships. Since we examined a preexisting feature of our subjects and related it to another variable, heart rate, it is more similar to what was described earlier as the correlational approach. In a strict sense, this example combined aspects of the correlational approach with an experimental approach. Such designs will be seen often in the descriptions of fear and anxiety research in the following chapters.

Field Research.   The preceding example was designed to illustrate how it is possible to obtain information on fear and anxiety in an experimental setting which attempted to parallel a real life situation. Even though our controls may have been sterling and our situation similar to a dental office, we cannot be sure that our subjects would have reacted exactly this way during a real dental experience.

We must yet ask the question: Can we generalize results found in our analogue setting to what occurs outside the laboratory? To the extent that we can demonstrate similar results in the real world, our results can be said to have *external validity*. To demonstrate the external validity of our findings we would have to replicate them in a real dental setting. In such experimental field research it is of course much more difficult to ensure that all subjects receive the same treatments or stimuli. Although such research is possible and some such studies will be described in the following chapters, it is quite costly in time expended and requires a great deal of planning and the close cooperation of subjects and experimenter. Because of these problems, the use of analogue studies is extremely valuable. They enable experimenters to identify potentially fruitful areas and to refine their procedures before exporting them to a dental office or any other interesting field setting.

In this section we have only briefly outlined a few of the research methods used to study fear and anxiety. Although many variations of these three basic methods will be encountered in later chapters, they all incorporate the basic elements described here.

SUMMARY

The emotional experience of fear and anxiety can at times be exceedingly restrictive and can impair or hinder performance. At other times it is of great value in avoiding harm and can serve as an important source of motivation. In order to limit its effects to the more positive, we need to understand its causes, its effects, and how to treat it.

Although it was noted that there was no universal agreement or differentiation between the terms fear and anxiety, I indicated that fear will be used to refer to a pattern of responses elicited by an identifiable and/or predictable source of threat. Anxiety will be used to designate a more chronic condition with similar responses but where the source of threat is unclear or unpredictable. Phobia was defined as an exaggerated, irrational form of fear.

Anxiety and fear are labels that we apply to others or to ourselves when one or more of their response components are observed. The three response components making up the construct include: thoughts (cognitive); activation of the ANS, particularly the sympathetic branch (physiological), and behavioral manifestations that serve to remove one from a threatening situation (overt behavior).

In order more fully to understand fear and anxiety, it was indicated that investigations need to abide by several guidelines including the use of operational definitions, objective observation, and measurement and that results of an investigation needed to be replicated by others. These guidelines are used in all investigative methods whether descriptive or experimental. Two descriptive methods outlined were 1) the survey techniques through which prevalence and incidence data are obtained from large samples of the population and 2) the correlational technique which is used to determine the extent to which two or more variables are related or tend to occur together. The descriptive methods provide general information about the phenomena of interest and are important sources of hypotheses which can be further investigated. Because the investigator can only describe what occurs with these methods and is not able to control the many stimuli that might be causing the observed relationships, cause-effect statements cannot be made.

The experimental methods, in which the investigator arranges and controls conditions presented to the subjects and measures the responses to these conditions, do permit cause-effect relationships to be studied. To the extent that extraneous conditions are controlled, an experiment is said to be internally valid. When an experimenter studies fear and anxiety under controlled laboratory conditions while attempting to approximate a real life setting, it is called an experimental analogue. In order for results obtained under controlled laboratory conditions to be held as representative of real life events, the effects need to be demonstrated in field studies under naturally occurring conditions. If results are replicated in field studies, they can be said to have external validity.

Chapter 2

PREVALENCE AND ORIGINS OF FEAR AND ANXIETY

Fear and anxiety are universal emotions experienced by virtually all humans and most lower animals as well. The native in the remote jungles of the Amazon who comes face to face with a leopard is as capable of experiencing this same emotion as is the modern urban dweller who is accosted by a mugger on a dark street. As such these emotional reactions are universal, natural, and can be adaptive should the victim need the increased energy mobilization to escape. The associated feelings elicited by these encounters typically diminish and disappear as the immediate threat of harm is reduced. For the most part, there is little enduring residual effect other than perhaps the exercise of greater caution when a similar situation is again encountered.

The focus of this chapter, however, is not on these everyday transient or reactive fears and anxieties. Rather, the topic is those fears and anxieties that are more persistent and go beyond the immediate threat to the extent that they present some level of problem for the individual. These problem-level fears can vary from the moderate apprehensions experienced by many people for instance at the thought of giving a speech before a group or of an impending dental appointment, to the more intense but relatively common fears in which a person takes active steps to avoid contact with the situation. At the upper extreme are the severe phobias and anxiety states that are immobilizing and severely restrict any semblance of normal functioning in everyday life. This chapter begins with an overview of the prevalence of these fear and anxiety problems as they occur in the general population and as they vary by age and sex groupings. Then the several theoretical positions that have been postulated to explain their origins will be described along with supporting data.

The information in this chapter consists of knowledge accumulated by psychologists over the past 60 to 70 years or more. Since it covers such a broad time span and varies widely in the methods used to obtain and to analyze it, the result is often less clarity than we might hope for.[1] Because of these limitations I will mainly present those studies whose methods and data appear most interpretable and that are most consistent with other information. With these limitations in mind, let us look at the overall prevalence of fear and anxiety problems in the general population.

PREVALENCE OF FEAR AND ANXIETY PROBLEMS

Throughout the life span few people are immune to developing some form of specific fear or anxiety problem. Fortunately, many of our fears diminish with age and maturity. Unfortunately, others do not just fade away. Yet new fears can develop at virtually any point in our lives. In one rather comprehensive study, Macfarlane, Allen, and Honzik (1954) found that of a group of children, studied over 12 years, 90 percent developed at least one specific fear during this period that was bothersome enough to be considered a problem.

Although a majority of these childhood fears diminish as the child grows older, many persist into adulthood. Jersild and Holmes (1935) found by interviewing a group of adults that 40 percent of the fears they had as children remained with them into their adult life. Similarly, Marks and Gelder (1966) found that among a group of adult patients seeking treatment for specific animal phobias that these fears had been with them for an average of 25.4 years, having begun at the average age of 4.4 years. Clearly, although many early fears come and go, others persist into adulthood and remain significant.

As might be expected, the prevalence of fears of phobic proportions is not as great as that of the more common fears which probably accounted for a majority of those in the studies cited above. In the epidemiological study noted in Chapter 1 by Agras et al. (1969) the prevalence of specific common fears was found to encompass greater than 40 percent of the population of this community. However, the percentage of persons in this study who were diagnosed as phobic was only 7.7 percent. Further, those whose phobias were judged to be severely disabling included only .22 percent of those surveyed. Although the less disabling specific fears appear to be quite prevalent, the severe fears are found with less frequency.

Two more recent national scale surveys found prevalence figures generally comparable to those of Agras. Uhlenhuth et al. (1983) found 5.5 percent of the adult population to qualify for the diagnosis of phobia. The second study reported phobia prevalence figures separately for each of three communities. These rates were 7.8, 9.4, and 23.3 percent (Robins et al., 1984). The first two rates are similar to previous estimates but the latter rate of 23.3 percent was unexpectedly large. Unfortunately, the more recent survey did not evaluate the prevalence of common fears as did the Agras study. Nonetheless, from these three epidemiological studies, it is clear that upwards of 7.7 percent of the US population suffer from a clinically diagnosable phobia.

Another anxiety-related problem of intensity equal to the severe phobias is that called *Anxiety State*[2] or *anxiety neurosis*. This condition is typically experienced as an intense and sudden attack of severe panicky feelings, rapid heartbeat, sweating, breathing difficulties, and fears of having a heart attack or dying. These attacks seemingly come out of nowhere. That is, they appear to have no obvious stimulus to which the person is reacting, as is the case with specific fears or phobias. Because of this lack of predictability in not being tied to an object, it conforms to our earlier description of anxiety. Various estimates of the prevalence of these anxiety disorders in the general population range from 2 percent to 4.7 percent (Marks & Lader, 1973; Robins et al., 1984). It has been further estimated that up to 14 percent of patients seen in cardiology practices are suffering such anxiety states.

The Uhlenhuth study noted above also included a category similar to anxiety states called Generalized Anxiety. They found 6.4 percent of their national sample to qualify for this diagnosis. Further, an additional 10 percent were identified as suffering from what they called High Psychic Distress. Those persons qualifying for this category largely showed anxiety symptoms but not severely enough to qualify for formal diagnoses.

When the prevalence of anxiety states is added to that of common fears and phobias, we see that a rather sizable proportion of the general population is directly affected by specific fear and anxiety problems. From the figures cited above it does not seem unreasonable to conclude that as much as 20 percent of the general population suffers from some form of significant fear or anxiety problem. And greater than 90 percent have at some point in their lives experienced at least one specific fear, but of lesser proportions.

The general prevalence rates just cited give us some indication of the breadth of anxiety and fear as problems. However, such general figures also obscure many variations that are important for a more thorough understanding of the distribution of these problems. Of particular importance is how the distributions of prevalence and incidence change with age and how they differ for males and females.

Age Distribution

One of the most salient characteristics of the distribution of specific fears is their changing nature with age and maturity. As early as the first three to four weeks of life, fear is recognizable in infants. Sudden, loud noises or loss of support typically result in behavioral manifestations of fear, such as crying, stiffening the body, and diffuse movements. Fear responses at this level are essentially innate reflexes and are probably best considered diffuse emotional reactions. From this rather rudimentary level of generalized fear, the number of stimuli to which a child responds with fear increases.

As the child becomes more aware of his or her environment and those in it, the objects and situations capable of eliciting fear change. For example, fear of strangers emerges during the second half of the first year and increases in frequency up to and through the second year (Scarr & Salapatek, 1970; Lewis & Brooks, 1974). However, it should be noted that these early fears are highly variable. They are not shown by all children and the specific response may be dependent upon whether or not a familiar person is present.

After the first two years and as children expand their horizons in terms of both physical and cognitive (intellectual) development, these initial fears of loss of support, noise, and strangers rather rapidly decline. However, other classes of stimuli begin to take on fear promoting qualities. Most notable is the highly consistent finding that fear of animals shows an increasing incidence from around three years of age, and by four or five comprises the largest category of children's fears (Angelino, 1965; Macfarlane et al. 1954; Jersild & Holmes, 1935; Maurer, 1965). Jones and Jones (1928) provided one of the most vivid demonstrations of the age-related nature of these specific animal fears. They placed children of various ages in an enclosure with a large harmless snake and observed their reactions. No fear was shown by children up to age two. But by ages three and four, caution and hesitation were evident. After age four, definite signs of fear were displayed. They noted that the signs of fear were even more pronounced in the adults than in the children. Holmes (1933) similarly found by observation that fear of snakes was shown more frequently by children between the ages of two and four than before or after that age.

As the child matures past the fourth and fifth years, there is often seen a slow decline in the number of specific animal fears which continues to decrease into the middle school years. However, new kinds of fears begin to emerge as children develop the capacity for active imaginations. These new fears involve more intangible or abstract objects or situations including fear of imaginary creatures, monsters, and the dark (Jersild & Holmes,

1953; Maurer, Agras, et al., 1969). For most, the fear of creatures declines rather steadily and becomes negligible after ten or eleven years for most children. Again, other types of fears and worries begin to enter the child's life that reflect his more immediate concerns. At this point, fears associated with school and social concerns become more prominent, such as fears of taking tests, and shyness and worries over social relations (Angilino, 1956; Marks & Gelder, 1975; Jersild, 1975; LaPouse & Monk, 1950; Macfarlane et al., 1954).

Although these data do show some rather consistent age-related patterns across the several studies, they must be considered only general trends since all children do not follow clear patterns of the waxing and waning of these specific fears. Many of these fears decline with increasing age, maturity, and, presumably, experience. However, these trends of decreasing prevalence in general obscure the fact that some also persist into adulthood.

Persistence of Fears.   As noted earlier in this chapter, as many as 40 percent of childhood fears persist into adulthood. Further demonstration of this persistence is illustrated in the previously mentioned epidemiological study by Agras et al. (1969). These investigators noted three different patterns of prevalence and incidence of specific fears over a broad age range. As in the other studies noted, they found the highest incidence of specific fears and phobias during childhood typically reaching their peaks before age ten. The prevalence rates, which reflect the accumulation over time, or persistence, showed three different patterns. One cluster of fears represented by fears of doctors, medical procedures (injections), darkness, and strangers, showed a peak incidence at about ten when the prevalence also peaked. From there a rapid decline in prevalence was seen during the adolescent and early adult years, becoming negligible by the sixth decade. A second pattern including fears of death, injury, illness, separation, and crowds showed a steady increase in prevalence up to age sixty, followed by a sharp decline. The third pattern involving fears of animals, snakes, heights, storms, enclosures and social situations, showed an increasing prevalence up to age twenty. From there it showed a more gradual decline over the next 50 years, suggesting that these fears tend to persist much longer than the others.

Another way of looking at age changes in fears comes by use of factor analysis. Through correlational statistical procedures, groups or factors of related fears are identified. In one such study involving children, Miller et al. (1972) found three distinct clusters of feared situations. The first factor or grouping was characterized by fears of physical injury, largely from man-made dangers such as being poisoned, dying, germs and illnesses, as well as of small animals such as snakes and spiders. The second factor was characterized by natural and supernatural dangers: dark, storms, strangers, and creatures. The third factor included more socially oriented fears such as being criticized, taking exams, going to school, and fears of doctors and dentists. The first and third of these factors are also typically found in factor analytic studies of adult fears (see Hersen, 1973). However, the portions of the second factor pertaining to supernatural events and dangers appear largely unique to children and suggest that for the most part they diminish with age. However, those fears involved in factors one and three begin in childhood and for many persist into adulthood. Many of the fears which persist (e.g., of injury, death, crowds, animals, heights) are those for which a number of people later seek treatment (Agras et al. 1969; Marks & Gelder, 1975).

The more severe fears, phobias, and anxiety states also show age-related patterns. Consistent with the previously presented data concerning the onset of animal fears between the fourth and fifth years, is the finding by Marks and Gelder (1975) that of a group of patients seeking treatment for fears of small animals, the average age of onset of the fear was 4.4 years. Further, among their admittedly small sample, they found none of the small-animal phobias to have begun in later life.

In this same study, other phobias were shown to have considerably later average onsets. For specific phobias involving heights and storms, the reported age of onset was 22.7 years but was found to be highly variable and could be most any age. Social phobias and extreme shyness had a mean onset of 18.9 years and for agoraphobia it was 23.9 years of age.

Sex Distribution

The population distribution of specific fears is frequently found to differ for males and females. In general, and particularly from adolescence on, females express a greater number and greater intensity of fears than do males.

The few studies that evaluated sex differences up to the early teens show relatively few differences between boys and girls in the number of specific fears (Maurer, 1965) and the percentage of each sex that express fears (Macfarlane et al., 1954). In this latter study, of those who had fears over a 12 year span, boys showed a slightly greater average percentage. However, at ages three and thirteen, a significantly greater percentage of females were found to have problem-level fears. In another study Lapouse and Monk (1959) interviewed a randomly selected sample of parents concerning their children's fears. The results showed that overall, girls were reported to have a greater number of fears than boys. In particular, girls had more fears of animals, bugs, strangers, and dirt.

This latter study by Lapouse and Monk also pointed out some important limitations of the use of surveys for identifying fears in young children. The data from these surveys are typically obtained from parents' reports of their children's fears. Consequently, one cannot be sure of the extent to which the mothers' biases and/or lack of knowledge of their childrens' fears distort the reports. To investigate this possible problem, Lapouse and Monk interviewed another sample of mothers and their children separately. It was found that mothers tended to report 41 percent *fewer* fears for their children than the children reported about themselves. This would suggest that the prevalence of children's fears is even greater than indicated by the previously mentioned studies in which parents were the sole informants.

As one moves beyond younger children, sex differences in fear expression become somewhat more clearcut. However, since the consistency of these differences varies according to how fear responses are assessed, they will be discussed separately for each of the three fear response components.

Self-Report. For most fears, particularly those involving small animals and medical/dental procedures, females consistently report a greater number and more intense fears than do males (Herson, 1973). For example, Kleinknecht and his colleagues in two separate surveys found females to report greater fear of dentistry at the junior high, high school, and college levels and in a sample of adult community residents (Kleinknecht et al., 1973; Kleinknecht & Bernstein, 1978).

Similar findings have also been reported for fear of snakes (Bernstein & Allen, 1969; Klorman et al., 1973), spiders (Katkin & Hoffman, 1976; Kleinknecht, 1982; Evans & Harmon, 1981; Bernstein & Allan, 1969) and for blood and mutilation (Klorman et al, 1973).

The above feared situations in which females report more fear than males all have the commonality that they portend possible physical harm. In contrast, reported fears associated with social situations show no differences between the sexes. In several studies, males and females reported similar degrees of fear and anxiety associated with speaking before a group (Bernstein & Allen, 1969; Klorman et al., 1973; Blom & Craighead, 1974). Similarly, Zimbardo (1978) reports that the prevalence of shyness, which is related to social fears and anxiety, does not differ greatly between the sexes, although a slightly higher prevalence of shyness has been found in males.

In general, while females report more fears than males, it is important to qualify this generalization by taking into account the type of situations that are feared.

Overt Behavior. Relative to the number of self-report studies investigating sex differences, those that involve observations of overt fear behavior are few. In those from which we can extract some meaningful conclusions, the results roughly parallel what was found for self-reports. Females have been found to be less willing than males to approach, touch, or pick up snakes and spiders (Geer, 1965; Speltz & Bernstein, 1976; Evans & Harmon, 1981). However, in a study observing overt signs of anxiety while giving a speech, no sex differences were found (Blom & Craighead, 1974).

In three studies that assessed fear of small animals, all noted

an interesting sex-related relationship in the degree of correspondence between the subjects' verbal reports of fear and their
avoidance behavior. It was found that females' reports of fear
were generally consistent with their demonstrated avoidance.
That is, if they reported being fearful, it was highly unlikely that
they would approach or pick up the animal involved. However,
the males' behavior was less predictable from their level of reported fear.

Physiological Responsiveness.   Although sex differences in
physiological responsiveness in the presence of feared situations
is somewhat consistent with results shown for the other response
components, the relationship is less clear. The several physiological measures are each highly complex and do not always yield
results that are clearly consistent even within a given subject.
Consequently, relatively few studies have investigated sex differences using this component of fear responsiveness. Nonetheless,
there is some indication that females exhibit greater palmar
sweating in dental settings (Brandon & Kleinknecht, 1982; Wei-
senberg, 1976). However, no differences have been found for
reactions to slides of spiders (Katkin & Hoffman, 1976) or while
giving a speech (Blom & Craighead, 1974).

Clinical Fears.   Since the data from the studies cited in this
section come largely from surveys and other experimental settings most of which relied on college students, the sex differences do not necessarily apply to persons with severe phobias
who actively seek treatment. Nonetheless, these studies which
report sex differences in patients seeking treatment are generally consistent with the research already cited. For example, in
one report of a series of phobic patients, Marks and Gelder
(1966) found females clearly to predominate for a variety of
phobias: Animal, 94 percent; Specific situations (storms &
heights), 75 percent; Agoraphobia, 87 percent; Social phobia
and shyness, 60 percent. These percentages are quite consistent
with other clinical reports of the sex distribution of phobic patients (see Marks, 1969). It is of interest to note that even with
these clinical phobias, that social anxiety and shyness showed the
least sex differential.

Sources of Sex Differences.   From the foregoing discussion
of sex differences it appears clear that for most fears, with the
exception of social ones, that females generally express more
fear than males. This is most consistent in the postadolescent
years. Although definitive explanations for these differences
have eluded researchers, two lines of theorizing have prevailed.
One line of explanation suggests that hormonal differences
might play a role in the differential responsiveness (Kopacz &
Smith, 1976). A second, and somewhat more prevalent line suggests that the observed differences are largely a function of sex
role expectations and training in which males have been expected to demonstrate masculine (fearless) behavior from early
on in their social development (Speltz & Bernstein, 1976). Marks
(1969) suggests that the observed differences may result from
some combination of physiological/hormonal differences and
social expectation factors.

ORIGINS OF FEAR AND ANXIETY

Fear and anxiety, like many other aspects of human behavior, can develop from several sources. These sources may act individually in some cases or they may act in combination to result
in a specific fear or anxiety state. This section will discuss the
various sources individually. Then a theoretical position will be
presented which attempts to integrate some of the sources.

The sources to be reviewed in this section include 1) biological influences, including both human and animal data, 2) environmental experiences such as learning, conditioning, and social
development, and 3) the theory of biological preparedness,
which proposes that we may have a biological predisposition to
develop certain fears which is activated by specific environmental exposures.

Biological Origins: Animal Data

The inclusion of data from studies of lower animals deviates
from our primary focus on human fears and anxieties. However, it is my belief that understanding animal behavior patterns

that appear similar to those seen in humans will help us to understand the basic behavioral processes. Fear and anxiety are good cases in point. We should be aware, however, of the fact that human behavior is considerably more complex, and may show only remote vestiges of some of the biologically related behavior patterns seen in lower animals.

Among many species of animals there appears to be an innate disposition to respond to certain stimuli or stimulus patterns with fear-like behaviors. It is as though there exists a "wired-in," automatic response that is activated when certain conditions or stimulus configurations are encountered. These fear response patterns typically involve some form of escape or avoidance response and appear to have clear adaptive or survival value for the animal. The animal that does not run or hide from its predators will not be around long and of course will not be able to reproduce its species.

One such purported phenomenon has been termed the "Hawk-Effect." Two prominent European ethologists, Tinbergen and Lorenz, investigated the observation that young ducks and geese responded with fear when they observed a hawklike image soaring overhead. The hawk of course would be a natural predator of small ducks and geese. They also observed that if the hawklike image were reversed so that its long tail portion became the leading image followed by the shorter end, the young birds did not react with fear. This reversed image was more like that of a goose flying which would not pose a predatory threat. These ethologists suggested that there is an innate fear mechanism in the brains of young birds that is activated when certain visual patterns are perceived that were associated with danger.

Further investigation of the hawk effect has qualified this conclusion. It has been determined that the fear response is probably not elicited by the hawk image per se. Rather, it appears to be the result of the pattern of rapid increase in visual stimulation which of course would be more likely to result from a hawklike image approaching with its short neck and wide wings followed by the narrow tail. The reverse image would show more gradual stimulation (see Schneirla, 1965). Other images swooped toward young chicks, which also result in rapid increase of visual stimuli, have been found to elicit the fear or escape responses as well.

Another stimulus which appears among some animals automatically to elicit fear-like behavior is a snake image. As was noted previously, fear of snakes is perhaps the most frequently observed specific fear in humans and was shown to be developmentally related, emerging around age four. Fear of snakes has also been widely observed in lower primates (e.g., various monkeys, chimpanzees, and orangutans). Among the various investigations and demonstrations, fear among primates has been seen in response to models of snakes, pictures of snakes on TV, and even large worms seen in the feces of cage mates. These fear responses are apparently as likely to occur in primates reared in captivity and presumably with no opportunity to learn that snakes are dangerous, as they are in animals born in the wild (Hebb, 1946). Although the specific characteristics of the snake or snakelike images that elicit these fear reactions has not been thoroughly investigated, it is likely, that as with the hawk-effect, it is not the snake per se which is feared. Most likely the more specific characteristics would include movement patterns, and other physical characteristics embodied in snakes.

A threatening face is yet another stimulus pattern shown to elicit fear and avoidance behaviors in young monkeys. In a now classic study, Gene Sackett (1966) investigated innate fear responses in young rhesus monkeys. These monkeys were reared in total social isolation from other monkeys or humans. By isolating them, Sackett was able to eliminate the possibility that they have an opportunity to learn to be fearful. Sackett's method involved projecting pictures into the monkeys' cages of a number of stimuli and observing their responses. The results indicated that the pictures showing another monkey presenting a threatening posture and facial expression produced significantly more disturbed, fearful, or withdrawn behavior in the subjects than other pictures showing infants playing, fearful monkeys, geometric patterns, or living rooms.

More importantly for demonstrating the innateness of the fear response to the threatening pictures, was the clear maturational or developmental effect. Up to age two months, the infant monkeys showed no fear or disturbance to the threatening pictures. In fact they appeared to enjoy the threatening pictures, and would press a lever in order to view them. However, by 2 to

2.5 months, the same threat pictures began to elicit fear and disturbed behavior. This fear behavior peaked at about three months and declined rapidly during the 4th month. During the 2.5 to 3 month period, they also drastically reduced their lever pressing to view these threat slides. But by four months of age, the lever pressing again increased.

These data rather strongly suggest that the pictures of other threatening monkeys "function as an 'innate releasing stimulus' for fear behavior" (Sackett, 1966, p. 1473) and that it is maturational in nature. This is similar to the suggestion noted earlier that snakes, or snakelike stimuli, might also function as an innate fear releasing stimulus.

The widely observed fear related phenomena called *tonic immobility* (TI) provides yet another way of looking at the biological basis of fear behavior in animals. Tonic immobility, also called *animal hypnosis* and "death feigning," results when an animal is physically restrained or held down. After about 15 seconds of initial struggle, the animal becomes motionless. When released, the animal will remain rigid except for muscle tremors in the legs and appears to be asleep or "hypnotized." Once TI is induced, it will last anywhere from several minutes to several hours. The duration of the response varies by species and can be manipulated by a number of experimental procedures.

This phenomenon has been implicated as a kind of fear response since many stimuli that produce fear also increase the duration of TI. For example, presenting electric shocks, loud noises, or injections of adrenalin all result in an increase in the length of time the animal remains immobile (see Gallup & Maser, 1977).

Being found in a large portion of the animal kingdom, from insects to reptiles, to primates, it has been suggested that TI has evolved as an innate defense against predators. Once captured by a predator, if the animal, after its initial struggle, becomes motionless, the predator often will lose interest and become distractible, allowing the prey to escape. Although it is a rather long inferential leap and there are no solid data to support the contention, some investigators have suggested that humans being "scared stiff" or paralyzed with fear is a human equivalent of TI seen in lower animals.

Genetic Transmission of Fear.   The previous section provided data suggesting that fear reactivity at least among lower animals may have a biologically adaptive function that serves to maintain the species. The various forms of fear response described were seen as generally characteristic of a given species, although similar responses such as TI are seen in a wide variety of species. It is also observed that there are within-species differences in fear reactivity. For example, some dogs appear shy and reactive whereas others appear quite fearless. To investigate these differences using a genetic approach, a number of researches have instituted *crossbreeding* in attempts to produce fear variations within a given species. The general procedure is first to identify several animals, some of which appear to be fearful and/or timid and others which appear fearless. That is, they identify animals that naturally possess the characteristics of interest. Some of the fear-related characteristics often sought are reactivity to new or novel environments, persons, or reactivity to noises, such as huddling, cringing, or the tendency to withdraw. Once the two types of animals are selected, they are bred with others who also have the same characteristics. If these fear characteristics are genetically transmitted, succeeding generations of fearful animals should become more similar to each other, and more divergent from their opposites, the fearless or nonreactives. In short, over successive generations, the two strains should become more and more dissimilar with respect to fear-like reactions.

A number of studies, using different species, have shown quite convincingly that through such selective breeding, fearful and fearless, (reactive and nonreactive) strains can be developed. Striking behavioral differences are evident within the first couple of generations.

One of the most elaborate and extensive selective breeding programs was carried out by Broadhurst (1960). Broadhurst initially selected two groups of rats that differed from each other in the number of feces pellets dropped when placed in a small open box. This box is called an open field test and has been used extensively to observe fear-like behavior in small animals. After breeding high feces droppers with low feces droppers, he then tested the two strains to determine whether they also differed in other signs of fear behavior.

Other fear measures found to correlate with high feces dropping were: less exploration or movement within the open-field box, faster escape from electric shock, and more reactivity to intense stimuli. All in all, it was shown that the emotionality being bred involved several aspects of fear behavior. That is, it was not a single behavior being developed (e.g., feces pellet dropping); what was genetically transmitted was a whole complex of fear reactivity.

Similar crossbreeding experiments have been conducted with other animals. For example, pointer dogs were bred to be highly responsive to loud noises and avoidance of men (Murphree et al., 1967). Chickens have been selectively bred for the duration that they stay in tonic immobility, suggesting that this fear-related response also has a genetic component (see Gallup & Masar, 1977).

With this brief review of some of the biological contributions to fear responsiveness, it is clear that among lower animals fear behavior has strong biological underpinnings. The reactiveness noted here may be seen as similar to trait anxiety seen in humans. Next we will look at the data available concerning the biological or genetic relationships of fear in human behavior.

Biological Origins: Human Data

As was shown with animals, humans also show wide variation in the propensity to exhibit specific fears and to react to situations with anxiety. In this section, data will be presented suggesting that at least some of this variation is a function of a person's biological or genetic makeup. That is, some people may be born with the predisposition to react to many situations with fear or anxiety.

However, it is considerably more difficult with humans to isolate experimentally the possible biological influences from those resulting from learning or environmental influences. Obviously we cannot rear humans in total isolation from others as Sackett did with his monkeys. Nor can we select persons with and without certain fear-related characteristics and crossbreed them to investigate the hereditary contribution of these response traits.

Consequently, we are limited in our study to investigating

humans as we find them, without experimentally controlling their backgrounds. Therefore, the data on biological influences on humans is largely correlational in nature and cause-effect conclusions must be taken as tenuous at best.

Further, since humans have few natural predators, we might not expect hereditary components to be as specific as they might be in lower animals. Rather, from an evolutionary point of view, we might expect to observe only remnants or vestiges of specific fears, such as fear of snakes. As we saw earlier, this fear is near-universal in nonhuman primates. And although it is perhaps the most prevalent of specific human fears, a majority (60 percent) do not express fear of snakes.

Rather than possessing a number of biologically determined specific fears, we see more of a general disposition to react to a variety of situations with fear or anxiety: something more akin to trait anxiety. Such general dispositions to respond with fear-like behavior or anxiety are identifiable in humans from very early ages. When referring to such dispostions with the implication that they are inborn personality patterns the term *temperament* is often used.

Parents, nurses, and pediatricians can all testify that children display distinctly different reaction patterns from the time of birth. To investigate these apparent temperament patterns, a group of researchers intensely studied 141 children over a number of years. Through periodic observation of the children and interviewing parents they were able to identify several distinct personality or temperament characteristics evident from the first two to three months of life. The patterns appeared to emerge independently of the parents' child-rearing practices and thus appeared to be inborn behavioral patterns (Thomas, Chess, & Birch, 1970).

Among the nine reaction patterns observed, one is particularly relevant to our study of fear and anxiety. This pattern involves the child's response to new objects or persons presented to them. Some children would respond to newness or change by withdrawing from it and displaying fear or worry-like behaviors. Others would show the opposite pattern of accepting changes and approaching new situations or objects.

Over the years these patterns remained relatively stable for many of the children. A child who, for example, at age six months, would react to a stranger's face with crying, was also likely to be shy and withdrawn at school several years later. These early identified reaction patterns tended to persist over the years, suggesting that these fear-like behavior patterns were inborn temperaments.

More recently, similar observations have been made that also suggest that extreme shyness may be inborn. Jerome Kagan (1984), a prominent child psychologist, also investigated a group of children over a period of years. He observed that children identified as shy and who tended to withdraw from unfamiliar events at twenty-one months of age also behaved this way in the ensuing years into adolescence and beyond. In his studies, Kagan found that many of these extremely timid children had high and stable heart rate responses when confronted with new situations. He further noted that approximately one-third of the children who were very shy as infants overcame their timidity with age. However, those who changed were not the ones who demonstrated the characteristic high heart rate in response to new situations.

These studies then suggest that there may be inborn patterns of general fearfulness of new or unfamiliar objects or situations tending to persist into later life. Further, it is of interest that this reactivity was expressed behaviorally by withdrawal and physiologically by the characteristic heart rate response that differentiated the timid children from the less inhibited.

Although these intensive, long-term studies of children seem to suggest that some people are born with a tendency to react to the world in fearful ways, it is not possible to identify the cause of these temperament patterns. We do not know if they are the result of particular genetic inheritances or from prenatal influences such as nutritional or hormonal variations. To look more precisely at possible causal factors we need to look at the results of twin studies.

Twin studies are particularly useful for exploring genetic-related behaviors. The typical behavioral genetic study procedure is to compare vis-a-vis some behavioral trait the similarities between identical or *monozygotic (MZ)* twins, who share the same genes. The degree of similarity is usually expressed as a correlation coefficient. This similarity between MZ twins is then compared with the correlation between sets of fraternal or *dizygotic* DZ twins who, although born at the same time, are genetically no more similar than regular siblings. If there is a high degree of similarity between the MZ twins, and much less similarity between DZ twins on the characteristic of interest, it is taken as evidence that the characteristic is at least partially a function of inheritance.

Lader and Wing (1966) used the twin study method to investigate the hereditary influence on patterns of autonomic nervous system reaction to certain stimuli. As we saw earlier, the ANS (particularly, the SNS) is the physiological response system most active during fear or anxiety. In this study the experimenters exposed two groups of twins (11 MZ, and 11 same-sex DZ pairs) to a series of tones and measured several kinds of ANS reactions to these tones. One measure was the degree to which the galvanic skin response (GSR, a measure of electrical changes in the skin) decreased or *habituated* over successive presentation of the tones. On this measure, they found that the correlation between the MZ twins was quite high (.75), while the correlation between DZ twins was considerably lower (.13). These results indicate that the ANS of MZ twin pairs tend to react quite similarly. For example, as one twin would decrease over time, there was also a tendency for the co-twin to show a similar decrease in GSR. In contrast, the similarity between the DZ twin pairs was substantially lower. One twin's response would not necessarily be related to how the other twin reacted.

A similar finding was reported for heart rate response. MZ twins again showed high similarity with a correlation of .78, while the DZ showed a dissimilar reaction. The correlation for the DZ was − .38. The negative sign here indicates that, to some degree, as one twin showed an increase in heart rate, the other might show a decrease.

Since there was the relatively high degree of similarity in physiological response between MZ co-twins who have essentially identical genetic makeup, and the considerably lesser degree of similarity between DZ twins, these results suggest that ANS reactivity is at least partially a function of genetic endowment.

Table 2.1
Correlations Between Twins on Social
Anxiety Proneness

	Gottesman, (1966) Social Introversion Personality Scale	Scarr (1965) Home Observation of Children's Shyness	Shields (1962) Introversion Inventory
MZ	.55	.88	.61[a]; .42[b]
DZ	.08	.28	−.17

[a]Twins raised separately.

[b]Twins raised together.

The degree of social introversion or shyness has also been shown in several similar twin studies to indicate a hereditary relationship. Table 2.1 shows the results of several studies of children, adolescents, and adults. The study by Shields (1962) is of particular interest since it controlled for the possibility that being reared together and therefore having similar learning experiences might confound the effects of similar heredities. In this study, Shields had two groups of MZ twins. In one group the twins were separated from each other at a very early age and reared in different homes. Similarities between these pairs would be less likely to be a function of common learning experiences, leaving mainly genetic influences to account for similarities. The correlation coefficient between their extroversion scores was .61. The MZ group that was raised together showed some, but less, similarity (.42). The DZ twins who were reared together had a low, negative correlation of −.17, indicating that to a small degree, they were actually dissimilar or opposite in social extroversion.

The twin studies just cited imply that some facets of anxiety, particularly those relative to social situations may have a genetic background. However, these studies did not necessarily relate to persons whose fears or anxieties were of sufficient intensities to pose significant problems. Other studies, however, have investigated the relationship of anxiety disorders between twins. In one study, Slater and Shields (1969) found that within a group of MZ twins, one of whom was diagnosed as suffering from anxiety neurosis or anxiety state, 41 percent of the co-twins also received that same diagnosis. Among the DZ twins, again when one was diagnosed as anxiety neurosis, only 4 percent of the co-twins received the diagnosis. When the authors broadened their diagnosis to include more general anxiety traits, which may not have been as severe as the anxiety neurosis, the percentages of similarity increased to 65 percent for the MZ group and to 13 percent for the DZ group.

In a recent family study of anxiety neurosis, similarly suggestive results were obtained (Crowe et al., 1980). In this study immediate family members of persons diagnosed as having anxiety neurosis were interviewed. Among 19 persons so diagnosed, 14 of them had at least one close relative who also received the diagnosis. In contrast, only 4 percent of the members of a comparable control group had close relatives who could be diagnosed as suffering from anxiety neurosis. These data suggest that although the relationship is far from perfect, there does appear to be some genetic contribution to anxiety reactivity and neurosis.

It is of interest that although the same phobias are often found among family members there are virtually no twin data suggesting a genetic relationship in specific fears or phobias. To the extent that genetics are related to the presence of fears and anxieties, the influence appears to be more of a propensity to be highly reactive to unfamiliar or stressful situations and/or to react with anxiety to a wide variety of situations rather than the inheritance of specific fears.

Even with the data suggestive of an inborn or hereditary component in fear or anxiety states, there are many cases where the relationship does not hold. And, as just noted, specific fears do not appear to be genetically caused in humans. To explain the development of specific fears and phobias we now turn to the contribution of our environmental learning experiences.

Learning and Environmental Origins

Although our biological makeup may well have an impact on the capacity to experience fear and anxiety, it is largely our environmental experiences that determine what we are fearful of and when our anxieties are manifest. In this section the processes and theoretical positions proposed to describe how these experiences lead to fearful or anxious behavior will be presented. These processes include classical conditioning, vicarious or indirect learning, and psychodynamic formulations.

Classical Conditioning.   The processes of classical conditioning have long been held one of the major methods by which anxieties, fears, and phobias are developed. The delineation of the conditioning procedures came from the pioneer experiments in which Pavlov conditioned dogs to salivate to the sound of a metronome or bell, among other stimuli. The basic processes involve simultaneously exposing the subject to two different stimuli. One of the stimuli must be of the nature that it automatically or reflexively elicits a specific response. This reflexive response is called the *unconditioned response*, or *UCR*. The stimulus that automatically elicits it is called the *unconditioned stimulus (UCS)*. The second stimulus is such that it initially has no effect on the response in question; that is, by itself it is neutral with respect to the response. It is called the *conditioned stimulus (CS)*. After several pairings of the CS with the UCS, the CS alone acquires the capability of eliciting the response previously caused by the UCS. When the response is elicited by the CS alone, it is called a *conditioned response (CR)*.

When applied to fear or emotional conditioning, the UCS is such as to cause an emotional reaction in the subject. In experiments, common UCSs include, for example, electric shock, or frighteningly loud noises. When these stimuli (UCSs) are paired with other, non-emotion arousing stimuli (CS), the CS alone can come to elicit an emotional, anxiety, or fear reaction in the subject.

One of the first and most influential proponents of the conditioning theory of fear and anxiety acquisition was John B. Watson, the founder of Behaviorism. Watson's impact on the conditioning view stemmed largely from an experiment in which he and Rosalie Raynor (1920) conditioned a young child to fear furry objects and animals. The subject of this experiment was an eleven-month-old child named Albert B., often referred to as Little Albert. At the time of the study, Albert lived in a foundling home where his mother worked.

As in any conditioning study, the first step was to demonstrate that the subject had no prior fear response to the objects to which he was to be conditioned. Consequently Watson presented Albert with a white rat, a rabbit, a dog, a monkey, masks, and a ball of white cotton. None of these caused any fear reaction in Albert and therefore were considered neutral stimuli with respect to fear.

The conditioning procedure that followed consisted of presenting Albert with a white rat which was to be the CS. As Albert reached for the rat, a steel bar was struck with a hammer just behind his head. This loud sound had previously been shown to cause Albert to cry with fear and therefore was the UCS which caused an emotional response. After six simultaneous presentations of the rat, (CS), with the gong, (UCS), the rat was presented alone as a test trial. At the sight of the rat, Albert began to cry and crawl away. Five days later, they again showed Albert the rat without the gong and again it elicited the crying and withdrawal. From this demonstration, Watson concluded that the rat had become a conditioned stimulus for the elicitation of fear in Albert.

They then went on to demonstrate *stimulus generalization*. Albert was shown a white rabbit, a dog, fur coat, cotton, and Santa Claus mask, none of which at this point had been paired with the US. Also to be recalled is that none of these stimuli had previously caused fear. Now, each of them, which were furry like the rat, elicited some fear in Albert. This demonstration of fear conditioning was taken by Watson and other psychologists as showing that fear and anxiety reactions were essentially directly acquired responses or were acquired by stimulus generalization.[3]

From this demonstration by Watson, coupled with Pavlov's experiments demonstrating the nature and extent of our capacity to acquire CRs to a wide variety of environmental stimuli, the conditioning theory of fear acquisition became established. These early studies were further bolstered by virtually thousands of subsequent fear conditioning studies that clearly showed that fear and anxiety reactions could be conditioned to previously neutral stimuli (see Prokasey, 1965; Kimble, 1961).

Despite the many laboratory experiments and demonstrations of classically conditioned fear responses, a number of problems have been identified that temper the earlier enthusiasm in applying this theory to the acquisition of human fears. Stanley Rachman, a prominent English psychologist, has outlined several arguments against the unqualified acceptance of conditioning as the only method of fear acquisition (1977). Rachman notes that there are numerous well documented cases in which one would expect fear conditioning to occur but in which it did not. For example, he cites evidence from the WWII bombings of London. Here the British were presented with numerous occasions of trauma and frightening experiences, yet very few developed fear reactions as would be expected from the conditioning theory.

Similarly, there are numerous instances in which people have received painful and fear-producing stimulation but fear is not conditioned to the perpetrator nor to other stimuli prominent in the situation. For example, many people have experienced trauma at the dentist or physician's office. Yet only a portion of them develop fear of these persons or situations (e.g., Bernstein & Kleinknecht, 1979).

A further problem with the unqualified acceptance of the conditioning theory is that attempts to replicate Watson's conditioning study of Little Albert have not been fully successful. Bregman (1935) was unable to condition fear in a group of young children to objects such as curtains or geometrically shaped blocks. Similarly, Valentine (1930, 1946) was unable to elicit conditioned responses to a pair of opera glasses. However, he did obtain signs of fear after pairing a loud whistle with a furry caterpillar. In yet another attempt, English (1929) was able to condition fear to a stuffed black cat, but not to a wooden duck. These demonstrations suggest that conditioned fear reactions, in children at least, can be obtained to some objects (e.g, furry creatures) but only with difficulty, if at all, to others.

A further point of evidence which serves to limit the general fear conditioning theory, is the observation that the distribution of fear in the population is far from what we might expect. For example, fear of snakes was shown to be the most prevalent of common fears. Yet very few people have been directly traumatized by them. On the other hand, fear of dentists is only half as prevalent as fear of snakes. Many people have received direct painful and noxious stimuli during dental treatment, but all do not develop conditioned fear reactions (Bernstein & Kleinknecht, 1979).

A final criticism of the general conditioning theory of fear acquisition comes from the reports of persons who experience fears and phobias. Table 2.2 displays the results of several studies that have investigated persons' reports of how they acquired their fears. Inspection of Table 2.2 shows that in some studies, fearful subjects recalled no conditioning experiences, while others, such as Wolpe (1981), found that 65 percent of his 40 patients seeking treatment for phobias reported a conditioning experience associated with the origin of this phobia. Öst (1981) found 57.5 percent to report such experiences. It is of interest to note here that those studies that investigated clinical-level phobias (that is, those for which patients were seeking treatment) showed a preponderance of their subjects to attribute their fears

Table 2.2
Reported Origins of Specific Fears

Author(s)	Sources of Subjects	Source			
		Direct	Vic.	Inform.	No Recall
Rimm et al. 1971[a]	45 students	35.6	6.7%	8.9%	28.9%
Murry, 1979	60 students (snake)	13%	—	majority	—
Öst & Hugdahl 1981	106 Clinic Patients	57.5%	17%	10.4	15.1
Wolpe 1982[b]	40	65%	—	40%	—
Kleinknecht	71 spider fearful	–0–	34%	61%	10%

[a] a "non-specific" undescribed category including the remaining 20%.

[b] percentages equal greater than 100%; since several subjects reported more than one source.

to conditioning. On the other hand, those studying persons with subclinical fears, typically college students who reported their fear on questionnaires, showed lesser percentages in this category. It has been suggested that the more severe phobic conditions may result from direct conditioning experiences, whereas the more common fears result from other means of information or communication, to which we will turn shortly.

The foregoing points of criticism do not disprove that conditioning may be one way in which fears and phobias are acquired. There are ample demonstrations, both clinical and experimental, that fear is conditionable. However, the numerous exceptions do limit the theory's generality. Consequently, one must look to other possible sources of fear development.

Vicarious Informational Sources.   Many people report fears of objects and situations that they have never personally encountered, nor been directly traumatized by. Consequently the conditioning theory of fear acquisition cannot account for the full range of fears.

A second process or series of processes by which fears and anxieties are acquired is more indirect than that of conditioning. Fears can be acquired by observational or vicarious means or they can be transmitted by direct instruction. That is, rather than experiencing a trauma or being frightened in the presence of a specific stimulus situation, a person can acquire specific fears by observing another person undergoing the trauma of being frightened. Just as children learn to imitate and take on the mannerisms or characteristics of their parents, they can also imitate emotional reactions seen in others.

There are several studies that show a significant correlation between parents' fears and children's fears. Since through twin studies it does not appear that specific fears are genetically transmitted, these parent-child similarities most likely result from the imitation process (e.g., Bandura & Menlove, 1968). In fact, this is what a number of fearful persons report. As shown in Table 2.2, vicarious factors are often reported as the source of fears. For example, one spider-fearful person in a study that I conducted reported:

> I was made to fear spiders when I was a child. My mother
> was afraid of them and passed it on—'There's a spider!' she
> would shout 'kill it.'

Similarly, many people, fearful of dentistry, have themselves
never been hurt by a dentist and many are fearful before they
ever experience dentistry firsthand. Another person I treated
for dental fear reported that her fear stemmed from her mother's emotional descriptions of the horrors of going to the dentist.
She reported that she vividly recalled her mother describing
how she became so frightened at the dentist that she fainted. After she fainted, the dentist filled her teeth while she was
unconscious.

Other sources of vicarious experiences include the mass media, such as movies and television. The passing of such horror
stories either in person or through the media, especially if described with emotion, is fertile ground for generating fear in
others.

Fear can also be established from direct instruction, much
of which includes large doses of misinformation. Direct instruction has long been one means of imparting information to children. Children are enjoined to stay out of the street, to avoid
strangers, not to play with matches. These of course are natural
hazards to children and they must learn at least respect for them
if not fear. However, the line between respect and excessive fear
is not always clear to children. Such well-intended instruction
can lead in many cases to misinformation that can result in unnecessary fear. Such a process was illustrated in the report of a
spider phobic's description of where his fear originated:

> I was given instruction by my mother as to the grave danger
> involved in the possibility of being bitten by some types of
> spider. In our yard she took all six children out and told us
> to stand back and beware. Then she looked in the ivy and
> carefully caught a black widow. She held it in a container
> telling how otherwise she would be bit and die . . . I saw my
> first tarantula at a zoo and was told it was capable of killing
> with one bite.

The transmission of fears through vicarious and informational sources appears to be one of the major means of fear acquisition. However, this theory too presents many of the same vulnerabilities noted with the direct conditioning theory. Many persons exposed to such information do not develop fears. Further, there has been very little laboratory-based experimental evidence demonstrating that significant fears or phobias can be acquired through these processes. However, there is ample evidence that fears can be eliminated by vicarious processes such as observing a fearless person exposed to the feared object or situation. This process of communicating to the observer that no danger is present appears to involve the same processes as fear development, only the information is reversed.

Taken together, the direct conditioning processes and indirect information or vicarious communication of fears appear to account for most of the cases of fears or phobias. However, there still remain some anomalies to be accounted for in these theories. Why, for example, were fears able to be conditioned to furry objects, but not to common blocks, geometric shapes, etc.? In an attempt to account for some of these questions a revision of the conditioning theory has been proposed.

Biology and Learning: Prepared Fears

In the previous sections it was noted that there may be a biological component that somehow predisposes persons to be fearful. It was also shown that some fears could be acquired by classical conditioning. However, neither of these positions by themselves adequately explained all of the observed data concerning the prevalence and characteristics of fears. Martin Seligman (1972) has attempted to integrate these two positions and thereby more fully account for the different prevalence of some fears. Seligman's proposal is that we may be biologically prepared to develop certain fears and less prepared to develop others. Seligman contends that certain kinds of stimuli that were particularly dangerous to pretechnological humans, through natural selection have become highly conditionable CSs. That is, we are biologically prepared readily to develop conditioned fear responses to stimuli that in our evolutionary past portended danger. Consequently, the ability readily to develop fear to these stimuli would help us avoid them and therefore survive. In particular, snakes and spiders have been suggested to be prepared fear stimuli (Seligman, 1972; Seligman & Hager, 1972).

This preparedness theory of fear or phobia acquisition has been used to explain the disproportionately high prevalence of certain fears, such as of snakes and small animals. On the other side we see relatively fewer specific fears of more posttechnical stimuli even though they are realistically a greater danger. For example, fear of hammers is rare. Yet, many persons have received severe or painful stimulation to their thumbs from hammers. Similarly, as previously noted, fear of dentistry is only half as prevalent as fear of snakes. Again, the likelihood of receiving painful stimulation from dentistry is considerably greater than being hurt by or even seeing a snake.

This preparedness theory of fears and phobias as proposed by Seligman further hypothesizes that 1) prepared fears are easily acquired with as little as a single conditioning trial, 2) once developed will be quite resistent to extinction, and 3) that the prepared conditioned fear will not be diminished by information (for example, that spiders are not very likely to harm one).

If these hypotheses were found to hold up on experimentation, it would provide an important element to our understanding of human fears. Several recent studies have investigated these hypotheses. Some portions of the theory have received support while others have been found lacking. The preponderance of the research investigating preparedness in human fear conditioning has been conducted in Sweden by a group of psychologists at the University of Uppsala. The investigators have employed the usual procedures for studying classical conditioning. A group of volunteers, taken one at a time, are presented with a series of color slides (CS). In their experiments they typically use slides of snakes and spiders. Immediately after the slide is withdrawn, the subject receives an electric shock to the forearm (UCS). All the while, the subject's skin conductance response is recorded as a physiological measure of fear or emotional response (initially, the UCR). After several pairings of the CS with the UCS, the slide is presented alone as a trial. It is then observed whether or not the subject shows a skin conductance response. If conditioning has occurred, observation of the slide itself will result in a response, (the CR). Extinction is then evaluated by observing how many presentations of the CS, without the UCS, are required before the subject ceases to respond to the CS.

Over a series of studies, Hugdahl and Ohman have shown that: 1) conditioned responses could be acquired to slides of snakes and spiders on a single pairing of shock; 2) that these CRs are more resistant to extinction than are CRs developed to more neutral CS such as flowers; and 3) telling the subject after conditioning that no shock will follow does not affect extinction (Hugdahl, 1978; Ohman et al., 1975; Hugdahl & Ohman, 1977). These results then are consistent with Seligman's hypotheses concerning spiders and snakes as being prepared fear stimuli.

In the studies cited above, the researchers compared the characteristics of CRs developed to snakes and spiders with those associated with stimuli that should have no biological significance for eliciting a fear reaction such as flowers, mushrooms, and geometric shapes. In a subsequent study they compared conditioning to snakes and spiders with that obtained using slides of electric plugs and wires. These latter stimuli would now be considered dangerous but we should not be biologically prepared to fear them. Differences in conditioning between these two potentially dangerous sets of stimuli, one a recent development, the other, from our pretechnical past, could be taken as evidence of biological preparedness. The results were only partially consistent with the prepared fear theory. The conditioned responses were as readily developed to slides of electric light plugs as to slides of snakes and spiders. However, they found that the CR to the snake and spider slides were considerably more resistant to extinction than were the CRs associated with plugs or with neutral geometric shapes (Hugdahl & Karker, 1981).

From the foregoing studies, the prepared fear theory has received some support. Conditioned fear responses to slides of snakes and spiders are found to be more persistent than CRs to slides depicting neutral or other dangerous situations. They do not extinguish with repeated presentations of the CS alone, and are not affected by telling the subject that no more shock will be given to them. The hypothesis that these assumedly prepared fear stimuli will be more readily conditionable, however, has not been supported.

Whether or not subsequent research will help to clarify the prepared fear theory or not remains to be seen. Also, it is unclear whether or not such laboratory analogues of human fear development can be used to explain fear development in the natural environment. Nonetheless, the idea is intriguing and continued research should help to increase our understanding of the nature of human fears.

Psychodynamic and Phenomenological Views

The final two views or theories concerning the development of human fears and anxiety depart rather radically from the biological, conditioning, and informational theories previously presented. These two approaches to viewing fear and anxiety development are also different from each other in many ways. However, they share the position that the locus of anxieties lies largely within the person rather than being developed primarily from inadvertent environmental exposures such as conditioning. The first of these positions to be described is the Freudian or psychoanalytic view.

Freudian View of Fear and Anxiety.   The psychoanalytic position concerning the origins and development of fear and anxiety was explicated by Sigmund Freud during the 1920s in a book entitled *The Problem of Anxiety*. Although Freud's theory has been revised and refocused by later analysts the theme presented here is basically Freud's.[4]

Freud saw anxiety as an innate, biologically based emotional state of displeasure. Anxiety itself was therefore a natural state. The experience of anxiety was seen as important in that it provided an occasion to learn how to deal with the vicissitudes of life. However, if the individual's early experiences were such that he or she did not learn to handle the inevitable anxiety appropriately the result was the problem of neurosis.

Anxiety, according to Freud, is experienced by infants, first at birth when they are rudely exposed to the intensity of stimulation associated with the birth process. Since the infant has not yet developed its personality, there is no means by which it can cope with the felt anxiety. That is the job of parents, to keep stimulation such as hunger within bounds. Another source of anxiety for the infant is that associated with the loss of its mother, who at that point is critical to the child's survival.

Toward the end of the first year the child begins to develop its ego. The ego's task is to mediate the biological urges and needs of the id, and the social or environmental demands of society, which at this point are represented by the parents. As the ego develops it also learns to recognize potential threats to the individual. The anticipation by the ego of threats or harm results in what is called *signal anxiety*. Early sources of this signal anxiety generated by the ego's perception of threat included situations such as loss of a loved object, and loss of an object's love (separation anxiety). In the next few years, as the child develops, other sources of threat result in anxiety including fear of injury to the genitals, which are a source of pleasure and comfort. This fear is later seen as castration anxiety. After the superego or moralistic portion of personality develops, the ego comes to fear punishment by the superego if it lets the id go too far in seeking gratification. These various sources of danger are perceived at an unconscious level of awareness.

Through these early experiences of anxiety associated with the exposure to the demands of society, and progression through the stages of psychosexual development, the ego and superego become more or less developed. In the relatively normal person, these structures are generally able to cope with the anxiety generated by perceived dangers or threats from the id. This is accomplished through the use of ego defense mechanisms. It is through these defense mechanisms that the ego defends itself against the anxiety associated with the id's incessant demands for immediate satisfaction of sexual and/or aggressive urges.

The ego defense mechanism most frequently used is *repression*. Repression works by keeping an idea or thought from becoming conscious so there is no felt anxiety. *Rationalization* is also used to keep the urges at an unconscious level. Here the thought or feeling is changed by constructing a plausible-seeming logic. The true thoughts remain in the unconscious and protect the person from consciously experiencing anxiety.

Projection is the process by which the ego consciously denies a problem or urge and attributes it to someone else. *Denial* is seen when a person will consciously ignore dangers, perhaps rationalizing that tragedies only happen to other people. Again the conscious experience of anxiety is avoided.

These and other defense mechanisms serve to handle the anxiety generated by id impulses in persons whose egos and superegos are reasonably well developed. However, if a person's early developmental experiences were such that he or she had all immediate needs taken care of, seldom experienced anxiety, and therefore never learned to deal with problems, a weak ego could result. Later on, if id impulses threaten them, such individuals are unable to keep the anxiety under control, or effectively repress it. They will then experience intense anxiety, that which was referred to in Chapter 1 as neurotic anxiety. Moral anxiety results from an overly strict superego. If the superego is constantly threatening the ego with punishment for even considering id impulses, moral anxiety is felt as shame or guilt.

Freud described three major forms in which neurotic anxiety could manifest itself. *Free-floating anxiety* is experienced as a chronic state of apprehension or anxiety where there is no specific external object or situation to which the person is responding. This would be like the high level trait anxious person who continuously feels anxious. The psychoanalytic interpretation of this is that the ego is in a constant state of fear of being overwhelmed by id impulses which may cause him or her to do something that would be unacceptable to the ego. The fear of the id is, of course, at an unconscious level. However, the resultant anxiety is felt consciously since the ego, being weak, is unable completely to defend against it.

Phobias are seen as due to similar processes as free-floating anxiety except that the anxiety response is more intense and focused on some object or situation. The phobic object does not represent a real external danger. The anxiety from the id impulse is controlled by detaching it from the real idea or situation that subconsciously generates the fear. It is then displaced to some other object or situation that is only symbolic of the real internal threat. Consciously, the real threat is then rendered less recognizable and the person can give a more or less plausible (rational) explanation of the fear. For example, a snake phobia might represent a fear of strong sexual impulses or fear of being castrated. The anxiety is displaced onto the snake which symbolically represents a penis; but such anxiety can then be rationalized since some snakes can be dangerous.

Panic attacks also result from strong, poorly controlled id impulses. The person experiencing an intense "rush" of anxiety which is not displaced or attached to other objects as in phobias. Rather it appears to come out of nowhere since the person is consciously unaware of the true source.

The foregoing summary of the Freudian position on the origins of fears and anxiety is rather oversimplified, a fuller analysis being beyond the scope of this chapter. However, in essence, fear and anxiety are seen as stemming from unconscious impulses from the id, demanding instant gratification of its desires. To the extent that the ego is unable to repress or satisfy these urges in socially acceptable ways, they are consciously felt as anxiety. In contrast to the learning views previously described, the origin of the anxiety or phobia is internal; that is, it comes from within the personality. The learning views, on the other hand, hold that fears and anxiety are acquired by external experiences such as conditioning, observing others undergo some trauma, or by simply acquiring information that certain situations are potentially harmful.

Phenomenological/Existential Views.   The existential view of the origins of fears and anxiety is the final position to be presented here. Although it is represented by many writers with differing views and theoretical outlines, I will note some of their common themes. In doing so, I will draw largely from Rollo May who is credited with being the American founder of existential therapy.

The existential analytic view is in many ways a fusion of the existential view of human life and of psychoanalysis, although it departs rather radically at certain points. The two views are similar in that both hold anxiety as the central concept in one's psychological being. However, they diverge on the issue of one's ability to control his or her destiny. The psychoanalytic position holds that the personality is formed or determined at an early age, whereas the existential position holds that one is free to make choices in the world and therefore is alone responsible for one's existence. Further, psychoanalysis sees the individual as being a formed personality. Existentialism sees the individual as a process of becoming, that is, of continually changing, growing, striving for meaning and values in life.

According to May (1978) and others, values and what they mean to an individual are the core of one's existence. When a value that one holds is threatened, the person experiences anxiety. Since all values are vulnerable to some threat, everyone will experience some normal anxiety. Further, this normal anxiety is seen as a prime motivator of change and personal growth. Anxiety can therefore be seen as constructive if it is confronted consciously, evaluated, and held open to change. This flexibility, openness for change or reformation of values is the essence of self-understanding and growth.

When these new challenges, signalled by anxiety, are not confronted, but avoided and blocked by repression and other intrapsychic processes keeping them from awareness, the result is neurotic anxiety. The person has narrowed his experiencing and has cut himself off from growth possibilities. Anxiety is seen, not as a sickness, but as a symptom of voided possibilities or opportunities for change and growth.

Another term often seen in the existential writings is *Existential Neurosis*. This term, popularized by Victor Frankl, is characterized by a lack of an inner sense of oneself and of meaning in life. From these voids come feelings of emptiness, worthlessness, and anxiety. Existential neurosis comes from a failure to experience life on one's own terms. Persons whose lives are directed solely toward satisfying society's demands or goals without creating their own personally chosen destinies are prey to existential neurosis.

This overview of the existentialist anxiety is a drastically simplified version of extensive philosophical writings. The emphasis, as we have noted, is on the processes of experiencing and evaluating one's own values and goals in life. To the extent that these processes are blocked or unused, the person experiences vague, ill-defined feelings of anxiety.

This position concerning the origins of anxiety is considerably less specific than the others presented in this chapter. This lack of definitive focus, however, derives from the tenet that each person has his or her own phenomenal world. In order to understand a given person's fears and anxieties, one must attempt to view the world as that person does. One's values and the meanings they hold for that individual are the units of analysis. Therefore it is considered impossible to target precise situations that will induce anxiety in all people.

SUMMARY

At the outset of this chapter it was noted that greater than 90 percent of children develop at least one specific fear during their formative years. While many childhood fears appear to wane as the child matures, others, particularly some fears of small animals, tend to persist. As the child grows older and develops other interests, the objects and situations that are feared change. As the child enters the school years, fears of imaginary creatures become more prominent. These too tend to give way during the middle school years to fear associated with school and social concerns.

During the preteen years, there are relatively few differences between the boys and girls in the number who express fears. However, from the teens on, females tend to express more fear than males. These sex differences are found in self-reports, behavioral indices, and in physiological reactivity. A notable exception to this trend is that no differences between the sexes has been found for fear associated with social situations.

A brief review of some of the data concerning the biological origins of fears among lower animals indicated that there may be an innate basis for fearing some objects or stimulus configurations that portend danger. These fear reactions were seen as adaptive for animals in that the associated behavioral patterns may help the animal avoid or escape from predators. It was also shown that animals could be selectively bred to express fear-like behavior patterns or to be nonreactive and fearless.

Although data concerning the biological basis of fears and anxiety in humans is less clearcut than with lower animals, there are some data that indicate fear-like behavior patterns, including shyness, may be inborn in some people. Twin studies of autonomic reactivity, anxiety proneness, and introversion suggest that MZ twins show considerably more similarity in these traits that do DZ twins. There is also some evidence that disorders such as anxiety neurosis may have some genetic basis. However, there are few data to suggest that specific fears or phobias have a genetic origin.

Classical conditioning was shown to be one way in which specific fears and phobias could be developed. However, it was also shown that this alone could not explain the occurrence of all fears. Many persons with specific fears are unable to recall any conditioning experience associated with the onset of their fears. There are many instances where one might expect fears to become conditioned but they do not. Other learning processes by which information is conveyed such as vicarious experiences and direct instruction were shown to be involved in the development of some fears.

The new theory was introduced which attempts to integrate the biological background with conditioning processes. The preparedness theory holds that we may be biologically prepared or predisposed to readily develop conditioned fear reactions to stimuli which had survival significance for us in our remote past. In particular, we may be predisposed to become conditioned to fear snakes and spiders and various furry creatures. Experimental data have given partial support to this theory.

Freud's theory centers largely on the presence of anxiety. According to Freud, neurotic anxiety is the result of the ego recognizing potential danger signals to itself. These dangers come from feelings emanating from id desires and urges which the ego must direct to socially acceptable channels of expression. If the ego is not strongly developed, and thus unable to defend adequately against these impulses, it can become overwhelmed with anxiety. This felt anxiety can take the form of free-floating anxiety, phobias, or panic attacks.

The phenomenological view of the origin of anxiety holds that excessive anxiety results from unmet or unaccepted challenges to one's values. If one does not consciously acknowledge anxiety and does not continue to grow, change, and develop as new opportunities arise, a chronic state of anxiety results. Stagnation, rigidity, and loss or lack of meaning in life may result in existential neurosis.

NOTES

1. For detailed critiques of this often discrepant literature, see Berecz, 1968, and Graziano, 1978.

2. Anxiety State as a diagnostic classification should not be confused with State Anxiety. The clinical descriptions will be discussed in greater detail in Chapter 4.

3. Watson was unable to conduct the second portion of this experiment in which he had planned to remove the conditioned fear response. Unfortunately, before the fear could be extinguished, Albert's mother took him away from the hospital where the study was being conducted.

4. The neo-Freudians, such as Fromm, Horney, and Sullivan, placed a greater emphasis on the cultural, social, and environmental determinants of anxiety than Freud, who stressed innate drives and urges.

Chapter 3

FEAR AND ANXIETY ASSESSMENT

In the same way that each of us experiences fear and anxiety, we are assessors of anxiety as well. When we experience the sensations associated with anxiety we do an informal survey of these sensations, noticing our heart rate increase, feeling tense, and saying to ourselves, "I am anxious;" or when we say that "Joan looked jittery before her big job interview" we are essentially assessing our own or others' states of anxiety or fear. The processes of psychological assessment of fear and anxiety are not really different, although of course the specific procedures used and the depth of involvement is typically greater.

In general, psychological assessment refers to the application of a set of procedures for describing, forming impressions, checking out hypotheses, and making decisions concerning a person or persons' pattern of psychological characteristics and emotional states (Sundberg, Taplin, & Tyler, 1983). This rather broad definition of psychological assessment can be readily adapted to the more specific concern here of fear or anxiety assessment. It essentially involves the systematic gathering of information concerning a person's actions and reactions which fall into the domain of fear and anxiety responses. This information may be used to form clinical impressions, to describe the person with respect to his or her anxiety state or trait, fears or phobias, to check out experimental hypotheses concerning the person and his or her reactions to environmental events. In a clinical setting this information may lead to decisions concerning appropriate diagnoses and treatment, if the anxiety or fear is of sufficient intensity or debilitating.

Whether one's purposes in conducting such assessments are to survey the prevalence of anxiety states, to test experimental hypotheses about the nature of fear, or to develop clinical impressions of a phobia, many of the same procedures would apply. In each of these situations, but particularly for research purposes, the assessor would be interested in measuring fear and anxiety responses and in determining those situations that elicit them.

It was stated in Chapter 1 that measurement and quantifications are requirements of the scientific method. In keeping with that tradition and its advantages, the purpose of this chapter will be to describe the various methods used to measure and quantify fear responses. Here the focus will be on measurement as it is typically done in research investigations. In the following chapter, the focus will be on the diagnosis and classification of clinical anxiety and phobic disorders.

RELIABILITY AND VALIDITY

Reliability

Before considering the specific methods used to assess anxiety and fear responses, we need to introduce two new concepts that are essential in evaluating the adequacy of measurement. The first concept is that of *reliability of measurement.* Reliability refers to the extent to which obtained information, whether it is one's verbal statement, a test score, or a physical response, is consistent, stable, or dependable. The basic question being asked is: "Can we accept a given score as representative of how this person typically responds?"

There are several types of reliability, each pertaining to different aspects of consistency. *Temporal Stability* refers to the extent to which a given measure or score obtained on one assessment occasion is likely to be reproduced under similar circumstances on a later occasion. The most common means of evaluating temporal stability is through the *Test-Retest* method. This involves, for example, administering a scale on one occasion and again under similar conditions at a later date. To the extent that the person's scores are similar or consistent on the two testings, assuming that nothing to change the scores has intervened, the test would be considered reliable or to have stability. If the two scores were significantly different, we would not know which one to believe, if either, and the measurement would be considered unreliable.

A second type of reliability focuses on the extent to which two or more persons agree on how to score or to classify an individual based on information each has received from the one being assessed. This type of reliability, called *Inter-rater* or *inter-judge* reliability, would pertain to situations in which two observers independently evaluated another and made judgments concerning the level of fear in that person. For example, two judges might observe others giving speeches and rate the degree of anxiety observed. The extent of agreement or disagreement over the amount of anxiety observed would be the degree of inter-rater reliability.

A third type of reliability, called *Internal Consistency*, pertains to the consistency of items within a given test or measurement scale. For example, if there were a scale composed of 30 items to measure fear associated with taking exams, we could relate responses of each item individually to scores on the rest of the scale to evaluate the relation of the items to the whole scale.

A related approach is to separate a single test into two parts. For example, we could split the test into two halves and evaluate if the responses or scores on the first half are similar to those on the second half. This would tell us if the scale were relatively homogeneous in content or is it stable in the sense of hanging together. This form is called *Split-Half* reliability.

To determine the extent of reliability, the most common numerical notation is the *correlation coefficient* referred to in Chapter 1 and is represented by the symbol, r. It will be recalled that the correlation coefficient is a numerical term that indicates the extent to which two observations or measurements go together or co-vary. When we use the correlation coefficient as a means of expressing reliability, it is called a *reliability coefficient*. Here, rather than indicating the extent to which variable X goes with variable Y, (i.e., r_{xy}), we use the notation r_{xx} to indicate the extent to which the score x correlates with itself or scores on one testing go with scores on a second testing.

Numerically, correlation or reliability coefficients range from -1.0 to $+1.0$. A reliability coefficient of $+1.0$ would tell us that the scores on test occasion 1 were identical with those on test 2, or indicate perfect reliability, whereas $r_{xx} = 0.0$ would indicate that there is no relation between scores on tests 1 and 2. An r between 0.0 and 1.0 indicates varying degrees of consistency between the two measures being compared. Reliability coefficients are rarely of the magnitude of 1.0, due to a variety of sources of error that can affect scores at any particular time. Typically acceptable levels of reliability are above .70. In evaluating the various measures of fear and anxiety to be presented in this chapter, we will consider their levels of reliability.

Validity

Validity of measurement addresses the issue of the extent to which the measures are in fact measuring what we intend them to measure, that is, fear and anxiety. Even though a test or a physical measurement may be highly reliable, with nearly identical scores obtained on each occasion, if they do not relate to what we mean by fear or anxiety, then they are not valid measures of these states. As with reliability, there are several types of validity measures. Essentially, validity of a measure is the extent to which proposed measures of anxiety relate to some aspect or criterion relevant to anxiety.

One way of describing the validity of measurement is in terms of a given measure's ability to predict other behaviors or scores. *Predictive validity* refers to the extent to which knowledge of one measure of anxiety or fear can predict how an individual or group would behave or respond at some point in the future. For example, if a person who scores high on a scale designed to measure fear of heights was found later to be unable to climb a fire escape, whereas another person who scores low could climb it, the scale would be considered to have predictive validity.

A similar form of validity, called *Concurrent validity* concerns the relationship between two independent measures taken at the same time. For example, if a test were given with the intent of diagnosing a phobic state and a person was independently diagnosed as phobic by a clinician, the test would be said to have concurrent validity. The major difference between predictive and concurrent validity is the time element, with predictive relating one measure to a future one, and concurrent relating two measures taken at the same time.

As with reliability, validity can be expressed with a correlation coefficient called *Validity coefficients*. A validity coefficient of + 1.0 would indicate, in the case of predictive validity, that the first measure would allow perfect prediction of what people would do on a later measure. A validity coefficient of 0.50 would indicate a relationship between the two measures, but less than perfect.

Construct validity has a special reference to anxiety or fear. As was noted earlier, it is not a concrete thing but rather a concept that we have constructed to explain a set of related observations. To demonstrate construct validity of anxiety, we need to show that a number of phenomena that theoretically relate to our conception of anxiety actually do go together or correlate with one another. For example, we would need to show that persons who score high on an anxiety test also show signs of anxiety such as physiological responses and perhaps avoidance behavior if a specific object or situation were involved. Further, we could also hypothesize that high anxiety decreases one's ability to concentrate on rigorous intellectual tasks. Therefore, persons who show high levels of anxiety should also perform more poorly than low scorers on difficult examinations.

To validate a construct such as anxiety, we need to demonstrate that all of the hypothesized features and effects of anxiety in fact tend to occur together. To do so requires a great number of studies, rather than a single one, as might be the case with predictive or concurrent validity. Many sources of converging evidence would be required to validate the construct of anxiety.

The remaining pages of this chapter, describing the several means by which anxiety can be measured and the relationships between the various measures themselves, can be taken as evidence with which to evaluate the construct validity of anxiety or fear. Measures from each of the three anxiety response components will be presented in turn.

FEAR AND ANXIETY MEASURES

The Cognitive/Subjective Component

It has often been said that the quickest way to obtain information about how people feel or think is to ask them. This is the basis of the self-report mode of assessment. In a clinical assessment situation this may take several forms: the interview and various paper and pencil scales or tests to assess a person's anxiety level.

Interview. Although the clinical interview is one of the most basic information-gathering procedures, it is not typically seen as a method of measurement per se. However, it does provide an opportunity for the person interested in fear or anxiety to acquire a broad spectrum of information concerning the fear directly from the individual that may not be attainable by other methods. Among the types of information that can be obtained in the interview are: descriptions of the situations under which the fear originated; specific circumstances under which the response occurs and does not occur; how the person responds when fearful, as in thoughts, actions, and feelings; and the effects of the fear or anxiety on the person's daily life. Since it is impractical to follow the person around for days at a time and it is impossible to see what goes on in their heads our only entry into this private domain is through direct questioning.

In the context of assessing fear and anxiety, the interview then provides the assessor the opportunity to enter into the more private and subjective experiences associated with fear. It enables him or her to delve into details in exploring the individual's conceptions of the history and origins, circumstances and effects of the fear. The interviewer obtains information to begin developing impressions of the individuals relative to their fears and anxiety, and this is a good starting point to begin to understand the nature of fear. This opportunity to develop a contextual picture of an individual's fear is particularly important in the clinical diagnostic process and will be discussed more fully in the following chapter on diagnosis of anxiety disorders.

Although not a measurement device itself, the interview can provide detailed information of use in assessment. To obtain this a researcher typically follows a structured interview which focus on specific questions of interest. This detailed probing for precise information is the primary means to obtain cognitive data on fear.

An example of the use of a structured interview for these purposes comes from a recent study by one of my students and myself (Richardson & Kleinknecht, 1984). We were interested in the possible differences in thoughts or self-statements that ran through the minds of fearful compared with nonfearful subjects while viewing a stressful film. We initially selected two groups of subjects, one of which reported earlier that they were terrified of going to the dentist, and the other which disclaimed such fear. Both groups were shown a videotaped portrayal of a dental operation in which the patient had a tooth filled, along with all of the attendant procedures such as receiving an injection of local anesthetic and drilling of the tooth. Immediately following the film, each subject was administered a short structured interview containing questions such as "What specific bodily sensations did you experience when you saw the hypodermic needle being injected?" "What thoughts went through your mind when the dentist began and continued the drilling on the tooth?" Based on the responses to these questions, each subject was classified into one of three categories: *copers*, those who said to themselves such things as "just relax, this will all be over in a minute;" *catastrophizers*, who focused primarily on the negative possibilities: "This really is awful; what if he hits a nerve?" and a group of *non-strategy users*, who reported no particular cognitive activity. As might be expected, those classified as "catastrophizers" were mostly from the group which had initially characterized themselves as terrified of dentistry, while most of the "copers" and non-strategy users were from the nonfearful group.

With all the advantages of the interview as a means of acquiring a broad range of information, and in some cases, as just noted, the only way, the interview also has several disadvantages limiting its utility, particularly as a research or measuring instrument. Among its limitations as a specific information gathering and measuring procedure is its relative lack of *Standardization.* Standardization refers to the factor that each time information is obtained, it is done in precisely the same manner. That is, if a question is worded a certain way on one occasion, it must be worded similarly on subsequent occasions if the procedure is to be standard. To the extent that an interviewer or different interviewers ask questions differently, this variation could well affect the responses which are the source of data. Small changes in the tone of voice, length of question, and the like have been shown to affect the type of responses obtained (Matarazzo & Wiens, 1972), which in turn would affect the reliability of the information.

However, it is also found that as an interview format is more structured and detailed, (i.e. more standardized) it becomes increasingly more reliable (Di Nardo, O'Brien, Barlow, Waddell, & Blanchard, 1983). As the interview becomes more structured, soliciting concrete responses to definitive questions, it becomes more similar to another form of self-report assessment, designed specifically to capitalize on the advantages of standardization. This is the paper and pencil questionnaire or scale which subjects can complete themselves.

Paper and Pencil Scales. The second means by which the cognitive component of fear and anxiety can be assessed and the one used most frequently for research purposes (Herson, 1973) is the questionnaire, test, or inventory. Generally, these scales take the form of a series of statements or questions asking how the individual feels, what sensations are experienced, and what objects or situations are feared or avoided. Such scales have several advantages over the interview for fear assessment. As noted, they are well structured and standardized, which enhances their reliability. Further, they allow for the derivation of a numerical score to indicate more precisely the level of fear or anxiety. This score then provides a quantitative measure for ready comparison to other scores or to the same individual's at a different time.

The increased standardization and metric endows the assessment with more objectivity than is possible through the less structured interview.

There are many ways of viewing and categorizing fear and anxiety, as noted in Chapter 1: there is state and trait anxiety and a number of types of specific fears and phobias. For purposes of illustration, I will first describe a sampling of those scales most often used to assess or measure trait anxiety. Then several state anxiety and specific fear inventories will be presented.

Trait anxiety was defined as a general persistent pattern of responding with anxiety to a wide variety of situations. It was seen as an enduring characteristic of the person—a personality trait. Consequently, the questions or statements that make up these scales are framed in general response disposition terms. Three such scales commonly used to assess trait anxiety and that illustrate the different formats in which questions are set will be described: the Taylor Manifest Anxiety Scale, (TMAS, Taylor, 1953), the Eysenck Personality Inventory (EPI, Eysenck & Eysenck, 1963) and the State-trait Anxiety Inventory, (STAI, Speilberger et al., 1970) introduced in Chapter 1.

The TMAS was one of the first paper and pencil scales designed specifically to measure anxiety. This scale was originally derived from items taken from the Minnesota Multiphasic Personality Inventory, a multifactorial personality scale. Taylor was looking for a reliable, valid, and economical means to select subjects having high and low levels of anxiety to test hypotheses about the effects of anxiety on learning and conditioning. The theory from which she was working postulated that anxiety was a drive or motivating force and that persons with high drive (i.e., anxiety) would develop conditioned responses more rapidly than low anxiety or low drive subjects. This prediction was in fact borne out in numerous experiments (e.g., Taylor, 1951).

The TMAS has since been used in hundreds of clinical and experimental investigations of anxiety and has been found to have good levels of reliability. For example, in her initial studies Taylor found test-retest correlation coefficients of 0.89 and .88 over retest intervals of 3 and 4 weeks respectively and .81 at intervals as long as 17 months (1953). These coefficients suggest

Table 3.1
Sample Items from the Taylor Manifest
Anxiety Scale

I sweat even on cool days (true)
I am often sick to my stomach (true)
I have very few fears compared to my friends (false)
I am very confident in myself (false)

Source: Taylor, J. A. (1953). Reproduced with permission of the author. Copyright © 1953, American Psychological Association.

that the same individuals respond quite similarly over extended periods of time and hence the scale is quite stable or reliable. Sample items from the TMAS are shown in Table 3.1.

Following the development and the recognition of the apparent usefulness of the TMAS, a children's version was developed by Castaneda, McCandless, and Palermo (1956).

A second measure of trait anxiety is the Eysenck Personality Inventory (Eysenck & Eysenck, 1963, EPI). The EPI comprises two scales to measure different aspects of personality; an extraversion scale that will not concern us here and the Neuroticism scale (N). The N scale was designed to measure the dimension of stability/instability, or neurotism. These two terms are generally equivalent to trait anxiety.

This inventory contains 48 items, 24 of which compose the N scale. The respondent answers "yes" or "no," depending on whether or not that question represents the way he or she typically feels or behaves. Four sample questions from this scale are shown in Table 3.2.

The EPI has been shown to have good reliability as measured by the split half technique, in which responses to the first 12 items are correlated with the responses to the last 12. Reliability coefficients of .88 have been reported (Eysenck & Eysenck, 1969) and test-retest coefficients of .82. This scale has been translated into several languages and also has a version designed for children as young as seven years: the "Junior EPI" (S.B.G.Eysenck, 1964).

The final measure of trait anxiety to be described here is the *State-Trait Anxiety Inventory* described in Chapter 1 to illustrate

Table 3.2
Sample Items from the Eysenck Personality
Inventory, Neuroticism Scale

	Yes	*No*
Have you lost sleep over your worries?	____	____
Do you suffer from "nerves?"	____	____
Do you worry about awful things that might happen?	____	____
Do you get palpitations or thumping in your heart?	____	____

Source: Eysenck & Eysenck (1963). Reproduced with permission of the publisher. Copyright © 1963, Educational and Industrial Testing Services.

the concepts of state and trait anxiety. The STAI, A-Trait portion includes 20 statements relating to tension, anxiety, and upset, or the polar opposites. As shown in Table 3.3, respondents indicate on a scale ranging from 1 to 4 how often each statement pertains to them *in general*. You will note that some of the items are reversed for scoring, such as "I feel secure" being scored in the direction of anxiety would be "almost never."

The STAI, A-trait has been shown to have good temporal stability. For example, test-retest reliability coefficients are essentially identical whether repeated at 1-hour intervals ($r = .76$

Table 3.3
Sample Items from the STAI-Trait Scale

	Almost Never	*Sometimes*	*Often*	*Almost Always*
I wish I could be as happy as others	1	2	3	4
I feel secure	1	2	3	4
I am a steady person	1	2	3	4
I feel like crying	1	2	3	4

Source: Spielberger et al. (1970). Reproduced with permission of the publisher. Copyright © 1970, Consulting Psychologists Press, Inc.

for males and .84 for females) or at 20-day intervals (r = .76). This indicates that individuals taking the scale at various time intervals tend to score quite similarly each time they take it. Of course, this is what would be expected if it were measuring an enduring personality characteristic.

Concurrent validity is shown by validity coefficients of .80 between A-trait and the TMAS mentioned previously. The degree of relationship between these two scales indicates that a person scoring high on one would be expected to score high on the other. In other words, the two scales appear to be measuring the same thing—assumedly, trait anxiety.

As with the EPI and TMAS, there is a children's version of the STAI (STAIC). This version is called the "How-I-Feel Questionnaire" (Spielberger, Edwards, Montuori & Luschene, 1973). There are a number of other scales that also measure trait anxiety. However, they are essentially similar to the three presented here and all tend to correlate with one another quite closely.

Understanding the level of trait anxiety gives us some indication of a person's anxiety across situations and over time. However, it does not tell us how the person would respond in specific circumstances, nor necessarily reflect state anxiety. To get to this more specific level we need to focus on specific stimuli or specific situations. There are several *state anxiety* and *specific fear scales* available to solicit such information.

One of the earliest such scales was developed by Walk (1956) to evaluate the amount of fear experienced by paratrooper trainees when taking their first practice jumps. To obtain the trainees' cognitively felt fear (state anxiety), Walk devised a numerical scale ranging from 1 to 10 arranged vertically on a sheet of paper and in the form of a thermometer, hence the name, *Fear Thermometer* (FT). Immediately prior to each jump from the training tower, Walk had each trainee make a mark on the FT to indicate how much fear was experienced.

This relatively simple fear assessment technique appeared to be a valid means of obtaining one's fear level. Walk found, as should be predicted, that the greatest level of fear was reported on the first jump, with subsequent jumps being rated correspondingly less fear-provoking. Further, it was found that as the number of jumps progressed, there was a clear relationship between fear level and the number of errors made by the trainees. Those who continued to report high fear made the greater number of errors in their jumps and vice versa. And those who failed to pass the airborne training program showed more fear throughout the training program.

This fear thermometer technique was a simple means of obtaining a measure of the cognitive aspect of one's fear and was also adaptable to a wide variety of different fear-provoking situations. For measures of state anxiety, reliability, particularly of the test-retest type, would not be a relevant consideration since the purpose is only to see how the person feels at a specific point in time and under specific conditions. Also, with repeated measurements in the actual situation, the exposure to the feared situation might be expected to reduce one's fear, as was the case with many of the trainees. Consequently, one would not expect the response to be stable over time.

The *Anxiety Differential* (AD) provides another means of assessing state anxiety that is adaptable to a variety of situations. The AD (Husek & Alexander, 1963) is patterned after the Semantic Differential, a technique for evaluating the connotative meaning of words and concepts, (Osgood, Suci, & Tannenbaum, 1957).

As shown in Table 3.4, the AD is composed of a series of bipolar adjectives, separated by seven blanks. The subject is also presented with a word, such as "fingers." The task is then to make a mark between the two adjectives to represent what the concept "fingers" means to them. For example, in Table 3.4, if one were very tense and anxious, the subject would be expected to mark the word "breathing" toward the "tight" end of the scale. Or if one were calm and relaxed, the mark might be made toward the "loose" end of the scale.

The AD is a rather novel means of assessing state anxiety in that it is not readily apparent to the subject what is being measured. In the development of the scale, Husek and Alexander administered the AD to one group of students immediately prior to a final examination. Another group took it during a regular part of their class with no examination in the immediate future. Those in the pre-exam group scored in the direction of being more state anxious than the non-exam group. Also, after

Table 3.4
Sample Items from the Anxiety Differential

			Fingers					
Straight	___	___	___	___	___	___	___	Twisted
	1	2	3	4	5	6	7	
			Breathing					
Tight	___	___	___	___	___	___	___	Loose
	7	6	5	4	3	2	1	
			Hands					
Wet	___	___	___	___	___	___	___	Dry
	7	6	5	4	3	2	1	
			Me					
Calm	___	___	___	___	___	___	___	Jittery
	1	2	3	4	5	6	7	

Source: Husek & Alexander (1963). Reproduced with permission of the publisher. Copyright © 1963, *Educational and Psychological Measurement*.

Note: Numbers indicate direction of scoring and are not found in the response form.

taking the AD, the subjects were asked to write down what they thought the purpose of the scale was. Only 8 percent of the control group and 32 percent of the exam group were able correctly to identify the purpose as measuring anxiety. Further, there was no relationship found between the subjects' scores on the AD and the ability to identify the purpose correctly. Consequently, the AD appears to be able effectively to measure state anxiety without most subjects being aware of it. Internal consistency reliability coefficients among items was found to range from .58 to .80.

A third state anxiety scale, and one most often used for research purposes is the state form of the STAI. This scale is laid out similarly to the trait scale previously described. It differs in that the respondent is asked to rate his or her feelings " . . . *at this moment.*" Also, most of the statements to which the subject responds are altered to correspond to immediate feelings. Sample

Table 3.5
Sample Items from the STAI - State Anxiety Form X

	Not at All	Somewhat	Moderately So	Very Much So
I feel calm	1	2	3	4
I am tense	1	2	3	4
I feel comfortable	1	2	3	4
I am jittery	1	2	3	4

Source: Spielberger et al. (1970). Reproduced with permission of the publisher. Copyright © 1970, Consulting Psychologists Press, Inc.

items are shown in Table 3.5. A children's version of this scale, the STAIC, is also available (Spielberger et al., 1973).

The general nature of the state anxiety inventories such as the STAI, AD, and FT make them highly adaptable to assessing anxiety in a variety of situations. However, their generality also limits their usefulness in certain situations and for certain purposes. They must be administered at the time the person is experiencing the fear or anxiety. Consequently, by their design, they cannot be used to predict how someone would respond in a given situation that may be encountered at some time in the future. State anxiety scales are not useful for assessment outside the feared situation.

To evaluate before the fact how fearful one might be, another type of assessment scale has been introduced—the *Fear Survey Schedules* (FSS). These scales contain a listing of a wide variety of objects and situations to which the respondent indicates on a 5- or 7-point scale of intensity how much fear each situation would cause them. Several versions of the FSSs have been developed (Geer, 1965; Lang & Lazovik, 1963; Wolpe & Lang, 1964). Table 3.6 shows several sample items from the FSS-II (Geer, 1965).

This version of the FSS has been shown to have good reliability, with internal consistency coefficients as high as .94 (Geer, 1965) and .97 (Herson, 1971). Test-retest reliability over a

Table 3.6
Sample Items of Fear Survey Schedule II

1 = None	3 = A Little	5 = Much	7 = Terror
2 = Very Little	4 = Some	6 = Very Much	

Being a passenger in a plane	_____
Blood	_____
Being alone	_____
Spiders	_____
Heights	_____
Closed places	_____
Snakes	_____
Speaking before a group	_____
Dark places	_____

Source: Geer (1965). Reproduced with permission from *Behavior Research and Therapy*. Copyright © 1965, Pergamon Press, Inc.

10-week period is also quite high with coefficients of .88 (Braun & Reynolds, 1969) and .90 (Cooke, 1966).

These scales also have received some validity support in that persons scoring high on specific items have also demonstrated active avoidance to the objects rated as being fear provoking to them (e.g., Lang & Lazovik, 1963).

Conceptually, a summation of the overall fear ratings on the FSS should be related to one's level of trait anxiety. A person high in A-trait would be expected to respond with anxiety to a variety of situations. In fact just such relationships have been reported. For example, Lang and Lazovik found FSS scores to correlate .80 with the TMAS. Others have reported similar results, although of somewhat lesser magnitudes (e.g., Geer, 1965). Since the report of fear to a wide variety of situations is related to, but not necessarily identical with A-trait, one would expect some degree of relationship but not a perfect correspondance between these two types of measures: one involving how you feel in general, the other how you feel about specific objects or situations. These two types of scales, while related to the same general concept of anxiety or fear differ in how the information is presented and also in the purpose for which they might be used.

If one were interested in obtaining detailed information concerning the overall intensity and various manifestations of a given specific fear, then the A-trait and FSS approaches are inadequate for these purposes. The FSS provides only the opportunity for a single rating from "no fear" to "terror" concerning a particular object. And a single item does not allow for clear specification of the various conditions and circumstances that may affect the intensity of fear of that object. For example, response to the question "How much fear would a snake cause you?" may depend upon the size, color, proximity, whether it was in an open field, in a cage, or loose in your house! The ambiguity of a single item or question such as this would be expected to affect the reliability of one's response (Lick & Katkin, 1976). One person might interpret it as a live snake in a field while another might interpret it as a caged snake. Clearly, these two situations would result in different responses. Although the stimulus word snake was standardized, the actual stimulus to which the persons were responding, that is, their interpretation of the word "snake," was not.

To address the problem of specificity and clarity of stimuli, a number of more detailed fear scales referred to as *specific fear inventories* have been developed. These scales can be used to assess in greater detail the various features associated with a potentially feared object or situation and the various ways in which a person might respond. Specific fear inventories have been developed for many of the more common fears and phobias. Several representative samples will be described below.

The Dental Fear Survey, (DFS) is a 20 item scale designed to survey various elements of three aspects of dental fear (see Table 3.7). The first area concerns avoidance of dentistry due to fear, asking the extent to which the person has ever put off making an appointment or cancelled an appointment due to fear. The second area assessed concerns the person's perceived physiological responses during a typical dental appointment such as changes in breathing, sweating, and heart rate. The third area assessed asks the respondent how much fear or anxiety is experienced during specific phases of dental treatment such as sitting in the waiting room, when the dentist gives an injection of local anesthetic, and during drilling.

Table 3.7
Sample Items from the Dental Fear Survey

Has fear of dentistry ever caused you to cancel or not appear for a dental appointment?

1	2	3	4	5
Never	Once or Twice	A Few Times	Often	Nearly Every Time

When having dental work done:
My muscles become tense:

1	2	3	4	5
Not at all	A little	Somewhat	Much	Very much

My heart beats faster:

1	2	3	4	5
Not at all	A little	Somewhat	Much	Very much

How much fear do you experience when:
Being seated in the dental chair?

1	2	3	4	5
None at all	A little	Somewhat	Much	Very much

When seeing the anesthetic needle:

1	2	3	4	5
None at all	A little	Somewhat	Much	Very much

Source: Kleinknecht et al. (1973).

Studies using this scale have found that persons who score high prior to a dental appointment, indicating strong fear, also actually cancel more appointments, report more state anxiety when in the office, and give greater sweating responses during treatment than persons who score low (Kleinknecht & Bernstein, 1978). Test-retest reliability coefficients over a 4- week period have been found to be between .75 and .84.

The *Snake Questionnaire* (SNAQ) is designed to assess fear of snakes (Klorman et al., 1974). It is composed of 30 statements concerning snakes to which the respondents answer "true" or "false" as it applies to them. As with the DFS, these statements address the areas of avoidance of situations where snakes might be present, physical responses felt while in the presence of a snake, and thoughts one might have about snakes. Table 3.8 shows some sample items from the SNAQ.

Reliability of the SNAQ appears to be quite high with reported internal consistency coefficients of .89 and test-retest coefficients of .78 over a month's period. Although the scale appears to be a valid means of assessing the various elements of the cognitive component of snake fears, it has not received much validity research at this time.

The Sex Anxiety Inventory (SAI) provides another example of specific fear inventories. This 25- item scale differs in format from those presented previously. It has a *forced choice* format which requires the respondent to select one of two response alternatives which completes a statement so that it most closely represents the person's view concerning sex. Sample items are shown in Table 3.9.

Reliability coefficients of this scale are .86 for internal consistence and .85 for 2- week test-retest. Although this scale is relatively new, the authors report some supportive validity re-

Table 3.8
Sample Items from SNAQ

	True	False
I avoid going to parks or on camping trips because there may be snakes about.	___	___
I shudder when I think of snakes.	___	___
Some snakes are very attractive to look at.	___	___
I enjoy watching snakes at the zoo.	___	___

Source: Klorman et al. (1974). Reproduced with permission of the publisher. Copyright © 1974, Academic Press.

Table 3.9
Sample Items from the Sex Anxiety Inventory

Sex:
   a. Can cause as much anxiety as pleasure.
   b. On the whole is good and enjoyable.

I feel nervous:
   a. About initiating sexual relations.
   b. About nothing when it comes to members of the opposite sex.

When I awake from sexual dreams:
   a. I feel pleasant and relaxed.
   b. I feel tense.

When I meet someone I'm attracted to:
   a. I get to know him or her.
   b. I feel nervous.

Source: Janda & O'Grady (1980). Reproduced with permission of the
      authors. Copyright © 1980, American Psychological Association.

search. For example, they found that scores on the SAI were
significantly related to respondents' actual sex experiences. That
is, those with less sex anxiety as indicated on the scale reported
more sexual activity (Janda & O'Grady, 1980).

The three specific anxiety or fear scales presented here
were chosen to illustrate the range of feared situations and objects that can be assessed and that different questionnaire formats can be used to get at the level of fears. These three scales
are but a small sampling of the many such scales available. Others that the reader might find of interest are listed in Table 3.10.

Problems with the Self-Report Method of Fear Assessment.
The self-report procedures just described can provide the assessor with some important information concerning the cognitive domain of anxiety and fear. As previously stated, this is virtually the only means of acquiring this subjective information.
However, inherent in the self-report method are several potential problems that may limit its reliability and/or validity, and
hence how much reliance one might place in such information.

Table 3.10
Specific Fear Inventories

Title	Format	Source
Death Anxiety Scale (DAS)	15, T-F items	Templer (1970)
Spider Questionnaire (SPQ)	31, T-F items	Klorman et al. (1974)
Mutilation Questionnaire (MQ)	30, T-F	Klorman et al. (1974)
Social Anxiety Inventory (SAI) ratings	166, 1-5	Richardson & Tasto (1976)
Test Anxiety Scale (TAS)	21, T-F	Sarason (1957)
Acrophobia Questionnaire (APQ)	20, 6 pt. range	Baker et al. (1973)
Agoraphobic Questionnaire Cognitions	16, 1-5 ratings	Chambless et al. (1981)
Bodily sensations	17,	

One of the major problems of the self-report method is that responses may be determined by factors other than or in addition to the specific item content. One such factor is called *response style* or *response set*. A response style refers to a person's tendency to respond in certain ways to all questions, regardless of their content. A common response style is called *acquiescence* and refers to a general tendency to agree with statements to which they can answer "yes" or "no." Persons with this response style are called *yea-sayers*. Others may take the opposite style of *nay-saying* and tend to disagree with many items. Scales or inventories whose format is of the yes/no or true/false type are particularly vulnerable to such distortions.

Social Desirability is another response style in which respondents tend to endorse items in a way that is considered socially desirable. However, the fact that someone does tend to respond in a socially desirable fashion does not necessarily mean that they are consciously attempting to fake their responses. The tendency may simply be a part of the person's general style of responding to others. Whether intentional or not, such tendencies do limit the validity of the self-report.

To reduce these response sets, the forced choice response format for questions has been successful. This is accomplished by constructing the two response alternatives so that they are equated in terms of social desirability, thus reducing the effects of this response style (Nunnally, 1970).

Other factors also enter into distortion of self-report data, particularly in clinical settings. For example, there may be a tendency for persons seeking treatment for anxiety disorders to attempt to impress upon the assessor just how serious their problem is in order to ensure that they get the desired treatment. This tendency would lead the person to exaggerate how fearful or anxious he or she feels, either through the interview or through paper and pencil scales.

On the other hand, when such persons are assessed after treatment, they may minimize the amount of anxiety that remains so as to make the therapist who has helped them see how much they have improved. These two effects, called the "hello-goodbye" effect (Hathaway, 1948), must be considered when evaluating the effects of fear or anxiety reduction treatments.

The various potential problems associated with self-report methods of assessment, such as response style, item ambiguity, and the general unstructured nature of the clinical interview, must alert us to be somewhat critical in our acceptance of these data at face value. As a further check on the nature and extent of one's fear or anxiety, we can also examine the presence of the physiological component to which we will now turn.

The Physiological Component

Assessment of the physiological component of anxiety or fear involves the measurement of the effects of activation of the nervous system, particularly the ANS. In Chapter 1 the ANS was described as being composed of two divisions: the Sympathetic division which is responsible for energizing and mobilizing the body for fight or flight to meet threats, and the Parasympathetic division which functions to conserve energy supplies. The SNS was described as the system which becomes most activated during fear and anxiety. Consequently, psychophysiological assessment focuses on measurement of changes resulting directly or indirectly from SNS activation. Other portions of the nervous system also become involved and can be measured: such as the electrical activity of the brain and of skeletal muscles.

Many of the changes in ANS activity are readily apparent to the casual observer, such as facial flushing, pulsing of arteries, pounding of the heart, and sweating. However, these casual observations do not lend themselves well to precise measurement and many other ANS functions are not readily observable without special electronic sensing equipment. This equipment, the polygraph, allows for the simultaneous recording and continuous monitoring of minute changes in a variety of organ systems. Although in practice, several systems are monitored at the same time, they will be described separately here and are organized by the various organ systems involved.

The Cardiovascular System.   The cardiovascular system involves the various functions of the heart and the extensive system of arteries, capillaries, and veins. This system, like other bodily systems, is exceedingly complex and not fully understood. For the present purposes, I will describe three measures of the cardiovascular system: the heart rate, blood pressure, and blood volume. Although these functions are affected by states of fear and anxiety, it should be clear that they are also affected by many other conditions. Although under control of the ANS, the cardiovascular system is also influenced by the CNS and the many endocrines of the body.

As a whole, the heart rate (H/R) is controlled by the PNS for its normal rhythmic pacing. Under stress or threat, the SNS becomes activated and inhibits PNS activity which results in an increase in H/R.

The measurement of H/R can be obtained in several ways. Perhaps the most common is the one we have all experienced at the doctor's office: taking a pulse by hand. The wrist is held to feel the pulsing of the radial artery and the number of pulses per minute is recorded. A more precise and less obtrusive measure of H/R is the *electrocardiogram* (EKG). The EKG is a recording of electrical activity of the heart muscles. Measured by electrodes attached to the body, the EKG gives a continuous record of heart muscle contractions or beats. The beats can then be converted to beats per minute (BPM) by another electronic device called a *cardiotachometer*. This device translates the time between contractions of the heart muscle into a rate that can be read out on polygraph or as a visual display.

The normal H/R for adults at rest is about 70 BPM. This rate of course fluctuates as a function of many conditions including fear. When extremely frightened or panicky, one's H/R can double the resting rate. As we will see in the following chapter, this rapid heartbeat, or tachycardia, is one of the major responses seen in anxiety disorders.

Blood pressure changes, also under the control of the ANS, is often taken as a measure of fear and anxiety. As with H/R, our blood pressure is typically taken at the doctor's office. An inflatable cuff, called a *sphygmomanometer* is placed around the upper arm to cut off arterial blood flow. As the cuff is gradually deflated, the amount of pressure present at the time a pulsing is first heard by a stethoscope is called the *systolic* pressure. This is the pressure with which the heart is pumping and is measured in millimeters of mercury (mmHg). As pressure is released further, the sounds from the artery disappear. The pressure at this point is called the *diastolic* pressure, the pressure of the blood when the heart is at rest or between contractions. Blood pressure measurement is expressed as systolic/diastolic. The average blood pressure for adults at rest is 120/80 mmHg.

A third measure of cardiovascular activity sometimes used in assessing fear is blood volume change. This is measured by a device called a *photoplethysmograph* which consists of a photoelectric cell sensitive to changes in light. The photoplethysmograph is attached as a clip to the fingertip or earlobe. On one side is a light which passes through the skin and is recorded on a photosensitive plate on the other. Changes in the amount of blood coursing through the finger or earlobe affect the amount of light: more blood, less light. In this way changes in volume can be detected and these changes then are converted to electrical signals recorded on the polygraph.

The Skin. A second common system of physiologic response involves electrical changes in the skin. These response properties of the skin are called *electrodermal activity* (EDA), referring to changes in the electrical characteristics of the skin. Another term previously used to describe these is Galvanic Skin Response (GSR). Actually, there are several kinds of GSR or EDA, each correlated with one another but also reflecting different phenomena (Edelberg, 1976; Venables & Christy, 1972). Changes in EDA, although not completely understood, are a result of changes in the vasomotor system (dilation/contraction of underlying blood vessels), electrical properties of skin tissues, and sweat gland activity. Sweat is largely composed of salt water which is an electrical conductor.

Specific measures of EDA include *Skin Conductance* (SC) or changes in the degree to which an externally applied small electrical current is conducted through the skin—between two electrodes. The reciprocal or inverse of SC, also used occasionally, is called *Skin Resistance* (SR).

Another form of EDA, *Skin Potential* (SP) can be measured without introducing externally applied current. The SP measure records through strong amplification of naturally occurring changes in the electrical potential of the skin.

These various measures of electrical activity and/or properties of the skin are both directly and indirectly under control of the ANS. The sweat glands in the skin, particularly those on the hands and feet, are under the direct control of SNS. Changes in sweat content of the skin then affect the electrical activity.

Another measure of skin reactance to fear arousal can be obtained by directly measuring sweat gland activity. These measures are referred to as the Palmar Sweat Index (PSI). One commonly used procedure to measure PSI is to apply a solution to the finger which has in it a chemical that withdraws from moisture (sweat). Also included is a plasticizing agent which dries quickly, leaving a plastic finger print. The print has holes in it representing open sweat pores. A direct count of the number of open pores per specified area serves as a measure of "arousal sweating" (Johnson & Dabbs, 1967).

Skin temperature can also be measured by use of a small sensitive thermometer called a *thermister*. Changes in skin temperature are largely a result of changes in the vascular system. When more blood is supplied to the skin, temperature is increased and vice versa.

Muscles.   Although not directly innervated by the ANS, muscle tension, as was noted earlier, often increases with fear and anxiety states as part of the organism's preparatory response to deal with threats. Muscle tension is measured by use of an *electromyograph* (EMG). As a set of muscles become activated for use, the muscles contract. The electrical changes in those muscles (muscle action potential) is recorded and amplified. As more and more muscle units become involved with increasing tenseness, the corresponding electrical activity shows up as changes in the EMG which is recorded on a polygraph.

Respiration.   When fearful, our breathing rate may change, increasing the amount of oxygen supplied to our blood stream and on to body tissues. Two basic methods are used to assess Respiration Rate (RR) changes. Perhaps the simplest method is to use a small thermometer called a thermister, taped beneath the nose. The air being exhaled is warmer than that being inhaled. Consequently, changes from warm to cool as it passes the thermister can be construed as number of breaths taken, per time unit.

A second measure is somewhat more direct. A stretchable tube placed around the chest will expand and contract with each breath and exhalation. A device attached to the tube called a strain gauge can record on a polygraph changes due to the stretching. In addition to the rate, this device can also provide information about the depth of an inhalation.

Other Less Commonly Used Measures of Physical Change. The foregoing measures of physical reaction are those most commonly used to study fear and anxiety. A number of others, however, can be used as measures of stress or as a means of investigating functioning of the ANS and bodily systems. These include: *pupilography*, measuring changes in diameter of the pupils—they dilate when fearful. *Gastrointestinal reactions* such as stomach acid secretions and stomach motility (peristaltic movement of the stomach and intestines) can be assessed. However, these measures are much more difficult and require restraint, swallowing measurement instruments, or attaching electrodes to the abdominal area. Measurement of electrical brain activity is another dimension of fear response that can be measured by Electroencepholography (EEG).

Recently, another set of physical response systems have been shown to change under fear conditions—endocrines. Some of the hormonal responses found to change when phobic patients are confronted with their feared object include plasma norepinephrine, epinephrine, insulin, cortisol, and growth hormone (Nesse et al., 1984).

The investigation of such hormonal changes is, however, quite intrusive, requiring that periodic blood samples be taken. Although these hormonal response measurements are somewhat restrictive, it is important that they be investigated along with other response systems more fully to understand the body's reaction to fear and anxiety.

Problems in Assessing Physiological Components. At first glance, measurement of physiological responses indicative of fear would appear to be the most reliable, valid, and "scientific" means of assessing the presence and level of fear and anxiety. It would seem to be a direct reflection of our body's reaction to fear stimuli, devoid of the many complications seen in the self-report method such as ambiguity and response styles. While it is true that physiological measures do not pose these same problems, they present others that limit their reliability as indicators of anxiety or fear. Several of the more common problems will be described. For further evaluation of these issues, several excellent presentations are given in greater detail elsewhere (see Andreassi, 1980; Hassett, 1978; Sternbach, 1968).

One such problem concerns the *"Law of Initial Values"* (LIV, Lacey & Lacey, 1967). This law states generally that the higher the level of arousal that one starts with (the pre-stimulus level), the less (upward change) increase is possible. This is equivalent to a "ceiling effect." If there is a limit, for example, to how high one's heart rate can go, a person who always has a high heart rate would not show as great an increase when exposed to fear stimuli as one who typically has a lower heart rate. In other words, there is less room for change. Consequently we might expect a person who is high in trait anxiety with accompanying generally high heart rate level to show less of an increase when exposed to a fear-producing situation than someone who has a low level of trait anxiety. This, of course, is the opposite of what we would expect, but is really an artifact of H/R level from which each person started.

A second problem is interpreting psychophysiological responses to fear-provoking situations involves differences in response profiles among the several physiological systems. That is, when placed in a fear-provoking situation, the body does not simply respond with corresponding increases in each of its systems. Each system, and even components within a system (e.g., H/R and B/P) may serve different functions, and do not respond with a uniform increase. Rather than expecting all functions to change similarly, what is seen, and perhaps is more important, is the pattern of changes among the systems. The patterns and specific responses may depend on characteristics of the situation to which the person responds and/or characteristics of the individual doing the responding.

A related factor associated with these different patterns is what the person is doing "cognitively." For example, an interesting pattern called *directional fractionation* has been proposed (Lacey & Lacey, 1959). It has been observed that when one's attention is focused inwardly as when concentrating on mental activities, a characteristic pattern of H/R and SC increase is found. However, when focusing attention outwardly to the environment, a H/R decrease along with SC increase was found. The direction of change in H/R was dependent upon where one's attention was focused. Considering these results in the context of fears, we can see the importance of not only what stimulus is present, but also what the fearful person does cognitively. If a fearful person were to focus on the fear stimulus, we might see a SC increase, but a H/R decrease. Conversely, if the person were to "cognitively avoid" looking and focus on his or her mental images and thoughts, the result might be an increase in H/R. Consequently, in assessing a fearful person's physical response we would need to know what he/she was thinking.

Another problem of interpretation is that different people respond differently to similar situations. Some people will have characteristic physiological responses to many situations. This *Individual Response Specificity* implies that some people may respond to a variety of stimuli with increases in H/R, but no significant change in EDA, for example. Another person may have quite the opposite characteristic pattern. Not only do we need to know where the person's attention is focused, we need to know the person's characteristic response pattern in general. A particular case in point involved physical response of blood or injury phobics. Such persons show a physical response quite different from other phobics: they faint. Recent research shows that there is a two-phase response when confronted with blood or pictures of injuries and the like. First they show a rise in H/R and B/P, as we might expect of a phobic from SNS activation. This, however, is quickly followed by a dramatic drop in H/R and B/P, which results in fainting if the person does not quickly escape from the situation or lie down (Öst et al., 1984; Vingerhoets, 1984).

Compounding these variables of interpretation resulting from patterning, directionality, and individual response specificity, is that many other factors independent of the stimulus that is present can affect physiological responses. For example, drugs, even common ones such as nicotine and caffeine, hormonal changes associated with menstruation, exercise, and physical condition may influence responses (e.g., Andreassi, 1980).

These various phenomena and conditions that may intervene in interpretation of physiological responding as an assessment of fear or anxiety point up the fact that physiological responses are not unambiguous measures of fear or anxiety. This of course does not mean that they are not useful in fear assessment; but only that they should not be taken by themselves to indicate the presence or absence of fear. When these are used, several physiology measures must be applied to ensure that at least one system in which all subjects are responding is included.

Further, one would want to obtain some measure of the cognitive fear component to go along with the physiological responsiveness. Ideally, to assess fear more completely, the third response component, overt behavior, should be included as well. Methods for assessing this dimension of fear will be described next.

The Behavioral Component

Direct observation of fear-related behavior comprises the third component of fear assessment. There are two basic forms of behavioral observation: 1) the *Behavioral Avoidance Test* (BAT) in which the degree of approach or avoidance to the feared object or situation is measured and 2) *Performance Test* in which signs of fearful behavior are recorded while the individual performs some fear-producing task (Bernstein, 1973).

Behavioral Avoidance Tests.   It was noted in Chapter 1 that most definitions of phobia and fear involve the element of avoidance of objects or situations. Accordingly, we see persons fearful of closed spaces walking stairs to avoid elevators, snake phobics detouring around grassy fields, and those fearful of flying, traveling by bus or train. Such observations demonstrate the behavioral response component of fear. When such avoidance is extreme, it classifies the person as phobic.

To assess more precisely the behavioral component, laboratory analogues have been developed in which fearful persons can be observed under standardized conditions. The prototype of the BAT was first described by Lang and Lazovik (1963). These investigators were evaluating the fear-reducing effects of a treatment procedure, systematic desensitization. To ensure they were assessing the full range of fear responses they needed a controlled means of assessing avoidance of the feared stimulus: snakes. To do this, they placed a snake in a covered cage at the end of a room. Subjects were brought to the door and told what was in the room and that they would be requested to approach the snake. They were then asked to enter the room and to walk toward the snake as far as they were able. The actual distance from the door that they were able to traverse was measured to represent their level or degree of avoidance. If they were able to approach the cage, the experimenter asked them to touch the snake, then to hold it. This same measure then was used before treatment to determine initial fearful avoidance, and again after treatment, to assess improvement.

The general procedures used in the BAT have been adapted to assess a wide variety of fear-provoking stimuli. Similar BAT analogues have been constructed for spiders, dogs, and other small animals. Assessment of fear of heights has entailed having subjects climb ladders, open stairways, and fire escapes.

The BAT has many advantages in assesssing the avoidance component of fears and phobias. It is relatively easily administered, can be well standardized so that each subject is exposed to exactly the same stimuli, and has been shown to be highly reliable in terms of interjudge agreement on the amount of approach (Borkovec & Craighead, 1971).

However, a major drawback is that it is not possible to bring all fear-producing situations into the laboratory for this type of assessment. It is possible, however, to take the assessment to more naturally occurring situations and there observe how a person performs.

Performance Test.   Performance observations were used by Paul (1966) to evaluate effects of fear reduction treatments on speech anxiety. Paul constructed a list of 20 observable behaviors thought to be direct indications of anxiety arousal. The 20 behaviors formed the basis of his assessment instrument called the *Timed Behavioral Checklist* (TBCL). The presence of each of the behaviors was observed and recorded at periodic intervals while subjects gave a speech in class. The behaviors included such signs as stammering, clearing throat, lack of eye contact, hand tremor, pacing, and perspiring (see Table 3.11 for examples).

The sum of the number of observation intervals in which any of the behaviors occurred was taken as the behavioral index of anxiety. To evaluate the reliability, two raters gauged each subject at the same time and found about 95 percent agreement.

The same procedures of recording anxiety-related behaviors while the subject is either performing a task or engaging in a feared situation can be applied to virtually any circumstance. Other applications include adult and chilren's behavior at the dental office (Kleinknecht & Bernstein, 1978; Melamed et al., 1975); social interaction anxiety such as talking with members of the opposite sex, and to being in the presence of feared animals (Fazio, 1972; Bernstein & Nietzel, 1974). Further, the TBCL can

Table 3.11
Sample Items from the Timed Behavioral Checklist

Behaviors	Time Periods			
1. Paces	1	2	3	4
2. Arms rigid	1	2	3	4
3. Hand tremors	1	2	3	4
4. Swallows	1	2	3	4
5. Breathes heavily	1	2	3	4

Source: Paul (1966). Reproduced with permission of the publisher. Copyright © 1966, Stanford University Press.

be used in conjunction with the BAT, to examine not only the specific avoidance but also other observable physical signs of anxiety such as trembling, hesitation, and perspiration.

Problems in Assessing the Behavorial Component. As with the self-report and physiological components of anxiety, the behavioral component is subject to several potential problems that may skew interpretation of results.

The first problem is that in controlled experimental settings, subjects can not morally or ethically be exposed to intensely anxiety-provoking situations. Consequently, in those situations amenable to standardized behavioral observation, we are not likely to see the full-scale, raw panic that may occur under more naturally occuring conditions. For example, in the case of BAT with snake, the subject knows the snake is caged and knows that he or she may stop and retreat at any point. The whole procedure is controlled and predictable. On the other hand, a snake phobic who encounters a snake in the woods is not sure it is safe, and the element of unpredictability with the reptile in this uncontrolled setting is additionally frightening. The fear behavior we see in controlled assessments may not correspond well to how one reacts in the natural environment (Lick & Katkin, 1976).

Another element found significantly to influence behavior of reported fearful subjects involves situational demands. To the extent that the person perceives what is expected of him or her in a situation, the person will often behave accordingly. This phenomenon referred to as the *experimental demand characteristics* of the situation (Orne, 1962) has been shown rather dramatically to affect fear behavior in the BAT. In one particularly illustrative study, Miller and Bernstein (1972) recruited volunteers from the community who reported being extremely fearful of closed, dark places. As part of the experiment, subjects were placed in a small dark box and their pulse and respiration rates continuously recorded. There were two experimental conditions introduced to study the effects of demand characteristics. Under one condition, subjects were told that they should stay in the box as long as they felt able to. This was the "low demand" condition. In the other condition, "high demand," they were told that the experimenter needed to study their pulse and breathing while in the box and that they should try to stay for the full 10 minutes allotted. Half of the subjects received the low demand first, then a second trial under high demand instructions. The other half received the reverse sequence.

The results showed quite clearly, under high demand instructions, whether first or second time, subjects stayed in the box longer than with the low demand instruction. In fact, one half of these self-reported highly fearful persons stayed closed in a small dark box for the full 10 minutes under the high demand condition, but only one-fourth did so under the low demand conditions. These subjects had reported being fearful of closed dark places and had avoided them in their daily lives. However, they were able to tolerate the dark box for a considerable period if they were given the high demand to do so by the experimenter.

The implications for assessing the behavioral component of fear are clear. Fear or avoidance behavior will depend upon what subjects are told to do and/or what they perceive is expected of them. That is, it is more than their degree of reported fear that determines their fear behavior. Had they been given only the low demand instructions, they would have appeared to be behaviorally quite fearful. However, if given only high demand instructions, they would not have appeared particularly fearful at all.

Relationship among the Measures

Assessment of each of the components that make up the construct of fear or anxiety provides a broad picture of an individual's fear. Due to the several potential problems associated with measuring each of the fear response systems themselves, it is critical that assessments include each of the areas. Total reliance on any single measure could lead to inappropriate conclusions concerning one's state or level of fear. For example, if only the behavioral component were assessed under high demand conditions, we might conclude that the person was fearless. We could not "see" how the person was responding physiologically, nor know what he was experiencing cognitively. Conversely, a person might report being "terrified" of snakes, if the word snake were interpreted as a poisonous snake, yet quite readily pick up a small harmless garter snake. Consequently, reliance upon only a single assessment mode can lead to inappropriate classification, whether it be for inclusion in research on fear or for clinical purposes to determine if or how best to treat a person's fear.

Even to the extent that assessment procedures are constructed to avoid many of the pitfalls noted, it is commonly found that the responses among the three components do not perfectly correspond with one another (Lang, 1968). The fact that these several measures are imperfectly coupled should not be too surprising. Although all three modes of response represent what we call anxiety or fear, it must be remembered that they are independent systems as well. Further, we should realize that each individual is biologically unique and each has a unique history of learning experiences. Consequently different stimuli will be perceived and reacted to differently. We need to recognize these differences as well as the commonalities and ensure that our assessment procedures reflect the complexity of human variation.

SUMMARY

Fear or anxiety assessment was discussed as the set of procedures for describing, forming impressions, checking out hypotheses, and making decisions concerning a person's characteristic pattern of responses to fear- or anxiety-producing situations. To assess these response patterns, measurements are needed to evaluate the relative levels of fear and anxiety. It was noted that these measures, to be useful, need to have adequate degrees of reliability or consistency. Several forms of reliability were described: test-retest, inter-rater, internal consistency, and split half.

Validity was described as the extent to which these measures are in fact measuring what we intend them to measure—fear and anxiety. Predictive, concurrent, and construct validity were described as the main means for demonstrating that the assessments were measuring what we call anxiety or fear. Since anxiety was conceptualized as a construct, made up of three general components, each of the three systems needs to be assessed.

To assess the cognitive component, the interview and paper and pencil scales were described. The interview, being a rich source of subjective information concerning how the person feels and reacts, also suffers from lack of standardization which in turn affects the reliability of the information gathered. Paper and pencil scales or inventories were shown to provide greater standardization. A sample of such scales were shown for assessing state anxiety, trait anxiety, and specific fears. These, however, have potential limitations due to individual interpretations of questions and response styles.

To assess the physiological responses, electronic recording devices are often used: the polygraph. The various physical response systems most often used to evaluate fear include: the cardiovascular system (heart rate, blood pressure, and blood flow); the skin (electrodermal measures, palmar sweating, and skin temperature); muscles (electromyogram) and respiration rate.

Although seemingly objective, physiological measures are subject to interpretive problems associated with the Law of Initial Values, individual response specificity, directional fractionation and are affected by many substances (e.g., alcohol, caffeine), hormonal levels, and one's cognitive activity.

The behavioral component is assessed by use of behavioral avoidance tests and performance tests constructed directly to observe how a person performs when confronted with their specific fears. Although these methods provide some direct data on fear behavior, responses can be affected by variables other than fear such as social or experimental demand characteristics.

Due to the various factors in addition to one's fear level, which can affect these measures, it is critical that responses from each of these components be included in an assessment package.

Chapter 4

ANXIETY DISORDERS

Where does one draw the line between normal and abnormal expression of fear and anxiety? Since everyone experiences these emotions in some degree of intensity this question is of considerable interest. Perhaps the simplest answer to this difficult question is: When the fear or anxiety is of sufficient proportions and persistence that it becomes a significant problem for the individual and interferes with what one wants or needs to do. Hardly a clearcut answer, this is probably as close as we can come. It is similar to another common experience, headache. When is a headache a problem deserving of treatment? This too depends on the intensity and persistence/duration and the degree to which it interferes with our daily functions. In both cases, the extremes are easy to identify but there is a lot of gray area in between. Nonetheless, as we saw in Chapter 1, it is estimated that as many as 11 percent of the US population suffer from one form or another of anxiety disorder sufficiently that it affects their day-to-day functioning. It is a problem of no small proportion.

In the preceding chapter, the various methods for assessing the degree of fear and anxiety were presented. Now we turn to the use of assessment information to aid in the description and classification of the several forms and patterns in which problem-level fear and anxiety are manifest. We are therefore talking of *diagnosis*: The determination of the nature of a disorder, illness, or abnormality, and its classification. Assessment was seen as the process of data-gathering to aid in diagnosis or classification. Diagnosis in turn leads to directing the appropriate treatment which will be the topic of the following chapter.

The classification of anxiety disorders to be described here is based on the American Psychiatric Association's *Diagnostic and Statistical Manual III* (DSM-III, APA, 1980). Within the DSM-III, two broad classifications are presented: Phobic disorders and Anxiety states. Each of these subclasses has several specific disorder categories which will be described along with illustrative case examples. Although the focus here is on those disorders in which anxiety and fears are the major problem, it is important to realize that these emotions are found as symptoms of various other mental disorders as well.

PHOBIC DISORDERS

Phobias are intense fears that interfere with a person's life adjustment (APA, 1980). There are five basic characteristics which differentiate phobias from common fears. First, phobias are *persistent*. A person phobic of heights cannot be cajoled or talked into climbing a fire escape. Second, the fear reaction is *irrational* in that it is clearly out of proportion to any actual danger. Third, the individual recognizes that his or her reaction is excessive and unreasonable. Fourth, even with this recognition, the person has an overwhelming desire to escape or to avoid the feared object or situation. Fifth, this avoidance causes significant disruption or limitation in the person's day-to-day functioning.

Each of these characteristics must be present to qualify for the diagnosis of phobia. For example, a person highly fearful of snakes who lives in New York City and therefore rarely, if ever, encounters one, might not be considered phobic. However, if that person were fearful of seeing even a picture of a snake and therefore avoided all magazines and newspapers or TV, the reaction would most likely affect adjustment and thereby be considered a phobia.

The term "phobia" comes from the Greek word for morbid fear—phobos. Phobos was a Greek god whom warriors called upon to frighten and rout their enemies. The Greeks also gave us the word "panic," derived from another of their gods: the fun-loving, capricious Pan who is said to strike terror into the hearts of shepherds in the fields and woods just for the sport. Given this Greek legacy for our terms, it is only fitting that our earliest written descriptions of phobias come from the Greek physician, Hippocrates. However, he did not use the term phobia. It was the Roman physician, Celsus, who is credited with first using this term to describe an effect of rabies—hydrophobia, fear of water (Errera, 1962).

It was not until the early 1900s that phobia came into common clinical use as it is today. Since then, however, hundreds of different types of phobias have been observed, described, and named. The name given to a particular phobia is a combination of the Greek word for the object or situation feared and placed before the term phobia. Table 4.1 lists a sampling of the phobias clinically described.

Research using factor analytic techniques mentioned in Chapter 1 shows that certain of the more common phobias tend to cluster (Arrindell, 1980; Hallam & Hafner, 1978). The various phobias within each cluster have a conceptual similarity and in some cases correspond in the age at which they are acquired and the course they take over time. The factors or clusters typically found are consistent with the DSM-III classification to be used here. These clusters include Agoraphobia, Social Phobia, and Simple or Specific Phobia.

Simple/Specific Phobias

The essential defining feature of the Simple Phobia is that the person exhibits a fear reaction to a single circumscribed object or situation which meets the five diagnostic criteria detailed above. Excluded are those fears that involve social situations, to be described later, multiple fears, and fears which are a part of other disorders such as schizophrenia.

Table 4.1
Phobias

Animals
  Acrophobia; entomophobia—
    insects
  Apiphobia; melisophobia—
    bees
  Arachneophobia—spiders
  Batrapchophobia—frogs
  Equinophobia—horses
  Ichthyophobia—fish
  Musephobia; murophobia—mice
  Ophidiophobia—snakes
  Ornithophobia—birds
  Zoophobia—animals

Natural Phenomena
  Acluophobia; nyctophobia—
    night, darkness
  Acrophobia; hysophobia—
    heights
  Anemophobia—wind
  Astraphobia—lightning
  Aurophobia—northern lights
  Brontophobia; kerauno-
    phobia—thunder
  Ombrophobia—rain
  Potomophobia—rivers
  Siderophobia—stars

Blood-Injury-Illness
  Algophobia; odynophobia—
    pain
  Belonephobia—needles
  Dermatophobia—skin lesions
  Hematophobia; hemophobia—
    blood

Pyrexeophobia; febriphobia—
  fever
Molysmophobia; mysophobia—
  contamination
Traumatophobia—injury
Vaccinophobia—vaccinations

Social
  Aphephobia; haptephobia—
    being touched
  Catagelophobia—ridicule
  Ereuthophobia—blushing
  Graphophobia; scriptophobia
    —writing
  Kakorrhaphiophobia—failure
  Scopophobia—being looked at
  Xenophobia—strangers

Miscellaneous
  Ballisphobia—missiles
  Barophobia—gravity
  Claustrophobia—confinement
  Dementophobia—insanity
  Dextrophobia—objects to the
    right
  Erythrophobia—the color red
  Harpaxophobia—robbers
  Levophobia—objects to the
    left
  Pediophobia—dolls
  Trichopathophobia; tricho-
    phobia—hair

Although most people with a Simple Phobia have only the one, the factor analytic research noted above shows that certain fears and phobias tend to cluster, indicating that some people with a certain phobia may have features of related ones. And the fears and phobias that appear to cluster often have similar onsets and causes. These studies generally find the following clusters of specific phobias: Animals, blood and injury, and natural phenomena. There is an additional group of other, less common, specific phobias which are not included in these clusters.

Animal Phobias.   This cluster includes a variety of animals, the most common of which are dogs, cats, snakes, worms, spiders, birds, mice, fish, and frogs. Although animal phobias, and fears as well, are probably the most common in the general population, they are seen only infrequently in treatment clinics. Assumedly, the disruption in one's life caused by these phobias is less than for other phobias and the individual can find adequate means to avoid them in many cases. Agras et al. (1969) found that animal phobias accounted for only 4 percent of the phobics seen for treatment at the University of Vermont. Similarly, Marks (1969) reports that of the phobics seen at Maudsley Hospital clinics in London only 3 percent are animal-phobic.

Animal phobias have several distinct characteristics that set them apart from other phobias and indicate that they have their own natural history. They tend to develop very early in life. Marks and Gelder (1966) found that the average onset is at 4.4 years of age and development is rare after age seven or eight. However, they can be acquired later if the person is exposed to some traumatic event associated with animals, such as being attacked by a dog. Marks (1969) suggests that the clear age-relatedness of onset indicates that there may be a facilitory age associated with one's biologic development during which such phobias are readily acquired. After that age, it may take a rather unusually traumatic experience to cause an animal phobia to develop.

Also common to many animal phobias is that they diminish with maturation. A five-year follow-up study of the phobics identified in the Agras community survey, found that of those under twenty years of age at the time of the original survey, 40 percent were symptom-free and the remaining 60 percent were improved after 5 years. However, those phobias which do not dissipate during childhood tend to persist. Of phobics over twenty years of age, only 23 percent were symptom-free, 42 percent improved, while 35 percent were either unchanged or worse after 5 years. Although the particular study combined all phobias, the pattern of early onset with persistence over years is quite characteristic of animal phobias (Agras, et al., 1969; Mark, 1969).

Significant gender differences are also evident with animal phobias. As was noted in Chapter 2, prior to adolescence, males and females show few differences in prevalence of fear, but later females' fears become more prevalent than males'. In adulthood this differential remains strong for animal phobics (Kirkpatrick, 1984). Marks (1969) reports that upwards of 95 percent of animals phobics are female.

Another characteristic of persons with animal phobias is that the phobias are generally highly circumscribed. In all other aspects of their lives they tend to be as well-adjusted as the population in general. They are no more trait anxious than others and their fear is quite specific to the animal involved (Marks, 1969). This monosymptomatic picture with generally good adjustment may be one of the reasons this group so infrequently seeks treatment. Seeking treatment is often precipitated by changing life circumstances which bring about more frequent contact with the phobic object. For example, John was a twenty-six-year-old popular radio announcer who had a phobia of fish. In all other aspects of his life he was active, happy, productive, and well-liked. Although he had the fish phobia as long as he could remember, he had hidden it from others due to his embarrassment over such a "silly thing." He simply found other things to do when family and friends went fishing, and avoided fish markets and pet stores.

However, he was stimulated to seek treatment when his parents invited him and his brother for a vacation in Hawaii. His brother had become an avid scuba diver and had plans for the family to explore the underwater marvels of the beautiful reefs and tropical fish. The mere thought of coming face-to-face with a fish, especially on the fish's own turf, caused him to cringe and shudder. He felt his choice became one of not going with the family or facing the embarrassment of openly admitting his irrational fear.

John's fish phobia was one with which he could live under normal circumstances. It became a significant problem for him only when his normal circumstances changed. Further, his problem, although significant to him, did not severely limit his daily functioning as long as he could successfully avoid fish.

The following case of Anna presents a more debilitating situation and illustrates the extreme proportions that even "simple phobias" can reach:

> Anna was housebound. Six months ago, the house next door had become vacant and the grass had become a rendezvous for the local cats. Now Anna was terrified that if she left her house, a cat would spring on her and attack her. At the sight of a cat, she would panic and sometimes be completely overwhelmed with terror. She could think of nothing else but her fear of cats. She interpreted any unexpected movement, shadow, or noise as a cat (Rosenhan & Seligman, 1984, pp. 200-201).

Blood, Injury, and Illness Phobias. This constellation of phobias concerns fears associated with bodily harm. Within this group are specific fears of having a serious illness, receiving an injection, being injured or seeing others with injuries, and the sight of blood. Although this group is one of the more prevalent of the classes of phobias, it has been the object of relatively little research. Survey studies indicate that it comprises the largest number of phobias in the general population. The Agras et al. (1969) study showed that 3 percent of their population sample was diagnosed as having illness or injury phobia and Costello (1982) found 4.5 percent in a sample of females. Among all phobics identified by Agras, 42 percent were of this type. Compared with animal phobias, these are also seen more frequently in treatment clinics. Marks (1969) reports that 15 percent of his series of Maudsley Hospital phobics were of this type, whereas Agras reported that 34 percent of phobics seen at Vermont sought treatment for illness or injury phobias.

Since there has been less research on this group of phobias, the nature of the relationship among the several types is not clear. Consequently, I will discuss separately some of the specific phobias within the group. *Illness phobia* is characterized by a person being chronically anxious and worrying over the possibility of having some specific disease. Such persons may constantly search their bodies for outward signs and overinterpret all seemingly odd sensations. They may also seek frequent medical examinations due to this fear. Goodwin (1983) notes that the specific illness feared seems to be whatever disease is most publicized at the time. Currently, cancer appears to be the most popular, whereas in previous decades it was tuberculosis and before that, syphilis.

Persons with such illness phobias may show some pattern of avoidance of doctors or self-inspection as noted. However, for the most part avoidance is difficult since the feared situation is not an external object. Rather it is something within the individual. Fear of doctors may also be a part of this phobia if the individual perceives the doctor as the source of confirmation of the illness feared.

This fear appears most prevalent among middle-aged and older persons, most often beginning after the age of forty. As with animal phobias, females appear to predominate with illness phobia, although the proportions are not as discrepant, with about two-thirds female, one-third male (Agras, 1969).

Phobias of receiving *injections* also tend to cluster in this group. In part, this fear may be a reason for fear of doctors and dentists, since many persons fearful of dentistry cite the local anesthetic injection as the reason they fear and avoid dental treatment (Kleinknecht et al., 1973). In some this needle phobia is highly specific, as was the case with Jennifer.

> Jennifer was a normal sixteen-year-old teenager who was in need of considerable dental treatment. She knew and accepted that fact with little apparent anticipatory anxiety. However, each time the dentist approached her mouth with the syringe to inject the local anesthetic her arms would reflexively jerk up to protect her face. Each time this occurred she felt badly and said she would try not to do it again, but each attempt met with the same protective arm movements.

Fear of injections, like Jennifer's, appear to follow a pattern similar to that of fear of doctors and dentists, with onset being typically before age ten or eleven with slowly diminishing prevalence to about age sixty (Agras et al, 1969; Kleinknecht & Bernstein, 1978). Information on sex differences for injection phobia per se are unavailable. However, for dental phobia, females clearly predominate at least by their reports (Agras et al., 1969; Kleinknecht et al., 1973; Kleinknecht & Bernstein, 1978).

Blood and Injury Phobia, although grouped with illness and injection phobia, presents a somewhat different picture from that presented above. This phobia too has received minimal research attention in the past but recently has attracted the interest of several investigators. The apparently unique feature of persons phobic of the sight of blood and injuries is that fainting often occurs. This response is in sharp contrast to other specific phobics in whom actual fainting in the presence of the feared object is rare (Connolly et al., 1976). Recall that the typical physiologic response in fear involves a sustained activation of the SNS with consequent increases in heart rate, blood pressure, and/or other systems. Fainting is mediated by activation of the parasympathetic system with a decrease in H/R and blood pressure. When blood is shunted from the peripheral to the internal organs, the blood supply to the brain decreases and the person looses consciousness.

In the case of blood/injury phobics, there appears to be a biphasic response involving an initial increase in H/R and B/P followed by a rather sudden decrease which results in the faint (Öst et al., 1984; Connolly et al., 1976).

Due to the paucity of research on these phobias, little is known about them. Consistent with reports of the larger group of illness/injury phobias noted previously, females predominate (Klorman et al., 1974; Öst et al., 1984), and many have family histories of similar reactions (Connolly et al., 1976; Öst et al., 1984; Yule & Fernando, 1980).

Also of interest is that fainting at the sight of blood or injury appears to be relatively stimulus-specific. That is, such phobics do not typically faint more than nonphobics in other situations (Connolly et al., 1976). Much remains to be learned about this interesting group of phobias. For example, it is unclear whether the drop in heart rate and blood pressure, with resultant fainting response is truly unique to this group or whether it is simply an exaggerated response to these stimuli which nonphobics also have, but to a lesser degree (Öst et al., 1984). Further, we do not yet know blood phobics' response to the pattern of other physiologic indices such as electrodermal activity and the like described in Chapter 3.

Like other phobias in this group, blood and injury stimuli are difficult totally to avoid. Who has not shed a drop of blood or seen someone else injured? Consequently, such a phobia can be limiting as it was for Jack (Yule & Fernando, 1980).

Jack was a sixteen-year-old student finishing a technical school course in motor mechanics when he sought treatment for his phobic reaction to blood and needles. He was concerned that his fear of blood, and his fainting when he saw it, would interfere with his work as a mechanic. Jack had fainted frequently during his biology classes at school and was about to begin a course of ambulance training. Fainting while working as a motor mechanic could be dangerous and, of course, an ambulance assistant who fainted at the sight of blood or injury would be of little use.

Although Jack's reaction was clearly of a phobic nature, in all other areas of his life he appeared well-adjusted and happy. It was also of interest, as is often found with blood-injury phobias, Jack had three close relatives who also had this reaction: his mother, brother, and an uncle.

Natural Phenomena Phobias. The phobias within this group primarily include storms with thunder, lightning, and strong winds. Some also find that fear of other natural phenomena cluster here as well. These include fears of darkness, heights, and deep water (Hallam & Hafner, 1978).

The only data on prevalence of these phobias comes from the Agras (1969) study which found that 1.3 percent of their sample were phobic of storms. This accounted for 18 percent of the phobias identified, second only to illness and injury phobias in prevalence.

The distribution of storm phobias over age groups suggests that onset is during childhood, with a slowly declining frequency with increasing age. Two recent reports of small series of patients under treatment for storm phobias are consistent with this age-related information. Liddell and Lyons (1978) found that seven of their 10 phobics had childhood onset while Öst (1978) found five of six patients seeking treatment to date their phobias from early childhood. It therefore appears that early onset is the typical pattern, but some can develop in adulthood as well.

In the three reports cited, all the persons identified as storm-phobic were female. This predominance of females identified in adulthood with storm phobias is of interest from a developmental perspective. During the ages of six and twelve, fears of thunder and lightning were found by LaPouse and Monk (1959) to have a prevalence of 38 percent and were equally prevalent among boys and girls. Apparently the maturation and/or socialization process differentially affects males and females with respect to losing fear of storms.

The prototype of this set of phobias involves fears of thunder and lightning. In many parts of the world, such a phobia can be severely debilitating, particularly during the summer months. Persons with these phobias typically spend a great deal of time organizing their lives so as to avoid being away from home and being caught out in storms. They must arrange their work, shopping, and outings to ensure that no storms are imminent. This typically includes continuous checking of weather reports and calling the weather bureau for updated forecasts. During a storm, behaviors such as uncontrollable trembling, crying, nausea, and rapid heart rate are common. Avoidance measures are taken as well, such as covering one's head with pillows, and hiding in closets or basements (Liddell & Lyons, 1978; Öst, 1978).

This pattern is well illustrated in a case report by Öst (1978):

> This lady was 64 years old at the time she sought treatment for her fear of thunderstorms. She recalled her parents being very fearful when a thunderstorm arose and took extraordinary precautions when a storm was forecast. As an adult she was unable to stay alone in her summer house or to enjoy being outside during the summer because a thunderstorm might arise. Her thoughts centered on thunder and lightning and she constantly checked the radio and TV weather forecasts. When a storm did come, she paced incessantly, was exceedingly anxious, had headaches, palpitation, and an urge to urinate.

Social Phobias

The second classification of phobias are those which involve other people. The essential element of the several forms of social phobias is that the individual feels he or she is the object of scrutiny by others. In this sense, these phobias involve a strong fear of being observed and evaluated by other persons. Although for many socially phobic persons, there is a relatively circumscribed situation to which they react, such as public speaking, it can take on broad and very limiting proportions. It is very difficult to avoid other people.

A variety of specific social situations may become the focus for a social phobia. Among the more common types of situations are the following: meeting strangers, speaking or performing in public, meeting authorities, being criticized or observed while working, use of public lavoratories or dressing rooms, eating in public, fear of vomiting, blushing, or fainting in public, and fear of writing one's name where others can observe. In each of these situations, the central issue is the fear that others will observe and negatively evaluate some aspect of the phobic individual. In most instances the individual's anticipatory anxiety over what *might* happen if they actually enter the feared situation leads them to avoid the situation altogether.

Some such feared situations are common and relatively easy for most to avoid without significant restrictions in their lives, such as public speaking. However, for others, this fear can be a significant hindrance to advancement in one's career, for example, if promotion to higher levels of responsibility requires giving speeches or presentations.

Estimates of the prevalence of social phobia are unavailable. As noted in Chapter 2, the social anxiety and shyness are relatively common, but such fears of phobic proportions are presumably relatively rare (APA, 1980). However, by the very nature of the phobia, avoidance of interpersonal situations, many such phobics may literally be hiding in the closet. Among phobics in the Maudsley Hospital services, social phobia accounted for only 8 percent of those seeking treatment (Marks & Gelder, 1966).

Social phobics have a relatively circumscribed age of onset. Typically the phobia begins in adolescence when teenagers are keenly self-conscious and concerned with peer evaluation. Occasionally, but less frequently, they begin after age thirty (Marks, 1969; Marks & Gelder, 1966).

In contrast to all other phobias, social phobia, like social anxiety, is relatively evenly distributed among males and females. This is the major male phobia (Arrindell, 1980; Marks & Gelder, 1966).

The following cases of "scriptophobia," fear of writing in public, illustrate some of the features noted above. These case studies described by Biren et al. (1981) involved three women who responded to a newspaper announcement of the availability of treatment. The onset of their phobias was during high school for two of the women and in the early thirties for the third. At the time they sought treatment, the phobia had persisted for between sixteen and twenty-one years.

All three were unable to write their names in public, which resulted in none of them being able to write checks, use bank cards, or vote. All three had accommodated to their avoidance by arranging for their husbands to handle all financial matters which involved writing. Two had avoided telling even their husbands of their fears. As is usually characteristic of social phobics in general, they experienced less fear if they were in the company of a trusted family member. The more formal the situation, the more anticipatory anxiety and fear they experienced.

When anticipating or encountering their feared situation, they experienced physiological symptoms of heart palpitations, shortness of breath, trembling hands, sweating, and dizziness. Cognitively, when confronted with having to write their names, they thought to themselves: "People will wonder what's wrong with me;" "I'll feel clumsy;" "People might think that I am not stable, that some thing is wrong with me" (Biran et al., 1981, p. 527).

Each of these women also experienced some anxiety when in other social situations, particularly where they felt they were being evaluated or observed performing some task. This more general social anxiety is often seen in addition to the reaction to the more specific phobic situation. However, it is not always the case as illustrated by the following case of George whose reaction was quite specific: he was phobic of using public restrooms.

George, who was thirty-seven years old at the time he sought treatment, dated the onset of his social phobia to his junior high school days. Being somewhat slower to mature physically than his classmates, he was very self-conscious at undressing, showering, and using restrooms at school when others were present. Even after he achieved puberty, his fears of being observed while in a restroom, in particular, persisted. Although he had accommodated to his fears for about 25 years, it was bothersome, restrictive, and made him ashamed of himself for being so silly. The phobia was most pronounced at the office where he held a responsible middle-management position. He would avoid using the office restroom if he thought one of his colleagues was present. If he miscalculated and happened into the restroom when someone else was present, he would become weak-kneed, his face would flush, his heart would pound, and he would be unable to speak. This reaction was worse if he was about to relieve himself and someone else walked in. His sphincter muscles would constrict and he would be unable to urinate. His evaluation fear was that if he could not urinate due to the constriction, the other person would wonder what was wrong with him. This anticipatory anxiety over wondering what others would say became part of the vicious cycle that led to his fear and in turn kept him from being able to urinate, further reinforcing his phobia.

In situations where he felt anonymous he had less difficulty, although he still felt some anxiety. At home, or when he was clearly alone, he had no fear at all. In fact his wife of some 16 years was totally unaware of his relatively circumscribed phobia. He was too embarrassed to tell anyone. His therapist from whom he sought treatment was the first person he ever told.

Agoraphobia

Agoraphobia, the third general category of phobias, is clearly the most pervasive, disabling, and complex. The term "agora"—from the Greek root meaning "market place" or "open spaces"—may well be a misnomer for this disorder. Al-

though most agoraphobics are indeed fearful of the market-
place (e.g., crowds and shopping centers) and some of open
spaces, the breadth of situations that elicit fear in agoraphobics
is much broader. Elements of many of the specific fears described previously as well as elements of social phobia are often
combined in this disorder. Complicating matters further is an
underlying theme which pervades agoraphobia: fear of fear itself (Goldstein & Chambless, 1978).

Agoraphobia in its more severe form leaves the persons af-
flicted virtually housebound. Their fear is so intense and pervasive that they cannot venture past their front door unless accompanied by a trusted companion, and then only with considerable
apprehension.

The constellation of situations most feared and avoided by
agoraphobics has been described with considerable consistency
by clinical and factor analytic research (Arrindell, 1980; Hallam
& Hafner, 1978; Marks, 1969). The most commonly reported
situations include: leaving home alone, strange places, travel by
train, bus, or airplane, crowds, large open spaces, enclosed
spaces, shopping centers and department stores, movies, eating
or drinking in public, crossing bridges or streets, and high
places. This list leaves few alternatives for the agoraphobic but
home.

This list of specific situations feared should not be taken to
suggest that agoraphobia is simply a compilation of specific phobias. Rather, these situations are elements of relatively distinct
patterns of fears that comprise a syndrome of their own (Hallam
& Hafner, 1978). Further describing this syndrome is that agoraphobics typically fear their reactions as well as the specific circumstances. These include fears of fainting and losing control in
public should they experience a panic attack. They not only experience fear in certain situations but also fear their reactions.
The fear of reactions also has a strong element of social fear.
They are fearful that if they should have a panic attack in public
they might faint or otherwise lose control which would cause
them to be the center of attention. Others will wonder what is
wrong with them and hence they will be negatively evaluated for
making fools of themselves. It is in this sense that agoraphobia
has been called fear of fear, or rather fear of the reaction which
in turn may draw attention to them and render them subject to

social evaluation. This fear of social evaluation is further illustrated by the common observation that many agoraphobics, if they go out, wear dark glasses and prefer to go out in darkness rather than the light of day. They feel less conspicuous.

Another feature often associated with agoraphobia and which differs from other phobias is that of depression. Although depression is seen in some other phobia, particulary social phobias, it is more prominent in agorphobia (Marks, 1969; Arrindell, 1980). An associated complicating factor is the presence of obsessions, which will be discussed separately in a later section.

Two recent national surveys investigating the prevalence of agoraphobia among other psychiatric disorders showed that between 1.2 percent (Uhlenhuth et al., 1983); and 4 percent (Robins et al., 1984) of the general population could be so diagnosed. Although this percentage is somewhat lower than for other specific phobias, its debilitating nature renders this disorder a significant problem, affecting millions in the US alone. As with most other phobias, agoraphobics are approximately 75 percent female (Marks, 1969; Uhlenhuth et al., 1983; Robins et al., 1984). Further, although agoraphobics account for only 8 percent of phobics, they represent fully 50 to 60 percent of those seeking treatment (Agras et al., 1969; Marks & Gelder, 1966).

The age of onset of agoraphobia is similar to social phobics with the majority beginning between the years of eighteen and thirty-five (Marks & Gelder, 1966).

To clarify further the debilitating nature of agoraphobia and how the multiple situations become fear-producing, I will describe some of the more typical features of the process of fear development. In the majority of cases, agoraphobia begins with a sudden panic attack, seemingly coming out of nowhere. The person experiences an intense attack of the physical symptoms of fear: extreme heart palpitations, weakness in the knees, lightheadedness, dizziness, and rapid shallow breathing which may lead to hyperventilation. This panic attack can last from minutes to hours. Since the person can identify no object or situation to cause this reaction, the typical explanation is that they are having a heart attack, or are losing their mind. It is not uncommon for the person to go straight to see a physician, who of course can find nothing physically wrong.

Although fewer in number, a significant proportion of

agoraphobics begins more slowly, with a generalized anxiety feeling of lesser intensity. These feelings persist, come and go, but create a similar result as for those who experience the intense panic attack. Eventually there is an increasing restriction of activities and a retreat to the more reassuring environs of home.

Those for whom agoraphobia begins with the sudden panic attacks will subsequently avoid the situation in which it occurred as well as similar situations. Eventually they may experience another attack in a different situation, which then adds to the list of situations to be avoided. Due to the unpredictable nature of the attack, the person begins to avoid many public situations for fear of having another attack. Eventually the person's world constricts further until home is the only remaining refuge. In many cases the person may be able to leave home, but only with a trusted companion, typically a spouse or close friend, or in some cases, a pet. However, even when accompanied, the person will only be able to go to certain places. These places must be such that the phobic has a ready escape route in the event of another panic attack. If they were to go to a movie, theater, or church, they would take great care to ensure a seat in the back on the aisle, for ready escape.

Accompanying the fear of having an attack is the fear of others seeing them having one. This social phobia then also serves to maintain the fear and avoidance of situations where there are large crowds and/or where the person feels conspicuous.

Since a large proportion of agoraphobics are married and many have children as well, the family must make many accommodations to this reclusive life-style. The spouse must do the shopping and handle all matters outside the home. The social and recreational activities would be severely limited. When the agoraphobic is on safe ground (i.e., home) he or she may well appear and feel perfectly normal. Visitors may suppose nothing is out of the ordinary. However, some agoraphobics may show high levels of pervasive trait anxiety.

The initial panic attack or the more gradual onset typically begins during periods of significant life changes and personal stress. One survey found that in 85 percent of the cases specific life stresses preceded the onset (Doctor, 1979). The most common stresses involved separations or losses, relationship or work stresses, and health problems (Doctor, 1979; Marks, 1969).

The situations in which the attack first occurred show a common theme as well. They typically occur in situations in which the person is physically confined or restricted. These include traveling by bus, airplane, or driving a car on freeways and bridges, and being in enclosed places such as elevators, theaters, churches, or restaurants. The feeling of being trapped with no escape available appears to be the common denominator of the circumstances in which the attack first occurs, as well as the precipitant of later attacks and subsequently of situations to be avoided.

In summary, agoraphobia is a pervasive fear of having a panic attack away from home where others might observe. This fear of fear and of being observed leads to a progressive restriction of mobility and subsequent confinement to secure refuges.

ANXIETY STATES

Panic Disorder (PD)

The essential feature of PD is recurring unpredictable panic attacks. For most, the panic attack seemingly comes out of nowhere. However, for some the occurrence may be more likely during particular activities such as driving.

The panic attack begins suddenly and the person is immediately overwhelmed with a flood of ANS activity. They experience intense heart palpitations, weakness in the knees, sensations of choking and smothering, parathesia (tingling in hands or feet), sweating with hot and cold flashes, and trembling. Cognitively they experience feelings that something horrible is about to happen. They may also feel that things are not real (derealization) and/or that they are not themselves (depersonalization). This experience is of course extremely frightening and the person often feels as if he or she is dying, having a heart attack, or losing their minds. These attacks, like those with agoraphobia, may last several minutes or, more rarely, for hours. The aftereffects of the attack are variable. Some people remain shaken for hours afterwards, while for others the symptoms subside as completely and suddenly as they arose, leaving them essentially as they were before the attack.

Due to the intensity and inexplicability of panic attacks not closely associated with environmental situations, many sufferers will consult a physician, fearing they have had a heart attack. Indeed, it has been estimated that between 10 and 15 percent of patients seen by cardiologists suffer from panic attacks (Marks & Lader, 1973). Most often, of course, no physical basis is found for the attack, and no signs of heart disease. However, some patients with panic attacks have recently been found to have a physical condition called mitral valve prolapse syndrome (MVPS, Wooley, 1976). This disorder involves a midsystolic prolapse of one of the mitral valves in the heart. The result is heart palpitations and other ANS reactions essentially identical to symptoms of panic disorder. One recent study found 38 percent of a sample of patients diagnosed as having PD also to have MVPS (Crowe et al., 1980). However, the significance of this finding is unclear. Approximately 5 percent of the general population has MVPS and the majority do not experience anxiety or panic symptoms (Shader, et al., 1982).

As with the phobic disorders, there is a predominance of females with panic disorder. Anderson et al. (1984) found that females comprised 71 percent of a sample of panic disorder patients; a finding generally consistent with other reports (e.g., Marks & Lader, 1973; Crowe et al., 1980).

The age of onset of PD appears to be quite similar to that reported for agoraphobia, falling within the sixteen- to forty-year-old range (Marks & Lader, 1973), with a mean in one study of 22.8 years (Anderson et al., 1984).

Generalized Anxiety Disorder

Generalized Anxiety Disorder presents a related but somewhat different picture from Panic Disorder. In contrast to those with PD, generalized anxiety disorder people do not experience the repeated panic attacks. Rather, their anxiety is relatively constant. Although they may experience occasional surges of high anxiety, they are constantly in a state of arousal, essentially equivalent to a high level of trait anxiety. Like the panic disorder, there does not appear, at least to the individual, to be a specific source of the anxiety. Consequently, this has been referred to as "free-floating" anxiety. This constant level of anxiety keeps the person on edge most of the time, although it typically causes only mild social or economic impairment.

The general defining characteristics include: 1) *motor tension*, such as being jumpy, jittery, or having tense muscles; 2) *ANS hyperactivity*, including sweating, rapid heartbeat, cold clammy hands, or feeling there is a lump in the throat; 3) *Apprehensive expectation* such as worry and ruminating that something bad will happen; and 4) *Vigilance and scanning*, meaning that the person is hyperattentive to what is going on around him. This in turn results in distractability, inability to concentrate, irritability, and insomnia (APA, 1980).

Like PD and other anxiety disorders, GAD shows a two-thirds majority of females (Anderson et al., 1984; Uhlenhuth et al., 1983). Overall estimates of the population prevalence of GAD range from 2.5 percent (Anderson, 1984) to 6.4 percent (Uhlenhuth et al., 1983).

GAD appears to have a more gradual and earlier onset than PD. Anderson and her colleagues (1984) report a mean onset at about sixteen years of age, nearly 7 years earlier than for their subjects with panic disorder. Further, in contrast to phobic disorders, with exception of agoraphobia, both PD and GAD may have a relatively strong familial/genetic component (Anderson et al., 1984; Crowe et al., 1980, 1983). These disorders in particular require a thorough medical evaluation to rule out physical problems which can produce the symptoms of anxiety.

Obsessive-Compulsive Disorders

This category has two related components: Obsessions, which are recurrent thoughts, ideas, or images, and compulsions which are stereotypic repetitive acts. As with common fears, most of us experience mild versions of these such as the tune or commercial that we can't seem to get out of our mind, or the thought that we forgot to turn the water off in the bathroom.

However, for the person with obsessive-compulsive disorder, the thoughts or actions do not go away so readily. In the more extreme forms, this can be the most disabling and immobilizing of the anxiety disorders.

Obsessions. In contrast to the recurring tunes or jingles that we may experience as nuisances, obsessions typically have a disturbing, morbid, or frightening quality to them.

Another defining characteristic of clinical obsessions is that they appear to be largely out of the person's volitional control. It is as if they are being forced upon the consciousness and therefore are seen as alien or foreign to one's personality. To describe this intrusive quality of obsessions, the term *ego-alien* is often used (e.g., APA, 1980). Attempts to ignore or suppress the obsessions are made but are typically unsuccessful. The resulting sense of lack of control may be as anxiety-provoking and disturbing as the content of the obsessions.

The most common content theme of obsessions concerns dirt and contamination. These obsessions, reported by up to 46 percent of a group of obsessive-compusive patients, center on thoughts and fears that they will develop some disease if they come into contact with virtually any object (Akhtar et al., 1975). This obsession can become quite debilitating, since one of the major sources feared is doorknobs. For example, a patient I once treated had this obsession with contamination and could not open a door with her bare hand. She would carry gloves or a clean cloth to drape over objects she needed to touch to prevent direct contact with any object. Ungloved, she could not shake hands. This particular obsession is typically associated with compulsive cleaning rituals as well. In fact, between 70 and 80 percent of persons with obsessions also have compulsions (Akhtar et al., 1975; Wilner et al., 1973; Emmelkamp, 1982).

The second common theme of obsessions involves thoughts or images concerning aggression or harm. Approximately one-quarter of obsessional patients report such themes, often involving loved ones being injured. This results in the persons constantly worrying about others and checking on their safety.

Concern with orderliness is also a common theme reported by 23 percent in one study (Akhtar et al., 1975) and 35 percent in another (Rachman & Hodgson, 1980). Less frequently reported are themes associated with religious and sexual issues. Approximately half of persons with obsessions report more than a single theme (Akhtar et al., 1975).

In addition to the different contents of obsessions, they also take different forms. An investigation by Akhtar and his colleagues (1975) revealed five different forms of obsessions. As with the different content themes, any individual may have more than one form of obsession. *Obsessive doubts* were the most frequent, being reported by 75 percent of the sample. These were characterized by the individual persistently worrying that some task had not been satisfactorily completed. Examples include doubts that a door had been locked, a window closed, water turned off. These doubts continued to intrude into awareness, even though the person rationally knew that in fact the act had been performed.

Obsessive thoughts were described by 34 percent as seemingly uncontrolled endless trains of thoughts. These thoughts typically concerned long scenarios of events that might occur in the future; or that germs were everywhere, and what would happen if the person were to become contaminated.

Obsessive impulses, described by 17 percent, involved powerful urges to perform certain acts that would seem silly and embarrass them, or that involved assaultive acts toward others. Common obsessive impulses described are: "I feel I will shout obscenities on the street," "I'm afraid that if I am around sharp objects, like knives, I will harm someone." A lawyer, described by Akhtar et al. (1975), had an urge to drink from his inkpot. Although this is a rather silly and mild obsession, the lawyer also felt frightening urges to strangle his son. Fortunately such urges, although bothersome and even frightening, are very rarely actually carried out.

Obsessive fears noted by 36 percent of the sample involved fear of losing control of oneself and perhaps doing embarrassing things. For example, a school teacher feared that he would tell his class about his unsatisfactory sexual relations with his wife. He of course did not want to do this nor did he have an urge to do so. But he feared that he might.

Obsessional images, reported by 7 percent, involve scenes of mutilated bodies, a loved one having a serious accident, or some-one being violently assaulted. Akhtar et al. describe one patient who on entering her bathroom experienced an image of her baby being flushed down the toilet.

Such scenes, impulses, and fears of embarrassment keep the person in a constant state of anxiety. And as noted previously, a majority of persons who experience obsessions also engage in compulsive acts which are related to their obsessions.

Compulsions.   In the same way that obsessions are intru-sions into one's cognitive activity, compulsions are intrusions into one's behavior. Compulsions are repetitive acts that one feels compelled to perform. Often these acts are conducted in a stereotypic and mechanical fashion. The acts are usually recog-nized by the person as being excessive and senseless. Although there may be a semblance of volitional control over the actions under some conditions (Rachman & Hodgson, 1980), the urge is so strongly experienced that in practice control is quite minimal. At least initially, the person also has a desire to resist the compul-sive act. Later, the person may just give in and go with it.

In as few as 6 percent of persons diagnosed as obsessive-compulsive, compulsions occur without accompanying obses-sions. When the two components occur together, as they do in about 70 percent of the cases (Welner et al., 1976) it appears that the obsession is causally related to the compulsive act (Rachman & Hodgson, 1980). That is, the content of the obsession is the source of the urge to perform the act. Two basic forms of com-pulsions were identified by Akhtar and his colleagues: *yielding* and *controlling*.

Yielding compulsions are the most common type, accounting for 61 percent of Akhtar's sample. In these cases, an obsessive thought drives the person to perform some act. For example, one of Akhtar's patients, a clerk, had an obsessive thought that he had an important document in one of his pockets. Although he rationally knew this was not true, he felt compelled to check his pocket repeatedly. The most common of the yielding com-pulsions is hand-washing. This is typically associated with obses-sions relating to dirt, germs, or more generally, fear of contami-nation and of ultimately contracting a disease.

Compulsive hand-washing can be exceedingly disruptive, time-consuming, and even painful when carried to the proportions often described. Marks (1978) relates a case of a woman who washed her hands up to 100 times a day. She spent hours each day at the sink and her hands had become raw and bleeding. Her fear of contamination also required her to use numerous bottles of disinfectant and bars of soap. When the cost of these items exceeded her available income, she resorted to shoplifting them. Finally caught for shoplifting, she was taken to the police station where they tried unsuccessfully to fingerprint her. She had virtually scrubbed them off!

An interesting and illustrative sidelight of this case demonstrates the irrationality of compulsive acts and how some can be highly specific. Although this lady washed her hands almost continuously, she would not wash the rest of her body or bathe for weeks at a time. Her body odor was described as unbearable to others around her, but did not bother her at all.

The less frequent *controlling compulsions* (6 percent, Akhtar et al., 1975) take a different form but can be as intense and limiting as those of yielding. These are acts performed to allow the individual to control or to resist an obsessive urge without giving in to it. In other cases the act serves to prevent some other incident from occurring (at least in the person's mind). In many cases, these are like superstitious rituals. An example of a preventive type of controlling compulsion was described by Cammer (1976). This concerned a lady who felt compelled to touch her venetian blinds four times and then all her pieces of art five times. Her reason for this touching was that it protected her brother from harm. The fact that he always came home safely proved to her that the touching-ritual worked. She also admitted that if she did not go through with the ritual, she started to stutter.

Another way of categorizing compulsions is by separating them according to the form of the act itself: what the patient does. Two basic types include the majority of cases: *checkers* and *cleaners*.

The lady described above who compulsively washed her hands was an example of a cleaner. However, not all cleaners are as specific as she, nor is the cleaning restricted to washing oneself. Also, as noted previously, cleaning compulsions typically involve obsessive fears of dirt and disease. And like the phobias, compulsive cleaners will go to great lengths to avoid becoming contaminated. Since complete avoidance of contact with other parts of the environment and other people is virtually impossible, the cleaner will never successfully avoid all "contamination." This then seems to impel them to attempt to restore themselves, or the objects or persons with which they are concerned, to a state of cleanliness (Rachman & Hodgson, 1980). In some of the more extreme cases, the attempted avoidance of potential contaminants and the continuous cleaning can be as debilitating as agoraphobia, leaving the person housebound. Even worse than with agoraphobia, however, is that the person has no really safe places; dirt and germs are carried in the very air.

Illustrative of such restriction is the following situation described by Rachman and Hodges (1980): "A 38 year old mother of one child had been obsessed by a fear of contamination for over 20 years. Her concern with the possibility of being infected by germs resulted in washing and cleaning rituals that invaded all aspects of her life. Her child was restrained in one room which was kept entirely germ free. She opened and closed all doors with her feet in order to avoid contaminating her hands" (p.111).

Compulsive checking involves stereotyped acts carried out with the expressed purpose, on the part of the checker, of ensuring the safety, security, or well-being of oneself, others, or possessions, or to verify the accuracy or security of situations or information (Rachman & Hodgson, 1980). Such checking rituals are seen as preventive of some future or potential problem or disaster.

The clerk who checked for the nonexistent document and the lady who touched her venetian blinds four times were examples of compulsive checkers. Other common checking compulsions involve checking with the police or the newspaper after driving to ensure that they had not caused an accident, and checking repeatedly all windows, water and gas taps, light switches, electric plugs, and doors for hours before retiring each night. For many checkers and cleaners, though not all, the carrying out of the rituals tend to reduce a felt discomfort and/or anxiety. However, the emotional reduction is not long lasting, as the discomfort will recur later.

Compulsive Slowness.   Another variant of compulsive behavior is compulsive slowness, or, as it has been termed by Rachman and Hodgson (1980), *primary obsessive slowness.* This rare condition is characterized by the individual taking virtually hours to complete relatively simple tasks, such as getting dressed, washing, and putting things away. Because it takes the better part of a whole day to prepare to leave home, these persons are largely nonfunctional.

Marks (1978) describes a typical patient of his who would begin preparation for his doctor's appointment the day before it was scheduled. He needed this time because it took 5 hours to get ready. Similarly, another patient described by Rachman and Hodgson (1978) would have to start his preparation to leave at 3 or 4 o'clock in the morning in order to arrive at work by 10 o'clock. Since preparation of a meal took so long, he ate at a restaurant. About 9 o'clock in the evening he would begin preparation for bed which he would finally complete around midnight.

These agonizingly slow processess obviously take most of the waking hours, leaving no time for other pursuits such as employment. Such compulsively slow behavior appears similar to the other compulsions, but is also different in several ways. Although the person persists at tasks, it is not typically accompanied by obsessive thoughts. Nor when prompted or pushed to hurry is there the felt anxiety or discomfort experienced by checkers and cleaners when their routines are interrupted.

Also, unlike other compulsive individuals, they are hard-pressed to give reasons for their slowness, such as fears or obsessive urges. It appears to be more of a generalized meticulousness and concern with getting things just right (Rachman & Hodgeson, 1980). Although the bulk of their lives are taken up with this slow, meticulous behavior, they can talk, walk, and eat at a normal pace. Due to these differences from other compulsives, there is some question whether they should be classified as obsessive-compulsive at all (Rachman & Hodgeson, 1980).

Obsessions and compulsions of the proportions described here are apparently relatively rare. Emmelkamp (1982) suggests that the general population prevalence is only .05 percent. However, the more recent national survey puts the prevalence between 2 and 3 percent (Robins et al., 1984). This makes them still the least common of the anxiety disorders.

Onset of the obsessive-compulsive disorders can occur at most any age, but most start in late adolescence and early adulthood. The typical onset is in the early twenties and by age thirty, nearly three-fourths have developed their symptoms.

Overall, males are as likely as females to develop obsessive-compulsive disorders. However, the type of disorder developed may be sex-related. Rachman and his colleagues found that while males and females are equally distributed among compulsive checkers, females clearly predominated among cleaners (Emmelkamp, 1982; Rachman & Hodgson, 1980). This correlation, according to Rachman, supports his view that cleaning compulsions are very similar to phobias, where females also are overrepresented.

Emmelkamp (1982) goes further to explain this preponderance of female cleaners. He believes that, since in our Western culture females are typically responsible for maintaining the household, and therefore cleaning, they would be more likely to develop cleaning compulsions, an overreaction to their domain of responsibility. On the other hand, behaviors associated with checking should have no particular sex-role relatedness and, accordingly, there is no sex difference in prevalence of checkers.

Due to the relative rarity of the obsessive-compulsive disorders, sufficient study has not yet been done to delineate clearly the full reasons behind these differences.

ANXIETY DISORDERS OF CHILDHOOD AND ADOLESCENCE

This final category of anxiety disorders focuses on children and adolescents. Although these younger age groups can experience the other disorders discussed, the three types to be described here are specific to children. However, as we will see, they clearly have variants similar or identical to those found with adults. The specific categories include: *Overanxious Disorder, Separation Anxiety Disorder,* and *Avoidant Disorder.* Also included with these categories is a description of school phobia, or as it is sometimes called, school refusal.

These categories are based on the diagnostic classification system of DSM-III and are not necessarily accepted by all research workers as being discrete entities (e.g., Morris & Kratcohwill, 1982). Indeed, early reliability studies investigating interrater agreement on classifying children into these categories was quite low, ranging from .25 to .44 (APA, 1980).

Overanxious Disorder

The overanxious child or adolescent is characterized by chronic and excessive worry and fearful behavior. Although similar in many ways to phobias, the anxiety or fear expressed is not focused on any specific object or situation nor is it a specific reaction to some life changes or events. The child will typically worry about future events, exams, being injured, other children, or chores to be done. There is often an element of perfectionist tendencies, obsessional self-doubts, conformity and approval-seeking from others, along with concern over what others think of them. This chronic worry results in continuous states of ANS activation including feelings of a lump in the throat, headache, stomachache, nausea, "nerves," and difficulty falling asleep. Behaviorally, the child may exhibit nervous habits such as nail biting, restlessness, and hair pulling.

This condition then has features similar to generalized anxiety disorder and social phobia. It is suggested that if this overanxiousness persists into adulthood, that it may become either GAD or social phobia (APA, 1980). Although figures are not available concerning the overall prevalence of this disorder, it is apparently more common among boys than girls (APA, 1980).

Avoidant Disorder

Avoidant disorder in children involves persistent shrinking from contact with strangers to the extent that it impairs social functioning and peer relations. When confronting a stranger the child becomes essentially mute or inarticulate. Such children typically lack self-confidence and social assertiveness and express a great desire for attention and affection from family members.

Fear of strangers is of course a normal part of development that most young children go through. However, in most cases, this normal fear begins during the first year of life, having an average onset of about eight months of age (McCandless & Trotter, 1977). Typically it begins to diminish by the end of the first year and, for most, is gone by the second year of age. This diagnosis is only considered after the intense fear of strangers has persisted well past the normal developmental phase (e.g. two and one-half years) and the avoidance is interfering with the child's social development and peer relations. Data are unavailable on prevalence and sex distribution of avoidant disorder. In adulthood, if the condition has persisted for years it may be considered in another category of avoidant personality disorder, or social phobia, whichever appears to apply.

Separation Anxiety Disorder

Separation anxiety, like the two previous categories of childhood and adolescent anxiety disorder, is in some degree a part of many children's normal developmental experiences. It becomes classified as a disorder when it is severe and persists beyond what is expected for a child's normal developmental level. Separation anxiety is characterized by excessive anxiety to the point of panic when separated from parents or parent figures, from home or familiar surroundings (APA, 1980).

The child will typically refuse to visit or stay overnight with friends, run errands, attend camps or school. This latter situation pertaining to school has been referred to as school refusal or school phobia and will be described separately.

When anticipating being separated, the child typically clings to the parents, and complains of numerous physical symptoms such as headache, stomachache, and nausea. When children with separation anxiety are separated from parents, they become preoccupied with obsessive worries and fears of accidents that might befall themselves or their parents.

This generalized anxiety with its cognitive (worry), behavioral (clinging and refusal) and physiological (aches and pains) manifestations appears to be a form of phobia: a phobia of being left, or of illness or injury. Further, these children often have a variety of other fears, as of animals, monsters in the night, of being kidnapped and of dying. In sum, it is a rather generalized phobic reaction to many situations, particularly involving being separated. As such it is akin to adult manifestations of agoraphobia. Consequently, this may result in somewhat of a diagnostic dilemma concerning whether to call it a phobic disorder or separation anxiety disorder.

Although prevalence figures are not available, separation anxiety disorder is apparently equally distributed among boys and girls (APA, 1980).

As noted, when the child becomes fearful of separation, refusal to go to school is typically involved as well. When this occurs, such children have been called school phobic. However, often the school refusal is part of the larger picture of separation anxiety. That is, it is not school that they fear, but separation from parents. In keeping with recommendations of DSM-III, it would seem more appropriate to retain the term school phobia for those cases in which the anxiety and fear reactions occur due to school per se. When school refusal is due to fear of being separated more generally, separation anxiety is the more appropriate term. The school refusal child will attempt to avoid school by convincing the parents that he or she is ill, and should be allowed to stay home. Complaints typically include stomachache, headache, and not feeling well. The anticipatory anxiety generated by the thought of having to go to school may in fact cause the child to have a stomachache, or even to vomit, which of course is rather convincing to the parent.

Physical complaints are typically most pronounced in the morning (before school). If allowed to stay home, the child will typically feel better by early afternoon, after the threat has passed (Weiner, 1982). However, it will return the next morning, or the next school day.

As with other phobias, school phobia does not go away with reassurance nor with minor changes in the school environment. Although school phobia can begin at virtually any grade level, including college, it appears to peak during periods of major transitions such as when first beginning school (five to eight years of age) and into junior high or high school (eleven to fourteen years of age) (Weiner, 1982).

Although prevalence rates are difficult to interpret due to the possible confusion with separation anxiety, school phobia has been estimated to involve between 1 and 2 percent of school-aged children (Weiner, 1982). Like separation anxiety, males and females are equally represented.

RELIABILITY OF ANXIETY DIAGNOSIS

In Chapter 3, the concept of reliability was introduced as a measure of the consistency with which observations or test scores can be made. Since diagnosis involves obtaining information about persons, evaluating that information relative to diagnostic criteria for specific categories of disorders and assigning the person a diagnosis, reliability of this process is also important. The type of reliability appropriate to diagnosis is inter-rater reliability. The typical procedure for determining diagnostic reliability is for two diagnosticians to evaluate independently a group of individuals. A reliability index is then calculated representing the percentage of cases in which the two diagnosticians agreed on the diagnoses. The specific measures used are either a percentage agreement or a type of correlation coefficient called the *Kappa coefficient* which represents the percent agreement but also includes a correction factor for chance agreements.

Since the current diagnostic system on which the classifications described here are based (i.e., DSM-III) is relatively new, few reliability studies are yet available. However, those figures which are published suggest that different diagnosticians can come to good agreement on anxiety disorder diagnoses. The reliability figures (*Kappa*) classifying individuals into the general category of anxiety disorders as opposed to other diagnoses, have been reported of .72 (APA, 1980) and .68 (Di Nardo et al., 1983). A *Kappa* of .70 or greater is generally considered to be satisfactory. Therefore, it appears that diagnosticians can achieve fair inter-rater agreement in categorizing patients as having anxiety disorder.

However, when it comes to determining into which subcategory of anxiety disorder an individual is to be assigned, there is considerable variability in agreement. In the study by Di Nardo et al. (1983) the *Kappa* figure for agoraphobia was quite high (.85), as it was for social phobia (.77) and panic disorder (.69). Other categories faired somewhat less well: obsessive-compulsive was .66; generalized anxiety disorder .47.

In general, most of these reliability figures are quite acceptable. However, we must be aware that they are less than perfect. The major reason found for those disagreements that did occur was that while the two raters identified the same clinical features or symptoms, they disagreed on just how to weight them (Di Naro et al., 1983). This often resulted from a given individual displaying characteristics of more than one disorder (e.g., phobia and obsessive-compulsive). The source of disagreement then became which of the two diagnoses to assign as primary.

Perhaps the most important finding was that for the most part these patients were consistently classified, even though in some cases there was disagreement on primary versus secondary diagnoses. To the extent that accurate diagnosis is necessary for determining the appropriate treatment, reliability becomes a critical issue. As will be seen in the following chapter, the treatment procedures can be adapted to several of the anxiety disorders. Most psychologically based procedures focus on observed symptoms rather than on diagnostic categories per se.

SUMMARY

Fear and anxiety of sufficient intensity to meet criteria for diagnosis as anxiety disorders affect a significant proportion of the general population. Large-scale surveys suggest that greater than 10 percent of the US population suffers from one or another form of anxiety disorder, while another 10 percent shows symptoms of high distress.

Phobias are among the more prevalent of the anxiety disorders. Simple phobias included fears of animals, fears of natural phenomena such as thunder and lightning, and fears of blood, injury, or illness. This latter group was notable in the distinctly different response from other phobias. Rather than the usual

SNS activation, blood phobics respond with an initial heart rate and blood pressure increase, followed quickly by a rapid decrease which often results in fainting.

Social phobia was the second class of phobias and it was noted that there was a strong element of concern with social evaluation—how others might see them. The various forms of social phobia included fear of public speaking, writing in public, using public restrooms, and meeting strangers. Agoraphobia was seen as the most restrictive phobia. Often beginning with a panic attack, the person begins to anticipate having another one and therefore avoids situations in which they might occur. Due to the fear and anticipation of having another panic attack, the person eventually becomes housebound.

Anxiety states include panic disorder, generalized anxiety disorder, and obsessive-compulsive disorder. Panic disorder involves recurrent panic attacks with intense SNS activity and feelings that something horrible is about to happen. Unlike phobias, these panic attacks do not occur in a predictable fashion nor in the presence of specific situations.

Generalized anxiety disorder is characterized by an intense chronic state of tension and anxiety. The person does not experience the severe panic attacks as in panic disorder and the anxiety is not clearly attached to specific stimuli. It is referred to as free-floating anxiety.

Obsessive-compulsive disorder involves either obsessions, intrusive thoughts, images or urges, or compulsions, repetitive, ritualistic, and uncontrollable acts. Most often, both obsessions and compulsions occur together, with the obsession leading to the compulsive act.

Anxiety disorders of children and adolescents include over-anxious disorder in which the child is chronically worrying and fearful. In some ways it appears to be similar to generalized anxiety disorder in adults.

In avoidant disorder, the child persistently shrinks from contacts with persons outside the immediate family and therefore is usually deprived of social and peer relations.

Children with separation anxiety disorder become panicky when separated from parents or familiar places. This often involves school refusal in which the child develops physical symptoms such as headache or stomachache to avoid going to school. This was differentiated from school phobia, a term better reserved for when it is school itself that is the object of fear rather than separation from home.

Reliability of anxiety disorder diagnoses was reviewed and the available figures showed that there is a good inter-rater agreement for most diagnostic categories. Reliability of diagnosis for agoraphobia was quite high while that for generalized anxiety disorder was relatively low.

Chapter 5

TREATMENT OF THE ANXIETY DISORDERS

Among the anxiety disorders are some of the most treatable of all psychiatric or psychological conditions. The phobias and particularly the specific phobias can be successfully treated in the vast majority of cases. Some reports show up to 100 percent treatment effectiveness (e.g., Bandura, Blanchard, & Ritter, 1969). Other anxiety-based disorders, however, are more refractory. For example, although numerous successful treatments of obsessive-compulsive disorders have been reported, many others have not yielded to current treatment methods (Rachman & Hodgson, 1980).

In this chapter I will describe some of the most effective psychological procedures used for treating the anxiety disorders, generically referred to as *Behavior Therapy*. More recently, with the increasing recognition of the role played by cognitive processes, this term has been expanded to *Cognitive-Behavior Therapy* or Cognitive-Behavior Modification.

The treatment procedures to be described are all aimed at uncoupling the ties between situations and the automatic fear or anxiety responses. These procedures attempt to accomplish this uncoupling by focusing on changing the three main response components. Although the several procedures have the same goal of reducing the anxiety or fear, they have different emphases. Some focus on attempting directly to reduce the physiological component by training in relaxation. Others focus first on eliminating the avoidance component by ensuring that the individual is exposed to the anxiety-provoking situation without escaping. Other approaches focus on the cognitive component. These approaches attempt to restructure or change anxiety-provoking thoughts and self-statements.

It should also be noted that most of the procedures to be described focus on alleviating the irrational and debilitating fear or anxiety responses, those which have little or no rational basis, such as the phobias. It would make little sense to attempt to eliminate all fear responding! And, even if it could be done, it would be highly maladaptive for a person not to respond with some fear to realistic dangers.

A general goal of these procedures is to instill in unduly fearful and anxious persons a sense of confidence that they can cope with the situation and develop a feeling of personal control over the responsiveness. After describing the various treatments, I will return to this issue in a discussion of possible unifying concepts.

TREATMENT PROCEDURES

Systematic Desensitization

Systematic Desensitization (SD) was the first of the behavior therapy procedures found effective in treating anxiety-based disorders. Developed by Joseph Wolpe (1958), SD has been validated in literally hundreds of experimental investigations (see Rimm & Masters, 1979; Rachman & Wilson, 1980). Although evidence of effectiveness has been demonstrated for almost all anxiety disorders, it appears to be most fruitfully applied to the phobias (Rachman & Wilson, 1980). Consequently, in the following discussions of this technique, I will use phobias as the prototypic example.

Wolpe theorized that neurotic disorders (i.e., anxiety-based) largely consist of maladaptive anxiety responses being tied to environmental events (objects or situations) through the process of classical conditioning (Wolpe, 1958). The task of treatment then becomes one of breaking the link between the stimulus and the anxiety response and/or substituting a new or more adaptive response to the stimulus. To describe this process Wolpe (1973) formulated what he called the principle of *Reciprocal Inhibition* which states: "If a response inhibiting anxiety can be made to occur in the presence of anxiety-evoking stimuli, it will weaken the bond between these stimuli and anxiety" (p. 17).

A number of responses have been shown to serve this purpose of inhibiting the anxiety response. Among those used are: eating, sexual stimulation, assertive behavior (for social anxiety) and relaxation (Wolpe, 1958; 1973). The one found most useful and versatile and hence most commonly used is relaxation.

The basic goal of SD is to enable the fearful or anxious person to relax in the presence of the anxiety-provoking stimuli. This is done in a stepwise fashion to facilitate the reciprocal inhibition process. The treatment begins by first training the person in deep muscle relaxation. Then, while deeply relaxed, the person imagines various scenes associated with the object or situation which elicits the fear reaction. Each of the steps and processes involved will be described in greater detail.

Relaxation Training.   There are many effective ways to attain a state of relaxation and for the purposes of SD it makes little difference which is used. However, the method most frequently used is one which Wolpe (1958) patterned after the Progressive Relaxation Training of Jacobson (1938). The training proceeds by having the person first tense specific muscle groups, one at a time. While tensing the forearm, for example, the person is asked to focus on the sensations of tenseness so they become very familiar. Then after 5 to 7 seconds, the arm is relaxed and the contrast between tension and relaxation is noticed. The alternate tensing-relaxing cycle allows the muscles a kind of running start to relaxing. Once one set of muscles has begun relaxing, it is allowed to continue to relax and another is introduced to the same sequence of tension-relaxation until the whole body is relaxed (see Bernstein & Borkovec, 1974, for a detailed step-by-step training program).

Although this or any other relaxation procedure is an integral part of SD, deep muscle relaxation is highly therapeutic in itself. There is ample evidence that such relaxation, even though directed at the muscles, results in overall diminutions in SNS arousal, such as lowered blood pressure, pulse rate, skin conductance, and respiration. Typically accompanying the physical relaxation is a calming of one's subjective state as well. However, there are some individuals in whom relaxation training causes subjective discomfort (Borkovec, 1984). An adequate level of relaxation can usually be achieved after a couple of weeks of training with daily practice.

The Anxiety Hierarchy.   The next step in SD is the construction of a list of situations that cause the person to become anxious or fearful. This list is then graded in terms of the degree to which each situation causes anxiety. The list of situations, ranked in order of anxiety arousal, is called the anxiety hierarchy. These are situations to be imagined later. An example of an anxiety hierarchy constructed for a person fearful of dentistry is shown in Table 5.1.

Table 5.1
Anxiety Hierarchy for Dental Phobia

Anxiety-Provoking Situation	SUD (0-100)
1. Being reminded you need a dental appointment	20
2. Calling for an appointment	25
3. Seeing the calendar that shows only 1 day left before appointment	32
4. Driving to the dentist's office	39
5. Entering the waiting room	45
6. Hearing the drill sounds while in the waiting room	54
7. Being taken into the dental chair	60
8. Seeing the dentist walk in	68
9. Dentist uses explorer (probe) to examine your teeth	73
10. Feeling vibrations from the drill on your tooth	80
11. Seeing the local anesthetic syringe	90
12. Dentist begins injection	95

The procedure for grading the hierarchy can be facilitated by having the person assign to each situation a number from 0 to 100 to represent the amount of anxiety it causes. These numbers are referred to as *Subjective Units of Disturbance* (SUDS) (Wolpe & Lazarus, 1966). According to Wolpe (1973) there should be no more than about 10 SUDS between adjacent items on the hierarchy. That is, there should not be a large jump in anxiety-provoking potential from one item to the next. Further details concerning development and characteristics of anxiety hierarchies with numerous examples can be found in books by Wolpe (1973) and Rimm and Masters (1979).

Desensitization Procedure.   Once the fearful person has attained skill in deep muscle relaxation and the hierarchy, or hierarchies if more than one is needed, are constructed, the actual procedure can commence. As noted previously, the task is to enable the person to imagine the anxiety-provoking situations from the hierarchy while maintaining relaxation. This is accomplished by first having the subject deeply relax. Then the therapist begins by presenting the least anxiety-provoking scene from the hierarchy for the subject to imagine. For example, from the hierarchy in Table 5.1 it might be "Imagine opening a magazine and seeing the word 'dentist'." If the person then experiences any anxiety, he or she is instructed to signal the therapist, usually by raising a finger. At the signal of felt anxiety the subject is instructed to stop imagining the word "dentist" and attempt to regain the full state of relaxation. Usually, a neutral or very pleasant scene, determined in advance, such as lying on the beach in the warm sun, is used at this point to facilitate relaxing and to give the subject something peaceful to think about. Once relaxation is regained, the anxiety scene is presented again. Each successive presentation typically results in a reduction in anxiety until the subject is able to remain completely relaxed while visualizing the scene. At this point, the second item is presented and the process is repeated for each item until the subject masters the entire hierarchy with no signs of anxiety.

The critical issue here is not just that the subject is able to imagine the scenes without anxiety; but rather, it is that the lack of anxiety response from imagining carries over to real life confrontations with the actual feared situations. This carryover or response generalization does indeed occur (Wolpe, 1958; Lang & Lazovik, 1963).

The exact mechanism by which the desensitization process works is still a matter of some theoretical controversy. Wolpe (1973) contends that it is essentially a counterconditioning process in which relaxing in the imaginal presence of the fear stimuli inhibits the fear or anxiety response. With repeated pairings of relaxation with the previous fear-provoking stimuli, the relaxation response becomes conditioned to those stimuli, i.e., counterconditioning.

Others have proposed that the anxiety-reducing effects of SD are due to an extinction process. That is, the presentation of conditioned stimuli (the feared situation) is made without experiencing the unconditioned stimuli (that which is frightening or aversive). For example, if one were shown a red light, followed by an electric shock, soon the light would become a conditioned stimulus and would cause an anticipatory anxiety response. However, if the light were then repeatedly presented without shock, the anxiety response would eventually diminish and disappear or be extinguished. Although the matter of whether the effectiveness of SD is a result of counterconditioning, extinction, or of neither or both, is unclear, it *is* clear that the process is highly effective for treating fear and anxiety problems.

Variations on the Desensitization Procedures

A number of variations of the systematic desensitization procedure have been investigated. These studies have extended the possible uses and efficiency of SD and have also called into question the need for some of the procedures originally described by Wolpe (1958). One of the first variations introduced was to examine the effectiveness of SD applied to *groups* of fearful persons, all with a common fear or phobia. Following Lazarus' (1961) first demonstration of group desensitization, a number of other investigators found the procedure as effective as when applied individually (e.g., Ihli & Garlington, 1969, for test anxiety; Paul & Shannon, 1966, for social anxiety; Sue, 1975, for snake phobia; and Rachman, 1966, for spider phobia).

A second variation was the use of *automated* desensitization in which the therapist's presence was not needed (Lang et al., 1966). After being initially introduced to the procedure by the therapist, the subject was given relaxation instructions from a prerecorded audio tape recorder. The anxiety hierarchy scenes were also presented on tape. The tape was programmed so that the subject could control which scene was presented, terminate the scene if anxiety was felt, and reset it to repeat scenes. Among the advantages of this type of automated procedure are minimal therapist time required once the procedure is set up, and availability for subjects to conduct their own treatment at home (e.g., Migler & Wolpe, 1967). In a highly innovative study, Donner and Guerney (1969) found automated group desensitization to be highly effective as well as efficient in diminishing fears.

Another variation on the standard desensitization procedures was introduced by Goldfried (1971). Goldfried conceptualized the desensitization process as one in which the subject learns to exercise self-control over his or her anxiety response in the presence of anxiety-provoking stimuli. In this variation subjects are not instructed to stop visualizing scenes once anxiety is experienced. Rather, they are instructed to continue to imagine the scene and attempt to relax away the tension experienced. By this process, the subjects gain practice in actively controlling and managing their own fear reactions.

Goldfried's conceptualization of SD also has theoretical implications. He suggests that the critical process is not just a passive counterconditioning or extinction but rather an active process of learning to control one's own reaction. Consequently, the attention paid to the graded anxiety hierarchy is seen as less important than the general practice in controlling one's anxiety by using relaxation in any situation.

In vivo desensitization is another variation on the traditional systematic desensitization procedure. In in vivo desensitization, the subject confronts the feared situation live or directly, rather than in imagined scenes. Depending on the nature of the stimuli, this direct confrontation can occur in the consulting office or the individual can be taken to the situation. The same SD procedure can be used: becoming relaxed, viewing or experiencing the situation until anxiety is felt, and then returning to relaxation. This in vivo exposure was also recommended by Goldfried (1971) as a situation in which self-control of anxiety could be practiced.

Wolpe (1973) recommends the in vivo approach particularly for subjects who are unable clearly to imagine their feared situation and/or for whom visualization does not generate sufficient anxiety to be realistic. In vivo desensitization has been shown to be at least as effective as imagined (e.g., Cooke, 1966) and when used in conjunction with the imaginal procedures, facilitates the desensitization process (e.g., Garfield et al., 1967).

The effectiveness of SD and its variants for reducing maladaptive fear and anxiety responses has been clearly demonstrated (see Rachman & Wilson, 1980; McGlynn & Mealia, 1982). However, the mechanism responsible for the anxiety reduction is unclear and the necessity for including some of the procedures described by Wolpe (1958) has been called into question. For example, it has been shown that presenting the hierarchy items in ascending order of anxiety provocation (i.e., from lowest to highest) may be unnecessary, at least for mild and moderate fears (e.g., Richardson & Suinn, 1973). Others have shown that anxiety reduction can be achieved by presenting the hierarchy scenes without relaxation training (e.g., Miller & Nawas, 1970). However, Schubot (1966) did find that for extremely phobic individuals, relaxation was necessary.

One element of the SD procedure, however, does seem essential: systematic exposure. Whether live or imagined, some exposure to the anxiety-provoking stimuli without the individual experiencing aversive or catastrophic consequences appears to be the common denominator of these treatments (O'Leary & Wilson, 1975). This element of nonreinforced exposure to feared stimuli is the basis for another set of anxiety reduction treatment procedures: the exposure techniques.

The Exposure Treatments

In contrast to SD, the exposure treatments are designed to generate high levels of anxiety or fear response in the presence of eliciting stimuli. Whether conducted in imagination or in vivo, the subject is exposed to his or her anxiety-provoking situation without escape. The subject experiences anxiety until it abates.

The theory supporting the effects of the exposure techniques is that repeated prolonged exposure to eliciting stimuli results in extinction of the conditioned fear or anxiety response. The process of extinction of fear responses was described in the previous section as an alternate explanation for the effect of SD. Repeated exposure to the CS without experiencing anticipated negative consequences leads to a reduction and eventual elimination of the CR. For example, an individual may have become phobic of dogs after having been attacked and bitten by one as a child. To treat this phobia with exposure, the person would be exposed to dogs which would elicit considerable anxiety. However, repeated exposure to the dogs, without being bitten again (UCS) would result in the extinction of the conditioned anxiety response.

In addition to the extinction of the CR another process contributes to the effectiveness of the exposure techniques. It has been noted that avoidance of the feared situation prevents extinction from occurring and maintains the fear. Escape or avoidance behavior was said to be reinforced because it removes one from an unpleasant situation. The exposure techniques also eliminate this component, extinguishing both the conditioned response and the avoidance behavior.

In this section I will describe three variants of the exposure techniques, all of which are structured to elicit anxiety or fear to facilitate extinction.

Implosive Therapy is an imaginal procedure for generating high levels of anxiety (Stampfl & Levis, 1967). In an attempt to maximize the anxiety during treatment, the therapist presents to the subject in a dramatic and exaggerated fashion images or scenes associated with his or her fear. The subject is encouraged to participate by getting into the role of experiencing the stimuli and the fear or anxiety reactions to the fullest. In addition to the typical cues that elicit the response (i.e., the specific object or situation feared) other "hypothesized cues" are incorporated as well. These hypothesized cues are based on themes derived from psychoanalytic theory (Freudian) which theoretically might be associated with fears and anxieties, but which have been repressed. The themes typically incorporated include hostilities and anger, feelings of being punished, and sexual and oral content (Stampfl & Levis, 1967). It is hypothesized that feelings associated with these themes are tied to the current problem, but since they are painful, they have been repressed from consciousness. However, since they may be tied to external stimuli and reactions to those stimuli, they must be brought out as well so the emotional content can be extinguished.

This technique as described by Stampfl represents an integration of psychoanalytic theory and behavior theory. However, the inclusion of the hypothesized psychodynamic material into the scenes has not been used by most researchers and may not be critical for the technique to be effective (Prochaska, 1971). Although a number of case and research reports indicate that implosive therapy can be effective in reducing fears (e.g., Hogan & Kirchner, 1967), the overall effectiveness of the technique has been questioned (e.g., Rimm & Masters, 1979).

Flooding also involves exposing the subject to the anxiety provoking stimuli. The exposure can be accomplished either through imaginal scenes or by direct, live contact with the anxiety-eliciting stimuli while preventing escape.

In recent years, flooding has been subjected to increasing research and application. It and its variants have been found to be effective in treating a wide variety of anxiety disorders including simple phobias, agoraphobia (Stern & Marks, 1973), generalized anxiety disorder (Girodo, 1974) and obsessive-compulsive disorders (Rachman & Hodgson, 1980). Indeed, flooding appears to be emerging as the treatment of choice in some of the more complex anxiety disorders such as agoraphobia and obsessive-compulsive disorders.

Because of increasing use and apparent efficacy of the flooding approach, I will describe some of the procedural variations found to contribute to its effectiveness. First, it has been generally determined that exposure sessions in excess of one to two hours are superior to a series of shorter sessions (e.g., Rachman & Wilson, 1980; Stern & Marks, 1973). In fact, short sessions of flooding, under 30 or 40 minutes, may result in increased anxiety. Consistent with the extinction theory, several studies have shown that during exposure, anxiety rises, peaks, then gradually diminishes. Foa and Chambless (1978) found this pattern with agoraphobics and obsessive-compulsives. For the agoraphobics, SUDS ratings of anxiety peaked at about 45 minutes into the session before tailing off. Had the sessions lasted only 45 minutes or less, the subjects would have been left in a heightened state of anxiety.

A second variation concerns the differential effectiveness of in vivo versus imaginal exposure. Although both forms have been found to be effective, most of the research shows the superiority of flooding in vivo, in which the subject directly confronts the anxiety-provoking situation (Stern & Marks, 1973; Emmelkamp & Wessels, 1975).

With in vivo flooding, the subject is taken directly to the situation that is feared. For example, with agoraphobia in which in vivo flooding is found quite effective, subjects may be directed to leave their house or the therapist's office and begin walking for a specified time or distance. Often they are assisted or accompanied by a therapist. In some situations, this type of exposure can be done effectively with groups as well (Hafner & Marks, 1976).

For some phobics, the anxiety and avoidance response may be so severe that they are unable initially to tolerate live exposure. In these cases, a few sessions of imaginal exposure might reduce their anxiety sufficiently to enable them to tolerate the live exposure.

A third procedure which appears to facilitate progress is self-directed practice between actual flooding sessions. This addition to the more formal sessions increases the amount of exposure and places subjects in a practice situation which they personally control (Mathews et al., 1977; Emmelkamp, 1982).

Another variant related to self-directed practice is *graduated exposure* in which the subject confronts the feared situation until considerable anxiety is experienced. The subject then retrenches and later tries to increase the time spent in exposure. This graduated, self-directed exposure appears to be at least as effective as intense immersion in the situation (Emmelkamp, 1982) and also offers the subject the sense of being more in control. The reader might note that this graduated exposure, controlled by the subject is quite similar to in vivo desensitization mentioned in the previous section.

Response Prevention is another variation of the exposure techniques. Used with obsessive-compulsive disorders, response prevention entails preventing the obsessive-compulsive subject from engaging in his or her compulsive ritual while in the presence of the stimuli that typically generate the urge and the behavior (e.g., Rachman & Hodgson, 1980). Response prevention, like exposure in general, typically results initially in intense anxiety, which in many cases precedes the compulsive ritual.

The anxiety generated from being exposed to the ritual inducing stimuli (e.g., dirt) eventually subsides as does the urge to perform the ritual. Response prevention and exposure are typically used together as a treatment package. However, many obsessive-compulsive disorders are exceedingly difficult to treat and these procedures are not universally successful when applied by themselves (Emmelkamp, 1982; Rachman & Hodgson, 1980). Another component of treatment found to be highly successful with fears and phobias, *modeling,* appears to add significantly to the overall treatment effectiveness (Rachman & Hodgson, 1980).

The Modeling Treatments

Observing a behavior of others is one of the primary means by which we learn. As noted in Chapter 2, fears can be acquired vicariously by watching others undergo frightening or traumatic events. Conversely, fear can be reduced by modeling or observing someone else perform a feared act or interact with an anxiety-provoking object. Fear reduction by observing others perform a feared act appears to operate primarily through the process of vicarious extinction, similar to the effects seen in the exposure treatments. However, several other elements may be operating as well to contribute to the effectiveness of modeling. Through observing others, one can obtain knowledge and information about the feared object and actually see what it is like. Further, the observer can see how to enact the required fearless behavior which had been previously prevented by avoidance.

As with the other fear and anxiety treatments, there are several variants of the modeling procedures and several factors that enhance their effectiveness. The modeling can be conducted in symbolic form or live. In *Symbolic Modeling* the model is presented on film or videotape. The observer (subject) simply views the film in which the model is depicted engaging in the feared actions. *Live Modeling* proceeds the same way except that the modeling is done in person. Although symbolic modeling could be most economical in time (not requiring another person always to be present), live modeling is generally considered more effective (Bandura, 1969).

Another dimension that facilitates the effectiveness of modeling is the perceived similarity of the model. That is, the greater the similarity that the fearful observer perceives between him or herself and the model, the more the observer can identify with the model and hence the greater the fear reduction (Bandura, 1969).

The use of multiple, as opposed to single, models also appears to enhance the overall effectiveness of modeling for fear reduction (Bandura & Menlove, 1968). With several models demonstrating the feared behavior, there is greater likelihood that at least one of the models will be perceived as similar to the observer. Multiple models also show the observer that not just one person can do it but several can.

The model's manner of dealing with the feared situation also appears to make a difference. The most effective demeanor of the model is one in which initial apprehension is displayed. Then the model progressively copes more and more effectively (less fearfully) with the situation. This use of a *coping model* has been shown to be superior to a *mastery model* in which the model demonstrates from the outset total control and no fearful behavior at all (Meichenbaum, 1971; Kazdin, 1974). The use of a coping model may be more effective since the initial apprehension displayed and subsequent attempts to cope make the model appear more similar to the subject, i.e., fearful. This may enhance the perceived similarity between observer and model.

A variation in modeling procedure, related to coping models, is the use of graduated sequences. In *graduated modeling*, the scenes modeled are presented in a fashion similar to the anxiety hierarchy procedure from SD. Beginning with mildly anxiety-provoking scenes, successive scenes are graded to be progressively more and more threatening.

For the most effective fear reduction, a combination of the above elements should be included in the procedure: that is, use of a live model similar to the subject who is shown to cope progressively with increasingly threatening situations. However, in this type of modeling, the subject is essentially a passive observer. Although such passive modeling has been shown to be effective in reducing fears and phobias, a more active form, *Participant Modeling* is even more effective (Bandura, 1977).

Participant modeling involves direct interaction between the therapist, who also serves as model, and the subject. As a general procedure, the model-therapist demonstrates each step of the feared behavior, beginning with relatively simple situations. After each step is modeled, the therapist invites the subject to try it. If the subject is able to perform the task, the next step is demonstrated and the subject is then invited to try this second one, and so on. If the subject is not able to do it alone the therapist might model the step again before inviting the subject to try. For example, for a snake phobic, the first step might be simply to enter a room with a caged, harmless snake. Then, with encouragement and support the subject may follow the lead of the therapist model and approach the cage, perhaps only a few steps at a time. Next, the therapist might open the cage, touch, pet, and eventually pick up the snake, inviting the subject to follow suit. The reader will probably note here that this procedure is similar to and combines elements of in vivo desensitization, graded exposure, and modeling, along with strong doses of support and encouragement to enable the subject to perform the feared act.

In addition to the above procedures, *performance aids* are often used to assist subjects in approaching the feared situation. Using the snake phobic example, gloves might be used initially to encourage subjects to touch the snake. After the subject becomes comfortable touching the snake with gloves on, the performance aids are withdrawn and the subject is encouraged to use his or her bare hands.

Another procedure used to encourage performing the feared act is direct physical assistance by the therapist. Again using the snake example, this assistance could take the form of the subject placing his or her hand on the therapist's hand who then touches the snake. Once this is accomplished, the therapist's hand is progressively withdrawn until the subject is touching the snake alone.

These forms of assistance to subjects are readily adaptable to the treatment of other disorders. For example, in treating an agoraphobic person fearful of entering a department store, the therapist or anyone who can provide comfort or a feeling of security could initially accompany the subject into the store. Then, after the subject became reasonably comfortable with assistance, the helper could gradually increase the distance from the subject. Eventually the assistant might wait outside while the subject goes in alone.

All of these active procedures designed to get the subject into contact with the feared object or situation are enhanced by encouraging the subject to practice on his or her own between treatment sessions (Bandura, 1974, 1977). It would appear to be important to the subject at one level to have successfully performed a previously feared behavior with the assistance of a therapist. The self-directed practice then takes subjects a step closer to mastering their fears. It not only demonstrates that they can do it with assistance, but that they can also do it alone. This sense of mastery over a previously threatening situation is seen by some as the central cognitive process that underlies behavior change (e.g., Bandura, 1977; Emmelkamp 1982). I will return to this issue of underlying processes in behavior change after presenting a final approach to fear and anxiety treatment.

The Cognitive Restructuring Approaches

There are several related treatment methods that fall under the general classification of cognitive restructuring. All have a common aim of effecting change in a person's thinking or cognitive processes. The assumption underlying these approaches is that emotional disorders result, at least in part, from inappropriate, irrational or self-defeating thoughts or beliefs. In this sense cognitions are seen as mediating between environmental events (stimuli) and fear behavior (response).

This mediation approach can be generally described as an S-O-R model where the O stands for organism, or more specifically refers to the individual's thoughts and interpretations of the meaning of stimulus events. Depending on the interpretation of the event, or what the person thinks or says to himself, the response may be one of fear and avoidance or of no fear and/or approach. In other words, how one thinks determines how one acts. Therefore, treatment is directed toward altering thought processes that are related to the cause or maintenance of fear or anxiety responses.

As noted above, there are several approaches that generally follow this cognitive model. For example, one of the first such theorists was Albert Ellis (1962) who developed what he called Rational Emotive Therapy. Aaron Beck (1976) independently developed Cognitive Therapy. The term cognitive restructuring came from the writings of Arnold Lazarus (1971) in which he described some cognitive approaches to behavior change as adjuncts to earlier behavior therapy procedures such as SD. More recently, Donald Meichenbaum (e.g. 1979), drawing in part from these other approaches, developed a cognitive restructuring procedure called *Self-Instructional Training* (SIT). Meichenbaum's SIT will be described here as a prototype of the cognitive restructuring approaches since it incorporates elements of the other cognitive approaches along with the other treatments described earlier. This procedure might best be seen as a general approach to treatment rather than a specific technique.

Self-Instructional Training is described by Meichenbaum as a three-phase therapy process. The phases are: 1) providing information and assessment of the relation between thoughts and anxiety or fear response, 2) trying out new alternative ways of thinking that fit the person and the problem, and finally 3) actual practice in using new self-statements in the presence of the anxiety-provoking situation.

In Phase I, the subject is provided with a conceptualization of the problem. This enables the subject to realize the relation between thoughts, emotion, and behavior; that it is not really the situation that causes the fear, but what the persons think and say to themselves about the situation. For example, the agoraphobic person who becomes exceedingly anxious at the thought of being out alone may say: "What if I have a panic attack?" or "What if I faint?" This thinking in turn leads to anticipatory anxiety and to avoidance of going out.

The goal then of Phase I is to have the subject realize this connection between thinking catastrophizing thoughts and the self-defeating anxiety they elicit. This may be done initially by having the person simply imagine him or herself in this situation and attend to the thoughts or self-statements that occur and the resulting anxiety. Also, homework assignments may be given, such as having subjects monitor and record thoughts and feelings they experience between sessions and note the relationship between them. Once the subject is able clearly to see the connection between his or her thinking processes and how they affect behavior, the next phase can be introduced.

Phase II involves developing and testing new things to do and to think that can prevent and/or counter the fear and anxiety responses. These new things would include learning relaxation techniques that could be used to help one prepare for and cope with an anxiety-provoking situation. Also, new self-statements and thoughts about situations could be tried and rehearsed. Here, Meichenbaum introduces another procedure that he calls *Stress-Inoculation Training*. In stress inoculation, the subjects develop statements to say to themselves prior to meeting the stressor such as "no negative thoughts, worry won't help," "just think about what you have to do." Then when actually in the situation, another set of self-statements can be used to keep the person on task and use coping skills: "take this one step at a time," "take a deep breath and begin relaxing," "you can do it, just hang on." These are designed to keep the person on task and remind him or her what to do. As the fear begins to develop the person then might say "it is only fear, it won't really hurt you," "let it come but keep it manageable."

Once the fear has passed, the person then needs to reinforce him or herself for having tolerated it and gotten through it: "you did it," "it worked." The development of these self-statements gives the person something constructive to do to cope with fear-provoking situations. They are then used to counter and challenge negative statements that creep into one's mind, and help keep the person on the task of working to reduce the response, rather than letting the anxiety-provoking thoughts take over.

Phase III of SIT can begin once the person has developed and tried out a series of new self-statements and coping skills.

Phase III is the actual use of these skills in feared situations. Here the full package of new skills, thinking, self-statements, and relaxation is put to use to enable the person to begin tolerating previously feared situations. Other procedures might also be enlisted to facilitate this process. For example, Meichenbaum would encourage subjects to use a variant of SD as described by Goldfried in which anxiety hierarchy scenes are visualized with the person coping with and attempting to reduce the felt anxiety. These scenes might actually involve the person visualizing himself being in the situation making coping self-statements and being able to tolerate it. In other words, this combines elements of SD, and covert or imaginal self-modeling, along with changes in self-statements.

Self-instructional training may then be seen as a treatment package incorporating elements and adaptations of other fear reduction methods. These methods are used to assist fearful persons to change self-defeating thoughts and to enable them to tolerate and cope with being in the presence of the feared situation until the fear diminishes.

Throughout this chapter, the reader will have noticed that the several treatment methods described progressed from a relatively structured set of procedures (SD, Symbolic Modeling) to more comprehensive and inclusive treatment packages such as participant modeling and cognitive restructuring. I believe this trend toward incorporating a broad assortment of methods reflects what therapists do clinically. That is, they draw upon established procedures and adapt them to the specific needs of their clients (e.g., Goldfried & Davison, 1976). What fits for some people or problems may not fit for others. This integration of the several treatments in practice will be further illustrated in the last section of this chapter where I will describe applications to specific anxiety disorders.

Another point that readers might have noticed is that the various procedures described were in some cases quite different or even apparently the reverse of one another. For example, the standard SD procedure attempts to insulate the person from feeling too much anxiety, while flooding attempts to *create* anxiety. Yet each of these techniques boasts substantial research support attesting to its effectiveness in reducing fears and phobias (e.g., see Rachman & Wilson, 1980; Rimm & Masters, 1979 for evaluative reviews). How do these seemingly divergent treatment techniques all produce significant reductions in fear and anxiety? Do they each operate through different mechanisms or is there some process common to all that can explain their effectiveness? In the following section I will present one theoretical position that attempts to account for the behavior change seen in all of these techniques.

Self-Efficacy Theory

Albert Bandura (1977a, 1977b) has presented a unifying theory of behavior change that attempts to explain the effectiveness of the various treatment procedures. According to Bandura, behavior change derives from a common cognitive process. This process is essentially the personal belief that the individual can perform a desired behavior (e.g., approach a feared stimulus). This belief, called an *efficacy expectation* reflects the extent to which an individual holds the expectation that he or she can perform a given act successfully. The greater one's efficacy expectation, the greater the probability that the person will be able to perform. Actual performance of course depends also on the extent to which the person wants to perform an act and expects that the outcome will be worth the effort.

With respect to fear behavior, a person phobic of snakes would be expected to have low *self-efficacy* concerning his or her ability to touch or pick up a snake. Accordingly, the probability of the person touching the snake would be correspondingly low.

The task of the several fear-reducing treatments according to Bandura is to increase the fearful person's sense of self-efficacy, which in turn will increase the probability that the person will perform the anxiety-provoking behavior. This sense of self-efficacy derives from a variety of sources. Bandura attributes the effectiveness of the seemingly different treatments to the fact that they all contribute to enhancing the fearful person's sense of self-efficacy. Although each of the techniques described previously are somewhat effective, some are more effective than others. Bandura believes that this differential effectiveness is due to differences in the extent to which the techniques enhance self-efficacy.

Bandura groups the various techniques according to the source through which each operates to provide efficacy expectations. The sources are: performance accomplishments, vicarious experiences, verbal persuasion, and emotional arousal.

Performance Accomplishments. The performance-based procedures in which the fearful person directly interacts with the feared situation are the most effective treatments. These include live exposure, participant modeling, and self-directed practice (e.g., Bandura, 1977; Emmelkamp, 1982; Rachman & Wilson, 1980). Their effectiveness is said to result from the fact that one's actual performance accomplishments, provided by these procedures, are the most dependable source of efficacy expectations. They are based on one's personal experience. Having successfully approached and touched a snake, even with aid and support, or having tolerated a session of intense exposure, is very strong evidence to an individual that he or she can do it again. This direct accomplishment strongly enhances one's self-efficacy which in turn increases the probability that next time, the person will be able to go even further in combating the fear.

Vicarious Experiences. A second source of efficacy information is provided by observing others perform a feared act such as in live or symbolic modeling. Although seen by themselves as providing less clear evidence that the observer can perform similarly, these vicarious experiences can enhance efficacy expectations. Observing multiple models who gradually but with persistence overcome their hesitations and are able to perform the feared act, can create expectations in the observer that he too can perform the act.

Verbal Persuasion. Techniques that involve verbal persuasion such as suggestion, exhortation, or attempts to convince a person verbally that he or she can perform a feared act are seen as relatively weak sources of self-efficacy enhancement. Although such efforts might encourage a person to try to perform the behavior, by themselves they do little to help one overcome intense fear. We recall that a defining characteristic of phobia was that a person could not be talked out of the fear.

However, verbal methods might be sufficient to convince

the person to make an initial attempt to overcome the fear. If this initial attempt results in some degree of success, the self-efficacy should be increased and should facilitate further efforts. However, if the attempt meets with negative consequences, the small amount of self-efficacy provided verbally is not likely to maintain persistent efforts. A common example is seen in persons fearful of dentistry. Often a fearful person will be persuaded by his or her spouse to make a dental appointment after years of avoidance. If the dentist is not cognizant of the extent of the person's fear and/or is not knowledgeable in fear treatment, a negative experience may well result. The person is unlikely to return for some time. On the other hand, if the experience with the dentist is positive and nontraumatic and the person finds he is able to tolerate it, his self-efficacy would be greatly enhanced and he would be likely to return. However, the major source of efficacy expectation here is from the fearful person's actual performance accomplishment, although the persuasion was important in getting the person into the situation to allow the accomplishment.

Emotional Arousal. The final source of efficacy expectations presented by Bandura is how persons sense themselves reacting physiologically. When confronted with a potentially threatening situation, the degree of fear and avoidance behavior shown may be partly a function of our perception of the physical arousal we experience. If our heart races, we are likely to label ourselves as fearful. On the other hand, if we find we do not become unduly physically agitated, we are less likely to label ourselves fearful. Thus the cues from our internal state provide information concerning whether or not we expect to be able to tolerate the situation. Treatment techniques that focus on reducing physical arousal then can contribute to one's sense of self-efficacy. These include relaxation-based procedures such as systematic desensitization and biofeedback as well as drug treatments that reduce physical arousal. (The issue of drugs in anxiety reduction will be discussed in Chapter 6).

According to Bandura, these treatments provide some information that enhances efficacy expectations. Through lowered arousal persons come to expect less fearful behavior in themselves which then allows them to approach or tolerate the feared situation. However, as with the method of verbal persuasion, the lasting effects of decreased arousal are won through enabling the person to enter the feared situation and ultimately to experience performance accomplishment.

In summary, Bandura's theory proposes self-efficacy as the common cognitive mechanism to explain the variable degrees of effectiveness of the several treatments. Any source of information that contributes to enhancing a person's expectations for success will contribute to overcoming fearful avoidance behavior.

This theory of behavior change provides a unified view or framework within which we can conceptualize similar effects from divergent treatments. It has a certain appeal and appears to make good sense. At this stage of our understanding of fear behavior, such a theory can be useful in guiding our thinking and research. However, as with any scientific theory, it will likely be questioned, evaluated, and revised.

Application of Treatment Packages to Anxiety Disorders

In this section I will describe the application of fear reduction treatments to specific anxiety disorders. As previously noted, in clinical practice several procedures are often used with the same subject to capitalize on the most effective elements of each and/or to adapt the treatment to the specific characteristics and needs of the individual client. The cases that follow were selected to illustrate how the various procedures can be effectively adapted and combined into comprehensive treatment packages.

Treatment of Dental Phobia

This case study illustrates the use of a combination of three treatment procedures to assist the subject in overcoming a long-standing fear and avoidance of dental treatment (Kleinknecht & Bernstein, 1979). The subject, Mrs. W., was a thirty-seven-year-old woman who had avoided dentistry for the previous 6 years.

However, several months prior to this treatment she had made an appointment to have her teeth cleaned. She was unable to complete the appointment due to a severe anxiety reaction. When in the dental chair, she experienced profuse sweating, shortness of breath, gagging, weakness in her knees, muscular tension, and nausea. Her reaction was so intense that even with the administration of nitrous oxide she was unable to tolerate having her teeth cleaned.

Mrs. W.'s fear reaction went far beyond being in the actual dental office. She was unable to call for an appointment either for herself or for her children. Her husband had to take the children to their appointments. Further, any time the subject of dentistry was brought up, it would later stimulate dreams in which her teeth shattered and fell out. Although Mrs. W. knew that her reaction was irrational, she was totally unable to control it. She clearly met the criteria for phobia.

Prior to beginning fear treatment, a series of assessments were completed to evaluate her fear reaction and to provide a baseline with which to compare treatment effectiveness. The assessment was conducted in a dental office but she was told no actual treatment would take place. While sitting in the dental chair, the cognitive component of state anxiety was assessed with the Anxiety Differential. Three measurements of her physiological arousal using the Palmar Sweat Index (PSI) were taken: 1) just as she entered, 2) just before receiving an anesthetic injection (she refused this injection), and 3) at the end of the assessment session. These assessment measures were taken again after treatment.

Following the assessment, the treatment began. It consisted of four components: training in muscle relaxation, symbolic modeling, graduated exposure to dental stimuli presented on videotape and self-paced live exposure practice in which she went to the dental office, and practiced relaxing while being exposed to the sights, sounds, and smells of dentistry.

This sequence of treatments was planned for Mrs. W. to reintroduce her gradually to dentistry. While being provided with a coping skill (relaxation), she also obtained information about how dentistry proceeds without her receiving negative direct experiences and by observing how several other people (models) coped with treatment. After viewing several coping models receive treatment her anxiety was lessened. Then the graduated exposure, also on videotape, allowed her safely to observe elements of dental treatment while she practiced remaining relaxed. Finally, on her own, she scheduled two sessions in which she went to the dental office to practice these skills. The first time she was instructed simply to sit in the waiting room, attend to the sounds and sights of dentistry, and practice coping with them. Once this step was mastered, her next appointment involved going into the dental operatory, sitting and relaxing in the dental chair, being exposed to the various instruments such as the drill, but without being actually treated. This live exposure, coupled with the previous information, allowed an informed, firsthand experience with dentistry that was nontraumatic. By taking it progressively, she was able to tolerate each succeeding step. The entire procedure took only 3.5 hours.

Following the successful completion of this program Mrs. W. scheduled a badly needed treatment appointment. At this appointment her fear responses were again evaluated. The posttreatment assessment was objectively more stressful than the pretreatment one since she was to have three teeth filled. In spite of the added stress, her AD score decreased significantly and her PSI showed a reversal of the pretreatment pattern. On the first assessment the PSI pattern showed progressively more sweating throughout the appointment. On the second session and during treatment, the pattern was one of decreasing sweating. Perhaps the most impressive evidence of treatment effectiveness was the fact that during the 12 months following treatment, she had five additional appointments at which she had a total of eight fillings, a root canal, a replaced crown, a fractured tooth repaired, and her annual cleaning.

Treatment of a Thunderstorm Phobia

This case study of a long-standing thunderstorm phobia was described by Öst (1978). The subject was a seventy-seven-year-old Swedish woman who had been phobic since childhood. Each spring, she would begin worrying about possible summer thunderstorms. She routinely avoided listening to weather forecasts since knowledge of impending storms would increase her anxiety.

During a storm she experienced chest pains, trembling, and felt panicky. She would crawl into secluded places in her house and bury her face in a pillow so she could not see the storm.

The treatment for this case included a two-stage process involving relaxation training, followed by a variant of systematic desensitization referred to by Öst as "self-administered desensitization."

Prior to treatment, a series of four assessment sessions were conducted in which fear reactions were measured. Since thunderstorms do not occur on demand, Öst constructed a laboratory analogue setting to simulate a storm. He played a tape recording of actual thunder synchronized with a series of slides depicting approaching storm clouds with lightning. Flashing lights were used to augment the realism.

While experiencing these sights and sounds, several fear measures were taken: self-report measures included a thunder and lightning phobia scale and a 1-10 point client rating of degree of anxiety experienced during the test. Also, heart rate and respiration were assessed throughout the simulated storm session.

After these initial fear measures were taken, the client was given five sessions of relaxation training with measurements taken during each session.

The self-administered desensitization was then introduced for an additional eight sessions. This procedure consisted of the client first listening to a tape recording of her favorite music while practicing relaxation for four sessions. Then for four more sessions the client listened to the tape of thunderstorms while trying to maintain relaxation. If she became too anxious, she could turn the tape off and relax again. Then the process could be repeated until she could listen all the way through without undue anxiety. Evaluation of treatment effects showed progressive decreases in each of the fear measures. Most of the reduction in the fear measures occurred by the end of the relaxation phase. The self-rated anxiety went from 8 during baseline to 4 during relaxation and to 3 by the end of the self-administered desensitization. Her heart rate showed a decrease from an average of 175.6 BPM to 69.76 BPM at the end of treatment.

During the 9 months following treatment, this client reported that for the first time in decades she was able to enjoy a summer stay in Italy even though she had encountered several thunderstorms and that she no longer worried so over the coming summer storms.

In this same series of case studies Öst (1978) described treatment of five other thunder and lightning phobics. He successfully used several different techniques with these cases including other variations on the systematic desensitization procedures, and Meichenbaum's self-instructional and stress inoculation training.

Treatment of Blood-Injury-Illness Phobia

Cohn, Kron, and Brady (1976) described an interesting treatment approach to relieving a twenty-eight-year-old man of his long-standing phobia of blood and injury. Their subject was a premedical student with a masters degree in chemistry who had his fear since he was four years of age. At the sight of blood or injuries to others he became light-headed and would faint if he did not quickly lie down. This reaction of course kept him from being a viable candidate for medical school.

Before treatment began, an assessment session was conducted to evaluate fully his physiological reactions. It has been noted that blood-injury-illness phobics show a response pattern quite different from other phobics; they have a drop in blood pressure and heart rate which results in fainting.

The assessment consisted of attaching the subject to an electrocardiograph to monitor his heart rate. He was then shown a series of slides of mutilated bodies along with a control slide of a cartoon. The slides were shown for varying lengths of time to observe how his heart rate changed. At exposures greater than 60 seconds, he reported feeling light-headed and his heart rate dropped from his normal rate of about 86 BPM to as low as 47 BPM. After 75 seconds, it dropped to 30 BPM, he fainted, and then it rose to over 100.

The initial treatment consisted of a variant of systematic desensitization. The subject was asked to lie down on a couch and relax. Then, while relaxed, he was shown brief glimpses of the mutilation slides which he could turn off if he became light-headed. After a session of this treatment, he was able to extend the length of time he could view the slides, but only a few seconds.

In the next session, the authors tried something different. They decided to seek a response that would be incompatible with fear but would keep the blood pressure up. Anger appeared to be such a response. Accordingly, with the subject's help, they identified several situations that aroused the subject to anger, e.g., his father, an argument with his wife and his college advisor. Then, while viewing the phobic slides, the therapists, playing the role of antagonists, aroused the subject to anger. Viewing the slides while angry was no problem. The subject was able to do so immediately for periods as long as 20 minutes and maintained his heart rate within the normal range of 70 to 90 BPM.

Following this successful session, he was given a homework assignment to practice on his own. He was given a medical textbook with pictures of mutilated bodies, asked to see horror movies, and to read books that had previously caused him to faint. He was to maintain his anger while participating in these tasks for several 30-minute practice sessions per week.

After 4 weeks of this successful practice he gave up the anger and pictures and became a volunteer worker in the emergency room of a general hospital. After 6 months, he had not fainted, despite his extensive exposure to the previously faint-inducing situation.

The authors of this report suggested that the treatment was probably successful due to two processes. First, by being angry, he did not identify so closely with the person injured. Secondly, the anger kept his blood pressure and heart rate up which prevented him from fainting long enough to allow himself to become habituated to the pictures.

Other studies have shown that a variety of techniques can be used to treat blood-injury-illness phobias successfully. Although the authors of the case study described caution against the use of systematic desensitization and relaxation, others have used it successfully (e.g., Elmore et al., 1980; Yule & Fernando, 1980;

Öst et al., 1984). However, these authors and others (Connally, Hallum, & Marks, 1976) all used some variant of in vivo exposure, with and without relaxation.

Treatment of Scriptophobia

The treatment of scriptophobia to be described is one of three such cases presented by Biran, Augusto, and Wilson (1981). The reader will recognize this case as one included in the description of social phobias in Chapter 4.

This subject was thirty-seven years old at the time of treatment and had been phobic of writing in public since she was sixteen years old. Due to her fear, she was unable to participate in any activity that required her to write in public such as purchasing items with checks or credit cards, or voting. Although she was working part-time as a typist, her work was impaired due to her phobia. She was less anxious, however, when in the presence of a trusted family member or was out of direct public view.

When in a situation requiring writing she experienced palpitations, shortness of breath, sweating, and shakiness, particularly of the hands. She avoided such situations over her concern that others would see her nervousness and would wonder what was wrong with her.

Assessment of her phobia included several cognitive self-report and behavioral measures. Before and after treatment she was given a Fear of Negative Evaluation Scale which showed her to be highly anxious over others' evaluation of her. The Rathus Assertiveness Scale indicated that she was quite unassertive.

A behavioral avoidance test was constructed which included a graded series of 13 tasks to be performed. Easier tasks included filling out forms in the therapy room with the therapist observing, and filling out forms alone in a hallway waiting area. More difficult tasks included purchasing items at a store with a check, a credit card, and with traveler's checks. The BAT score was the number out of 13 of these situations the subject was able to perform. During the BAT, she also gave a subjective rating of her anxiety on a scale from 0 to 10.

Since two different treatment procedures were to be tried in this single case study, a multiple baseline assessment procedure was used. She received five separate assessments: 1) pretreatment, 2) after treatment 1, 3) after treatment 2, 4) at 1 month follow-up and 5) at 9 months follow-up. By this procedure, the therapist could separately evaluate effects of each of the two treatment procedures.

Since scriptophobia involves both a strong cognitive component (anticipatory anxiety and worry over social evaluation) and a behavioral component (avoidance of writing in public) these authors felt that treatments should be chosen to focus specifically on these two areas. The first treatment was cognitive restructuring. As described earlier in this chapter, the procedure involved explaining to the subject that it was not the situation per se that caused anxiety, but what she thought about it. She then observed her own thinking to see how her thoughts and self statements initiated her felt anxiety. Then, more realistic non-anxiety producing thoughts were identified and practiced to replace the negative thoughts. These were practiced in imagination and in role playing with the therapist. Then she was encouraged to practice on her own between treatment sessions.

Following five sessions of cognitive restructuring the BAT was readministered. There was essentially no change in the number of tasks she could perform; four on both occasions. Her subjectively rated anxiety while performing the BAT was also unchanged.

At this point, five sessions of graded in vivo exposure treatment were initiated. The situations worked on were those from the BAT. However, performance at each level of task was assisted by the therapist. For example, for purchasing items from a store using a check, the therapist initially was present, which made it easier. As she was able to accomplish this task, the therapist then moved further and further away while she wrote checks, until she was eventually able to do it totally on her own.

After five sessions of this therapist-assisted exposure, the subject was reassessed on the BAT and was now able to perform all 13 tasks. Her subjective anxiety during these tasks dropped from a pretreatment average of 4 to an average of 1. One month following treatment she was still able to complete all 13 tasks and her subjective anxiety was virtually nonexistent. However, the assessment 9 months later showed conflicting results. Although she was still able to perform all 13 BAT tasks, her subjective anxiety had returned almost to her pretreatment level. Despite the return of some of the subjective anxiety, this subject was able to maintain her behavioral gains. She became employed full-time, was able to shop with checks and credit cards, and to endorse checks at the bank, none of which she was able to perform prior to treatment.

The results of this case were generally consistent with the other two reported in this series of case studies. That is, it appeared that the graded exposure treatment was most effective in reducing the behavioral avoidance component of social phobia. The cognitive restructuring appeared to have minimal effect. Also, at 1 month post-treatment all showed significant drops in subjective anxiety, but at 9 months, it had returned to near pretreatment levels.

Treatment of Agoraphobia

Of the phobic disorders, agoraphobia is the most debilitating. It deprives persons of most every aspect of life outside the home, leaving many housebound and totally dependent on "safe" others for excursions beyond the front door. In many cases the fear is so great the person is unable to come to clinics for treatment. In light of this difficulty, the treatment program to be described took the treatment to the clients. In this novel and successful series of case studies the subjects were given a self-help treatment manual while the therapists served primarily as consultants and advisors (Mathews et al., 1977).

The subjects in this study were 12 married women whose agoraphobia had persisted from 1 ½ to 20 years with an average of 9.3 years. All were disabled to the extent that they were unable to leave home alone to visit neighbors or to shop.

Prior to introducing the treatment programs, there was a 3 week period of baseline assessment. The measures included a self-rating of symptom severity, ranging from 1, which indicated very little restriction, to 5, which indicated severe incapacitation. The average pretreatment rating was 4.

A diary was also kept in which subjects recorded the amount of time they spent outside the home. Before treatment, this averaged 5 hours per week.

A third measure to evaluate treatment effectiveness was taken from a graded hierarchy of situations constructed during the baseline phase. With the aid of the therapist, 14 situations for each subject were listed as targets that the subject would work toward being able to achieve. The number of these target situations the subject was able to accomplish was taken as a behavioral measure of treatment effectiveness. Low hierarchy goals included such things as walking alone to a friend's house or walking to a local bus stop. More difficult situations were walking to a local shop and taking a short bus ride. Items at the top of the list included taking a bus trip to a nearby town and visiting a social club.

The subjects were tested at three points to see how many of their 14 situations they could complete. They were tested during the baseline period, after 4 weeks of treatment practice, and 6 months following treatment.

After baseline evaluation, the therapist met with each subject and her husband at their home. At this meeting they went over the detailed treatment manual and discussed procedures for implementing a graded exposure practice program. The manual described how to begin setting up short treatment goals, allowing oneself to be exposed to a situation until anxiety subsided, and then going to a more difficult goal.

An important ingredient in this program was that the husband had to be totally involved in the treatment process. The husband and wife had to work together to plan the specific treatment steps, and to carry them out. The husband was also given a manual to assist him in helping his wife. He had to participate in each of the 1 hour per day practice sessions and to record the time spent and work accomplished.

The therapist served primarily as advisor through the 4 weeks of the program. His role was to assist the husband and wife in setting practice goals, provide advice and support, and answer questions concerning the manual and program. He was present at only the first actual practice session, but met with the couple a total of 8 times over the 4 weeks to help them work through the program.

Following the 4 weeks of the actual treatment portion of the study, 11 of the 12 women had been able to enter at lèast one situation from their hierarchy that they had not been able to tolerate during the pretreatment assessment. Also, their self-rated severity of symptoms had declined to an average of 2.8 and the amount of time spent outside the home had more than doubled to an average of 11 hours by the end of the 4 weeks.

At the 6-month follow-up assessment these gains were either maintained or had increased. While the time out of the home remained at about 11 hours per week, the severity rating had further decreased to 2.3, a level indicating no significant restriction due to symptoms. By 6 months the subjects had achieved an average of 8.8 of the pretreatment hierarchy items and 9 of the 12 had been able to take shopping trips alone to nearby cities.

This study is quite encouraging in that it suggests that significant reductions in housebound agoraphobics' anxiety and avoidance behavior can be accomplished with minimal therapist contact. In this case, the average contact time was only 7 hours per subject. Another recent study replicated these successful results and spent an average of only 3.5 hours direct contact time (Jannoun et al., 1980). This home-based, self-help approach to treating agoraphobia appears to be both effective and efficient.

I should note here that another recent attempt to replicate these treatment effects met with failure (Holden et al., 1983). This study was similar in design, using a self-help manual for clients to work on their own to increase exposure to fear situations. The therapists maintained weekly phone contact to answer questions. However, this study, in contrast to the two successful homebased programs, did not actively enlist nor require a spouse or trusted companion to work closely with the subjects. This element of having a helper to work with who provides motivation, support, and general assistance in difficult tasks is probably a critical element in agoraphobic treatment. After it became apparent that little progress was being made alone these authors introduced therapists to participate actively in subjects' exposure practice. With this added assistance, significant progress was made in five of the six subjects.

Treatment of an Obsessive-Compulsive Disorder

Obsessive-compulsive disorders are some of the most resistent anxiety disorders. The following case is illustrative of these difficulties. Although treatment was largely successful, the subject was not completely symptom free.

The subject of this case study reported by Robertson et al. (1983) was twenty-three years old at the time treatment began and had been obsessive-compulsive since age ten. At the time of treatment she had been virtually housebound for the past year and spent most of her time in bed occupied by her obsessive thoughts and compulsive rituals. Her obsessive thoughts centered on the fear that harm would come to her parents on whom she was totally dependent. To protect them from harm she engaged in superstitious rituals of counting and touching things a set number of times over and over. While performing these rituals she would utter to herself "good" thoughts in order to avoid intrusive "bad" thoughts. Her "good" thoughts consisted of self-deprecating statements, while "bad" thoughts involved harm that might come to her parents.

As with most obsessive-compulsive disorders, the thoughts of harm led to an urge to conduct the compulsive rituals which in turn reduced the anxiety associated with the thoughts. The treatment approach then was to focus on breaking this sequence of events. First, response prevention was introduced, followed by attempts to disrupt the obsessive thoughts and restructure her maladaptive cognitions.

Before treatment began there was a 10-day period in which the subject was allowed to become accustomed to the hospital setting in which the treatment was to be carried out. Also, pretreatment baseline data were gathered to assess the frequency of her thoughts and rituals. She was asked to record each occurrence of her motor rituals and obsessive thoughts. Initially she reported an average of just under 400 motor rituals and just over 200 cognitive rituals per day.

The first treatment introduced was response prevention.

The subject would be reminded and encouraged to resist carrying out her motor rituals of touching things over and over and to allow the experienced anxiety to decrease. This was highly effective in reducing the motor ritual to about 20 per day. However, with the decline of motor rituals came a sharp increase in cognitive rituals, up to nearly 400 per day.

To combat this increased cognitive activity, an exposure technique was introduced in which her bad thoughts were played to her over and over on a tape recording. Unfortunately, this exposure was unsuccessful since the subject managed to avoid listening to the tape recording. Next, two cognitive procedures were introduced. A procedure called *Systematic Disruption* was used to interrupt her "good" thoughts which had kept out the "bad" thoughts. The therapists would contaminate her good thoughts by repeating to her content from bad thoughts. This procedure prevented her escaping from or avoiding the bad thoughts and allowed them to habituate.

Concurrent with this disruption was the introduction of cognitive restructuring. This focused on helping her see the senselessness of her fears that harm would come to her parents and the lack of necessity for her superstitious thinking. Also, the therapists worked at expanding her social activities and associations to reduce her dependence on her parents, which was seen as a large part of the source of her obsessive-compulsive behaviors. The tactics focusing on the cognitive activity resulted in a significant decrease in her cognitive rituals. These decreased from about 400 to about 20 per day by the end of treatment.

Following treatment, there was still some level of cognitive and motor rituals being performed. However, these were no longer severe enough to impair her functioning. She was able to leave the hospital, and within 6 months was working full-time and living on her own. However, over time there was an increase in symptoms and after 2 years she was readmitted to the hospital for another treatment session.

The techniques used in the treatment of this case are those generally found most effective in reducing obsessive-compulsive behaviors. Response prevention focuses on the behavioral rituals while the cognitive disruptions and restructuring are aimed at changing the obsessional components. (See Rachman &

Hodgson, 1980, for thorough review of obsessive-compulsive disorders and their treatment.)

Fear and Anxiety Reduction without Professional Intervention

Having just reviewed some of the more effective methods for treating anxiety disorders an important question should be addressed: Do people with anxiety disorders require professional treatment? Can people overcome anxiety disorders on their own? These questions have been the subject of much debate and some research. I will briefly review two issues pertinent to this question. The first concerns the issue of *spontaneous* remission rates or, the extent to which symptoms remit or improve without professional treatment. The second is the effectiveness of self-help books or manuals in assisting persons to overcome anxiety and fears.

Over 30 years ago, Eysenck (1952) concluded that as many as two-thirds of neurotic disorders (anxiety based) get better in 2 years, with or without treatment. Although these figures have been disputed by some (Bergin & Lambert, 1978), other recent evaluations of this literature tend to concur with these figures (Rachman & Wilson, 1980).

Whether Eysenck's two-thirds or Bergin and Lambert's 50 percent figure is correct, it is clear that a large proportion of persons with anxiety disorders do get better with or without treatment. It will be recalled from Chapter 2 that as many as 90 percent of children develop some specific fear, and that these fears tend to dissipate with age, maturation, and increased experiences. Also, Agras et al. (1972) found that among the clinical phobics identified in their 1969 community survey virtually all of those under twenty years of age were greatly improved 5 years later. Only 43 percent of those over twenty were so improved.

To investigate some of the possible reasons for untreated improvement, I conducted a survey of a group of persons previously fearful of spiders but who at the time of the survey were tarantula enthusiasts (Kleinknecht, 1982). Those who had overcome their spider fears attributed their improvement to the same factors included in the treatments described earlier in this chapter: increased and accurate information, vicarious exposure to others who were not fearful (modeling), and various forms of exposure. However, I do not know how severe these fears were. It may be that milder, nonphobic fears are more subject to change under these informal "treatment" conditions than would be the case for more severe anxiety disorders. We do not have reliable data on spontaneous remission rates as a function of disorder type and severity although there is a suggestion that obsessive-compulsive disorders are quite resistant to these effects (Rachman & Wilson, 1980).

We can conclude that between one-half and two-thirds of anxiety disorders may remit without formal treatment. However, much remains to be learned about the differential changes as a function of disorder type, age, severity, and the factors responsible for this change.

The second issue related to behavior change without professional intervention is the effectiveness of self-help books found on the shelves of bookstores. Do they work? The answer to this question, based on current research, is both yes and no. Unfortunately, most of the research on the effects of self-help books has been conducted on college students with subclinical fears. In reviewing the research on these effects, Glasgow and Rosen (1978) concluded that up to 50 percent of the subjects report some positive effects from self-help manuals. However, a major drawback in using these manuals is that 50 percent of the participants fail to complete the program laid out. So, while there may be some positive effect from self-help books for some people, adherence to the program is a major problem.

For many people, and perhaps for most of those with severe problems, some therapist contact appears to be important. Recall that the self-help study of agoraphobics by Holden et al. (1983) found virtually no effect when subjects were left on their own to complete a detailed program. However, when the therapists eventually became more actively involved, five of six did show improvement. This was similar to the two home-based treatment programs described which included more therapist contact and had the assistance of a spouse (Jannoun et al., 1980; Mathews et al., 1977).

At this stage of refinement of self-help manuals, I believe it is reasonable to conclude that some people, particularly those with milder anxiety conditions, can benefit without direct professional intervention. However, for more severe disorders such as agoraphobia, some skilled professional intervention may be necessary.

SUMMARY

The behavior therapy and cognitive behavior therapy procedures have been found highly effective for treating most anxiety disorders. Simple phobias have been most responsive to treatment while obsessive compulsive disorders have been somewhat more resistant. The therapy procedures described focus on changing the three response components of fear and anxiety: cognitive, behavioral, and physiological.

The first of the effective treatments for anxiety disorders was systematic desensitization, developed by Joseph Wolpe. In this procedure subjects are initially taught deep muscle relaxation. Then an anxiety hierarchy, composed of a graded list of anxiety-provoking situations, is developed. The subject then imagines him or herself being in each of the situations while remaining relaxed. With repeated pairings of the anxiety scenes and deep relaxation, the images lose their ability to generate anxiety. This imagery-based desensitization carries over into actual situations involving the feared stimuli.

Several variations of SD were described including using these general procedures as self-control training. SD was also noted to be effective when conducted in groups and when automated by use of tape-recorded presentations of the procedures.

The exposure treatments were described as anxiety-eliciting procedures. In these treatments subjects are exposed, either in imagination or in vivo to the sources of their anxiety. If exposed to anxiety for periods over an hour, the anxiety response diminishes. Exposure treatments can be presented gradually (small doses at a time) or with complete immersion. Self-directed practice between formal therapy sessions appears to enhance anxiety reduction effects.

Response prevention was seen as a variant of exposure

treatments applied to cases of obsessive-compulsive disorders. Here, the individual is prevented from engaging in the compulsion rituals until the resulting anxiety diminishes.

Modeling treatments involve observation of others, either on film or live, enacting the feared behaviors. Modeling appears most effective when the fearful observer perceives the model to be similar to him or herself. Coping models who are initially apprehensive but who eventually demonstrate coping with their fear are most effective.

In participant modeling, the therapist can act as model and as an aid to encourage the fearful subject to enact the feared behaviors. Performance aids are also used to enable subjects to begin to take steps toward achieving the behavioral goal of interacting with the feared object or situation.

Cognitive restructuring approaches focus on changing what subjects say or think to themselves. Subjects are taught that it is not the situation that causes the fear but what they tell themselves about the situation. Through self-instructional training, subjects are taught to develop a variety of means to help them cope with stress-inducing situations.

Bandura's self-efficacy theory was described as a unifying theory to help explain the effectiveness of the several treatment procedures which appear quite different from one another. It was theorized that any procedure which enhances a person's belief (efficacy expectation) that he or she can successfully perform a feared act will increase the probability that that act will be performed. Among the sources that contribute to enhancing self-efficacy are performance accomplishments, vicarious experiences, verbal persuasion, and emotional arousal.

Case studies using treatment packages incorporating components of each of the described anxiety-reduction techniques were presented. These included cases of dental phobia, blood-injury phobia, social phobia, agoraphobia, and obsessive-compulsive disorder.

Chapter 6

PSYCHOBIOLOGICAL RELATIONSHIPS AND FUTURE DIRECTIONS IN ANXIETY RESEARCH

In the preceding chapters anxiety and fear were described largely as psychological phenomena. I described the learning processes thought to be important in fear development, the psychological methods of assessment, descriptions of anxiety disorders, and psychological treatments for these disorders.

In this final chapter, I will attempt to round out the fuller picture of these phenomena by describing some of the biological/physiological and biochemical aspects of fear and anxiety.

It is important to realize that as humans we are both psychological and biological beings. To focus on one aspect to the exclusion of the other will provide an incomplete picture. Although for the sake of illustration we can describe psychological and biological factors in anxiety, in most cases they are difficult to separate. Our biological make-up may affect our psychological states and our psychological states may in turn affect us biologically. It appears most meaningful to use the term *psychobiological* to describe these interactional relationships. This chapter will briefly outline two areas in which psychological and biological factors interact with one another. The two areas to be discussed are psychopharmacologic treatments of anxiety disorders and the relationship of anxiety to pain. The final section of this chapter outlines some of the areas pertaining to fear and anxiety which remain to be clarified. These are areas in which the reader can expect to see future research directed.

PSYCHOTHERAPEUTIC DRUGS AND ANXIETY DISORDERS

In recent years psychotherapeutic drugs have been increasingly used in the treatment of psychological disorders. The national survey referred to previously by Uhlenhuth and his colleagues (1983) found that 16 percent of the adult population in the US had used one form of psychotherapeutic drug within the year prior to the survey. The most commonly used drugs and those most relevant to this book are referred to as *antianxiety* agents; being used by 11 percent of the sample.

In this section I will describe some of the drugs used in treatment of anxiety disorders, some of the research concerning the effectiveness of these drugs, and some of the postulated mechanisms thought to be responsible for their effects. Although many of these drugs have been shown to be useful in treating some anxiety disorders, it should be noted that exact biochemical mechanisms through which they exert their effects are currently unknown.

Further, as will be seen, these drugs are often used in conjunction with the psychological treatments described in Chapter 5. The three classes of drugs to be described are: the antianxiety agents, sometimes called "minor tranquilizers," antidepressants, and beta-adrenergic blocking agents.

Antianxiety Agents

The class of antianxiety agents most widely used in anxiety disorders is called the *benzodiazepines*. This class of drugs includes a variety of related compounds. All have similar antianxiety effects, but vary from one another in potency and length of time they remain active in the body. The most widely used of the benzodiazepines are diazepam (Valium) and chlordiazepoxide

Table 6.1
Antianxiety Agents: The Benzodiazepines

Generic Name	Trade Name
Alprazolam	Xanax
Chlordiazepoxide	Librium
Clorazepate	Tranxene
Diazepam	Valium
Lorazepam	Ativan
Oxazepam	Serax
Triazolam	Halcion

(Librium) (Blackwell, 1976). Other drugs within this class are shown in Table 6.1.

The benzodiazepines were introduced into the US market in the early 1960s: Librium, 1960, Valium, 1962. They immediately became extremely popular among prescribing physicians and patients alike and ultimately became the most widely prescribed drugs in the world. By 1973, Valium was the single most prescribed drug in the US and Librium was third (Blackwell, 1973). Part of the popularity of these drugs was due to the variety of conditions for which they appeared useful. In addition to treating anxiety states for which they are most commonly prescribed, they are used as skeletal muscle relaxants, as epilepsy control agents, in anesthesia, and as presurgical medication. However, it is tension and anxiety-related problems that account for the majority of prescriptions. As has been noted throughout this book, anxiety is perhaps the most prevalent of psychological symptoms.

These drugs affect anxiety through their action as general central nervous system depressants. That is, they tend to reduce the excitability of brain functions. After taking these drugs the anxious individual experiences physical and mental calmness, a reduction in felt tension, greater ease in falling asleep, a general feeling of well-being, and often a feeling of being better able to cope with stresses in their lives.

For most people, these effects are quite immediate and dramatic. However, these anxiety-reducing effects have been likened to the effect of aspirin on fever (Licky & Gordon, 1983). Aspirin clearly reduces the fever, but does nothing for the cause of the fever. Both are generalized treatments of symptoms. This of course is true of all psychotherapeutic drugs. They do not cure the problem (Rickels et al., 1978). They only make the person feel better while the drug is active in the body.

Numerous clinical and experimental studies have documented the anxiety-reducing effects of the various benzodiazepines (e.g., see Klein et al., 1980; Greenblatt & Shader, 1974; Chouinard et al., 1982). In particular, many authorities suggest that they are most effective in reducing generalized anxiety as seen in generalized anxiety disorder and various forms of anticipatory anxiety (Rickels et al., 1978; Klein et al., 1980). In contrast, some reports indicate that the benzodiazepines were not particularly effective in treating panic attacks as seen in agoraphobia or panic disorder (Rickels et al., 1978; Klein et al., 1980; Sheehan et al., 1980).

More recently, however, two studies have appeared that show that benzodiazepines may indeed reduce panic attacks as well as more generalized anxiety. Noyes and colleagues (1984) found diazepam (Valium) to be equally effective in reducing panic disorder, agoraphobia, and generalized anxiety disorder. Similar results were obtained using Alprazolam (Xanax) in another recent study (Chouinard et al., 1982).

Thus far these antianxiety agents do not appear by themselves to be effective treatment for obsessive-compulsive disorders nor are they effective for simple phobias. However, there are clinical reports that they can be useful adjuncts to treating phobias. For example, Wolpe (1982) reports the use of Valium to assist in the treatment of agoraphobia. Valium was taken to enable the patient to begin a graduated exposure treatment. With Valium, the patient was able to venture alone from home and to drive. Once this was established the dosage was decreased until he was eventually able to manage these situations in a drug-free state. The antianxiety drugs appear to offer some beneficial effects for anxiety disorders, both when used alone for generalized anxiety, for panic attacks and agoraphobia, and when used as part of an exposure treatment.

The physical and psychological effects of these drugs ap-

pear to come from general calming and tension reduction properties rather than from specific action affecting specific symptoms. That is, they are not specific anti-panic drugs. It appears
that they reduce the general excitability of the person, which in
turn may allow him or her to gain exposure to the feared situations.

The biochemical mechanism by which these drugs exert
their calming effects has become the subject of considerable research and theorizing. One proposed mechanism is that the benzodiazepines facilitate some naturally occurring neural inhibi-
tory processes in the brain. It has been hypothesized that they
interact with and facilitate the effects of the neurotransmitter,
gamma-aminobutyric acid (GABA). GABA serves to inhibit
nerve transmission. The benzodiazepines are thought to facilitate this inhibition, rendering the brain less excitable. Therefore
the person is less likely to react with anxiety or fear (see Licky &
Gordon, 1983, for lucid description of this theorizing).

Although these antianxiety drugs are useful in treating
some of the anxiety disorders, they are not without their drawbacks. Being CNS depressants, they affect other brain functions
as well. For example, negative side effects include decreased
psychomotor coordination and cognitive functioning (Kleinknecht & Donaldson, 1975). Further, long-term use of these
agents can lead to physical dependency and result in withdrawal
syndromes if abruptly terminated (e.g., see Rickels et al., 1978).

Antidepressants

The second class of drugs used in treating some anxiety disorders are called the antidepressants. Although developed for
and highly effective in the treatment of depression, these drugs
have also been shown to affect certain of the anxiety disorders,
particularly panic disorders.

There are two subclassifications of antidepressants, both of
which are capable of reducing panics. These include the *Mono-
amine Oxidase Inhibitors* (MAO-I) and the *tricyclic* compounds. Examples of each of these types of drugs are shown in Table 6.2.

The mechanism by which these drugs affect anxiety disorders is currently unknown, although it has been hypothesized

Table 6.2
Antidepressants

Monoamine Oxidase Inhibitors Generic Name	Trade Name
Isocarboxazid	Marplan
Phenelzine	Nardil
Tranylcypromine	Parnate

Tricyclics Generic Name	Trade Name
Imipramine	Tofranil
Desipramine	Norpramin
Amitriptyline	Elavil
Nortriptyline	Aventil
Doxepin	Sinequan
Protriptyline	Vivactil

that like the benzodiazepines, the GABA systems are involved (Sheehan, 1980). It is rather confusing to think of a drug which is used for treating depression also to be effective for anxiety. Further, the two types of antidepressants are shown to operate differently at the neural level. Yet both types have been shown in most studies to reduce panic attacks whether in panic disorder, or agoraphobia with panic attacks (Kelly, 1980; Klein & Fink, 1982; Sheehan et al., 1980; Zitrin, 1983).

Compounding the picture further is the finding that at least one type of tricyclic antidepressant appears to reduce obsessive-compulsive symptoms as well (Stern, 1983). However, they are apparently ineffective in treating the simple phobias (Kelly, 1980; Zitrin, 1983) and some feel they do not affect generalized or anticipatory anxiety. It has been suggested that anxiety and depression may be related and/or coexist in certain patients. If this were the case it might be that the reduced anxiety is effected by decreasing depression (e.g., Marks et al., 1983; Stern, 1983). However, most researchers believe that the antianxiety effect is not due to reduced depression but to some more specific effect on the mechanisms that cause panic attacks. Indeed, it has been proposed that the antidepressants may not be effective for treating anxious persons who are also severely depressed (Kelly, 1980; Zitrin, 1983).

These drugs appear to have their major effect on reducing more or less "spontaneous" panic attacks (those not associated with specific stimuli) and to have little affect on anticipatory anxiety. In cases such as agoraphobia where both types are seen, some suggest using antidepressants to reduce panic attacks, along with a benzodiazepine to reduce the generalized anticipatory anxiety (e.g., Kelly, 1980).

As with the antianxiety drugs, the antidepressants also have unpleasant side effects. In studies by Zitrin (1983) investigating the anxiety-reducing effects, as many as 29 percent of the subjects dropped out due to difficulties from the side effects. Because of these unpleasant effects and since the behavior therapy procedures noted in Chapter 5 are quite successful in treating phobias, Zitrin (1983) recommends that these drugs only be used in cases that have not responded to the psychological treatments.

The Beta Blocking Agents

The third class of drugs used for treating some anxiety disorders is quite different from the two previously described. The beta blockers do not exert their effect through brain neurons. Rather, they block the effect of certain peripheral nerves which compose portions of the sympathetic nervous system. The neurons that they selectively block are those that use the transmitter adrenaline or epinephrine. These directly affect the heart rate. Consequently, these drugs have been observed to block the rapid heart rate and some related functions experienced during intense anxiety or panic attacks. The beta blockers such as propanolol (Inderol) appeared to hold great promise as yet another drug which could effectively treat anxiety disorders.

Tryer and colleagues (see Tryer, 1976) performed a series of studies to evaluate these drugs. Although he found them to reduce the physiological component of anxiety, they appeared to have little or no effect on the cognitive component. In a trial comparing the effects of the beta blocker propranolol to the antianxiety drug diazepam, he reported that propranalol was the superior treatment for chronically anxious patients whose primary response was physiological, whereas diazepam was superior for patients whose primary symptoms were psychological or cognitive anxiety.

However, this matter of different drugs for different manifestations of anxiety is far from settled. In a recent study, Noyes and colleagues (1984) compared the effects of diazepam and propranolol on a group of patients with panic disorder, agoraphobia, and generalized anxiety disorder. They found diazepam to be highly effective for 20 of 21 patients, whereas the propranolol resulted in improvement in only 10 of 21. Further, diazepam was more effective than propranolol in reducing both the physiological reactions of the panic attacks and the cognitive components.

The results of drug treatment for the anxiety disorders, although showing promise in some cases, is far from conclusive. While some highly positive effects have been reported for all three classes of drugs, problems remain. Many patients are unable to tolerate the side effects and they are not necessarily effective in all cases. Given these variable effects and the fact that for some people there is a risk of abuse and physical dependence with the benzodiazepines, Zitrin's (1983) recommendation of using behavior therapy procedures as the treatment of choice would seem to have considerable merit. For those cases in which psychological approaches alone do not appear sufficient, then drugs should be considered as an adjunctive treatment.

Further, evidence supporting the use of behavior therapy approaches as the treatment of choice comes from a recent study by Barlow and colleagues (1984). They used relaxation-based procedures along with cognitive restructuring to treat successfully a group composed of both panic disorder and generalized anxiety disorder patients. It is these types of disorders for which drug treatment is most commonly used, largely due to the absence of demonstrations showing effectiveness of psychologically based treatments.

Pain and Anxiety

The experience of pain is in many ways similar to that of fear and anxiety. In this section I will describe some of the points of similarity and how these two states can affect one another.

What is pain? Is it a physical sensation, a psychological perception, or both? It is clearly a complex phenomenon. Numerous definitions and theories of pain have been presented by researchers and philosophers over the centuries (Melzack & Wall, 1982). None were fully able to capture the many aspects of pain since most saw pain as a purely physical sensation similar to the sense of touch. More recently there has come a greater understanding of pain as a psychological as well as a physical state. The committee on taxonomy of the International Association for the Study of Pain (1979) has presented a definition that clearly illustrates the complexity of pain: Pain is ". . . an unpleasant sensory and emotional experience associated with actual or potential tissue damage. Pain is always subjective. It is unquestionably a sensation in a part or parts of the body, but it is also always unpleasant and therefore also an emotional experience. This definition avoids tying *pain* to the *stimulus*. Activity induced in the nociceptor or nociceptive pathways by a noxious stimulus is not pain, which is always a psychological state, even though we may well appreciate that pain most often has a proximate physical cause" (p. 250).

In this definition we see that pain is much more than a simple reflexive response to physical injury. It is a subjective emotional experience: a psychological state. Although there are many psychological aspects of the experience of pain, I will focus here on the relationship between acute pain and anxiety or fear. Acute pain is that experienced in proximity to a clearly specified physical cause. It tends to be experienced concurrently with tissue irritation or damage and typically diminishes as the immediate cause diminishes and/or as damaged tissue heals.

Chronic pain, on the other hand, is pain that persists for long periods of time (e.g., greater than 6 months). Although chronic and acute pain are clearly related, most chronic pain having begun as acute pain, they are quite different in many ways. Since anxiety and fear appear most closely associated with acute pain response, I will not discuss chronic pain, which appears to be more closely tied to depression (see Fordyce, 1976; Melzack & Wall, 1982).

Pain Response Systems

Like anxiety, pain must be considered a construct. Although we have all experienced pain, we have never seen it. Rather, it is a psychological or emotional state. Its presence is inferred by observing the same three general response systems used in assessing anxiety.

The Cognitive or Subjective Component of Pain.   The cognitive component of pain is the private subjective experience. Since others cannot see it, its features can only be known by the individual's self-report. A variety of means have been used to evaluate this component of pain response.

One of the most widely used self-report instruments is the McGill Pain Questionnaire (MPQ) developed by Melzack (1975). This questionnaire is of particular interest and value in that it recognizes the complexity of pain and allows assessment of several relevant dimensions of the pain experience. In addition to an overall rating of pain intensity, the MPQ allows respondents to note which of a number of adjectives best describes the pain they feel. The adjectives are clustered into three main types. There are *sensory* descriptors which can describe specific sensory qualities of the pain such as hot, sharp, pinching, and the like. A second dimension is called *evaluative*. Adjectives here are those that relate to intensity of the pain, such as from merely annoying to unbearable. The third dimension is composed of *affective* terms; those which describe the emotional qualities of the pain. Adjectives on the affective scale include: fearful, terrifying, and vicious.

The MPQ allows a broad assessment of what the pain means to the person. It has also been of interest to show how individuals with pains of different origins differently describe their pain. For example, Melzack (1975) has shown that pain from toothaches is described quite differently from the pain associated with childbirth. These two types of pain were rated quite differently, particularly on the sensory and affective dimensions. Labor pain was described with more sensory adjectives and showed a stronger affective and fear component than toothache pain. This scale's incorporation of an affective dimension into pain description points out the important relationship between emotions such as anxiety and fear and the experience of pain.

The Physiological Component of Pain.   Since pain is a response to a real or perceived threat (i.e., damage or potential damage) we would expect the ANS to be involved. Indeed it is, as with anxiety or fear. Studies investigating the effects of pain on the ANS responding typically show patterns similar to that seen in response to fear stimuli such as increased heart rate, blood pressure, and sweating (Sternbach, 1968). This similarity in physiological response should be expected. Fear or anxiety often coexist in pain, particularly in clinical pain situations as noted in the previous section on cognitive components of pain. In the same way that fear results in mobilization of physiological systems to prepare to deal with a threat, pain is a threat signal as well. We should also expect pain to affect behaviors that reduce the intensity of the aversive experience.

Behavioral Components of Pain.   Pain behavior is how we communicate to others how we feel. Specific behavioral signs that signal the presence of pain are commonly seen such as crying, moaning, and facial grimaces when we hit our thumb with a hammer. Then we quickly remove it, grasp it, and may jump around. These behavioral signs of pain are similar to those assessed on instruments such as the Timed Behavioral Checklist for performance anxiety.

Other pain behaviors can be seen as avoidance responses, displayed to reduce pain. For example, limping on a sore foot relieves or reduces pain, or simply not using parts of one's body if use results in pain. Such avoidance responses are, of course, adaptive to reduce pain in the same way that avoidance of fear stimuli reduce fear.

Variability of Pain Response Components

These response modes are part of the defining characteristics of pain. As with fear, however, each of these components may be affected by a variety of external or situational factors. For example, some people do not always demonstrate the behavioral aspects of pain, even though they may emotionally or cognitively experience pain. The injured athlete who does not want to be taken out of the game may avoid limping so as not to let the coach know he is injured.

On the other hand, a person who is only mildly injured may react as though he or she has been mortally wounded. Further, the same individual may react quite differently under different circumstances. A football player may receive a kick in the shins during a game and hardly attend to it. The same person seen to bump his shin on a coffee table at home would most likely react with pain expletives, jumping about, and limping. From these common occurrences which most of us have seen or experienced personally, it is clear that focusing solely on the physical stimulus causing pain cannot account for the tremendous variability in pain perception and response. Psychological factors must be taken into account to explain the full range of pain perception and behavior (e.g., Melzack & Wall, 1982; Fordyce & Steger, 1979). Among the psychological factors affecting pain is the topic of this book: fear and anxiety.

Pain-Anxiety Relationships

The role of emotions such as anxiety has long been known to affect pain (Beecher, 1959; Melzack & Wall, 1982). However, the experimental study of these relationships stems in large part from some observations by Beecher during the Second World War (Beecher, 1959). He noted that about 70 percent of severely wounded soldiers did not ask for pain medication and reported little or no significant pain. On the other hand, among civilian patients having surgical wounds of comparable severity to those of the soldiers, 80 percent asked for pain relief. The difference between the soldiers' and the civilians' reactions was seen as reflecting the emotional significance of the wound. To the soldier, it meant he was alive and would be leaving the battlefront; it was a safety signal. To the civilian, the wound was associated with worry and anxiety over what it meant, concern with recovery, and possible continued pain.

These observations then led to numerous experimental studies of the psychological aspects of pain and in particular the relationship between anxiety and the intensity of pain experienced. Most such studies have clearly demonstrated that the more anxious the person is, the greater the felt pain (e.g., Bowers, 1968; Kelpac et al., 1980, 1982; Melzack & Wall, 1982; Sternbach, 1968). Illustrative of this relationship were the results of one of my recent studies investigating the fearful and nonfearful dental patients undergoing dental treatment (Kleinknecht & Bernstein, 1978). Patients who, prior to their dental appointment, reported being fearful of dentistry subsequently experienced greater pain than their nonfearful counterparts during the treatment.

Although, in general, anxiety enhances pain perception, this relationship is subject to certain situational variation. In particular, there has been found to be differences between laboratory versus clinical settings. Dworkin and Chen (1982) investigated these differences by submitting a group of subjects to electric shock applied to their teeth. Each subject experienced identical levels of shock on two occasions, once in a dental clinic and once in a psychological laboratory. The shock experienced in the dental clinic was rated by all measures as being more intense than that in the laboratory. In the clinic, relative to the laboratory, subjects reported lower levels of shock as painful and were able to tolerate less shock.

The only difference between these two conditions was the context in which the subjects received the shock. More specifically, it was what the context meant to them. After the experiment, subjects reported that they were more anxious in the clinic than in the laboratory. This study clearly shows that equivalent levels of stimulation to the same individual can be perceived as painful or not, depending on how much anxiety the situation provokes.

A related issue found to affect response to pain stimulation is the degree of control the person believes he or she has over the source of the stimulation (Thompson, 1980; Miller, 1979). Typically, when one has some means of controlling the negative stimulus or believes that control is possible, less pain will be experienced. Uncertainty, lack of control, or perceived lack of control tend to heighten anticipatory anxiety, which in turn affects pain perception.

The relationship of perceived control over an aversive, painful stimulus and anxiety was examined in an interesting study by Geer and colleagues (1970). The subjects were told they were participating in a study of the effects of electric shock on reaction time. They were to receive a series of 10 painful shocks of 6 seconds each, and were asked to press a button as quickly as possible following each shock. During the experiment, their anxiety level was assessed by monitoring their skin conductance throughout the session. After the first series of 10 shocks, half of the subjects were told that if they pressed the button quickly enough on the next 10 shocks, the duration would be shortened to 3 seconds. In other words, they were led to believe they could control the duration of shock by a quick reaction.

The other half of the subjects was simply told that the shocks would be decreased to 3 seconds with no implication that they could control it. Although all subjects received the same number and duration of shocks, those who were led to believe they were in control showed significantly less anxiety as measured by skin conductance than those not led to believe they had control. In this study the sense of control over the painful stimulation, even though they had no control, in fact resulted in less anxiety. Additionally, there was a strong trend indicating that following the experiment the level of shock reported as painful became higher in those subjects who perceived themselves to be in control.

This study and others like it demonstrate that pain, especially if one does not feel in control, increases anxiety and that increased anxiety enhances the perception of pain. Other studies bearing on this issue have shown that by decreasing one's anxiety level by psychological procedures, aversive stimulation is perceived as less painful and higher levels of stimulation can be tolerated.

Pain Reduction through Anxiety Reduction

The previous section illustrated the relationship between anxiety and the perception of stimuli as painful. As a logical extension of these findings, a number of studies have also evaluated the effects of anxiety reduction procedures on the perception and tolerance of pain. The goals of this research are to develop psychological procedures that may be useful in assisting patients better to tolerate pain in clinical situations. The methods used to reduce perceived pain can be classified into two general categories: those which attempt to reduce anxiety and those which attempt to direct one's attention from the pain stimulation (Turk et al., 1982).

Psychological methods found effective in reducing reactivity to pain and in increasing one's tolerance for painful stimulation are essentially the same as those described in Chapter 5 for treating anxiety disorders. For example, relaxation training has been found to reduce reported pain and distress experienced during exposure to painful stimulation (Clum et al., 1982).

Others have found that combinations of procedures may be even more effective than those presented singly. Klepac and his colleagues (1981) found a combination of relaxation training and practice exposure with the pain stimulus (arm shock) was highly effective in enhancing pain tolerance. A similar finding was reported by Hackett and Horan (1980).

Cognitive-oriented strategies as described by Meichenbaum (1977) have also been found effective in reducing pain. Among the cognitive strategies found useful in mitigating pain is diverting one's attention from the pain stimulus by focusing on pleasant images. For example, Clum and others (1981) trained subjects to imagine being exposed to the pain stimulus, then to imagine leaving the situation and going outside on a bright sunny day. Another cognitive strategy called *somatizing* is described by Turk (1975). Here the subjects dissociate themselves from the part of the body receiving the pain. Rather than thinking it is their arm that is being hurt, they try to think of it as if it belonged to someone else.

Recall from Chapter 5 that Meichenbaum (1977) described a comprehensive approach to anxiety reduction by combining a variety of procedures into what he called Stress Inoculation

Training. He and his colleagues have also applied this general package to dealing with the reaction to pain. Although applied to pain, the general procedures are identical to those for treating anxiety. Phase one involves providing the person with a conceptualization of the relationship between anxiety and pain. By reducing one's anxiety and controlling the emotional component, pain can also be reduced. Central to this conceptualization is that the person can control his or her reaction and in turn control the pain.

Phase two involves training the person to use a variety of coping procedures such as those described previously. These coping strategies would include relaxation training, attention diversions, and coping self-statements. The individuals would be given the opportunity to practice these techniques and select those that seem best suited to them. Once the person has developed these skills, phase three can be implemented: actual practice in using these procedures in the pain situation. A detailed description of SIT applied pain tolerance and treatment of pain disorders has recently been published by Turk, Meichenbaum, and Genest (1982).

FUTURE DIRECTIONS

The foregoing material presented an overview of the current state of knowledge of fear and anxiety. It is apparent that a large proportion of this information has accumulated in only the past 10 to 15 years. This suggests that the study of fear and anxiety is an area of current interest and rapid advancement of knowledge. Although much has been learned, a great deal remains to be clarified. In this final section, I will outline some of the areas still in need of more definitive research. By pointing out directions that future research will take, I hope to orient the reader to what can be expected to appear in the literature in the coming years.

One of the ultimate goals of this research is to understand more fully the nature of fear and anxiety. This understanding is not simply meant to satisfy scientific curiosity but to enable practitioners to apply this information for the betterment of human lives. In the short run, the goal is to develop more effective treatments for anxiety disorders. In the long run, as we come to better understand the nature of fear and anxiety, the goal becomes one of prevention of anxiety disorders.

Epidemiology

Historically as well as currently, one of the first steps toward conquering health-related problems is a thorough understanding of their epidemiology: obtaining a clear delineation of the distribution of the problem within the general population. This requires knowledge of the incidence of the disorder (newly developing cases) and prevalence (total numbers affected in the population). More specifically, it is not simply the overall rates of incidence and prevalence that are of interest, but how these figures vary among different segments of the population. Differentiating those characteristics of people in whom the disorder is most prevalent from those in which it is less prevalent, can help determine risk factors associated with development of the disorder. Knowledge of risk factors can tell researchers where to concentrate their efforts to best understand the disorder.

Through the preceding chapters, some of the current epidemiological information concerning anxiety disorders was presented. It was noted that, for the most part, fears, phobias, and anxiety were more prevalent among younger persons and females. These two factors emerge as possible risk factors. Further, it was noted that certain anxiety disorders tend to run in families, particularly panic disorder. Currently there is little more definitive knowledge of risk factors beyond these variables.

Other areas requiring more investigations as possible risk areas include: more detailed work on familial and/or genetic relationship, early developmental experiences, and cultural and geographic differences. Some data on these issues are currently being collected on a nationwide scale, and should provide useful information in the near future (Robins et al., 1984). As these data accumulate, a sharper picture should emerge of who is at risk and what factors differentiate them from nonrisk persons. From this data, more definitive hypotheses can be formulated to focus the search for causal factors, and ultimately for preventive efforts.

Origins of Fear

Chapter 2 presented several theoretical explanations for the origins of fears and anxiety. There were theories involving biological predispositions, conditioning, vicarious learning, personality dynamics, and existential-phenomenological views. Taken separately, these theories would appear to have little in common with one another. Yet each boasts experimental data or clinical experience in support of its validity. And each has its staunch followers.

If one assumes that each theory has some validity for explaining some parts or kinds of anxiety states, attempts at an integration would seem fruitful. It may well be that some theories are better suited for explaining some aspects of fear or anxiety than others. Further research might well be directed at theory testing to determine which theory or theories best explain which specific phenomena. The result might also be some interactive integration of several points of view. For example, certain anxiety disorders might be best explained by a combination of physiological and psychological factors. Certain people, perhaps on an hereditary basis, may be predisposed to react with anxiety or shyness to new or novel situations. Such persons, being more highly aroused, might then be more susceptible to developing conditioned emotional responses when exposed to fear-provoking circumstances. Other elements, as yet less clear, might combine to explain other anxiety disorders such as obsessions and compulsions or generalized anxiety disorders.

To the extent that various risk and etiological factors are identified, it should become possible to formulate a predictive model. Such a model would incorporate the relative contributions of specific risk factors and their combinations and lead to predictions of who is vulnerable under what conditions to develop which disorder.

Assessment and Description

In order to construct a comprehensive model of anxiety and its disorders, another necessary condition is that each of the disorders be clearly and unambiguously described. First it must be demonstrated that all of the conditions subsumed under the heading anxiety disorders indeed have anxiety or fear as their core. Then each type of anxiety disorder must be differentially described so that characteristics that diagnostically define one disorder are not also found in others. Such diagnostic clarity requires careful and precise assessment of each element of the disorder so that important similarities and differences can be distinguished.

The classifications of disorders presented in Chapter 4 approach these requirements but several points remain to be clarified. How, for example, does a simple phobia of dirt and germs differ from obsessive-compulsive disorders involving obsessive concern with dirt and compulsive cleaning rituals? There are differences between such obsessive-compulsive disorders and dirt phobias, but there are many similarities as well.

Another example of the need for more descriptive clarity concerns how blood-injury phobias should be classified. It was noted in Chapter 4 that the response pattern of blood injury phobias was biphasic. That is, it involved an initial rise in SNS arousal followed by PNS activity which resulted in lowering of blood pressure to the point of fainting. This physiological response pattern is quite different from that seen in other phobias and as some researchers have shown, treatments such as desensitization which are highly effective for other simple phobias may not be effective for blood phobia. The question then can be raised whether this blood-injury reaction should be classified as a phobia at all. Further research must be conducted to describe more fully this reaction and demonstrate its relation to anxiety disorders in general and phobia in particular. Until a clear and consistent descriptive classification system is available, a comprehensive theory of anxiety and anxiety disorders can have little foundation.

Treatments

It was noted earlier that a short-term goal of research was development of effective treatments for the anxiety disorders. The procedures described in Chapter 5 and the beginning of Chapter 6 suggest that tremendous progress has been made in treating anxiety disorders in general and phobias in particular.

While this progress is clearly evident, it should be clear that for the most part the treatment procedures are not disorder specific. That is, the effective elements such as relaxation training and exposure are applied to several disorders. Further, because we do not have a thorough understanding of the origins of anxiety and fear disorders, nor the processes that maintain them, we do not know the underlying mechanisms by which the treatments work. In fact, it is somewhat surprising that we are able to treat anxiety as well as we can, given our level of understanding of the basic processes involved. If we better understood the basic mechanisms of fear and anxiety we should be better able to formulate even more effective treatments.

One new direction for making treatments more precisely suited to specific anxiety problems was recently reported by Öst and colleagues (Öst et al., 1982). These researchers attempted to match treatments which focus on specific characteristics of the anxiety response components to patients who primarily respond in a particular mode. After careful and comprehensive assessment of a group of claustrophobic patients, some were found to respond with large heart rate increases but minimal behavioral response when placed in a small closed chamber. These patients were called physiological responders. Another group was identified who showed little heart rate change but who responded behaviorally to being enclosed. Half of each group were treated with applied relaxation training and half with exposure to small confined places. The results showed clearly that relaxation training was the most effective treatment for the physiological responders, while exposure was superior for the behavioral responders.

In this study, patients' primary mode of response was found to be logically related to the focus of the treatment procedure. This matching of patient characteristics to specific treatments appears to hold promise in making treatments more effective and more efficient. Further refinement of assessment and delineation of patient response characteristics should result in significant advances in matching the best treatment to specific patient needs. Given the current rates of treatment success and the encouraging advances just described, there is room for considerable optimism. However, such advances, current and prospective, are of little avail if they do not reach the population who needs them. A recent national survey has indicated that less than 23 percent of persons with diagnosable anxiety disorders seek or receive treatment for them (Shapiro et al., 1984).

Although treatments for anxiety disorders are less than perfect, they are effective for large numbers of persons. Consequently, another area in which treatment research could fruitfully be directed is toward enabling those in need to obtain services available.

It is likely that a significant proportion of those not receiving treatment may have been agoraphobic. As we have seen, the very nature of the disorder may preclude the person's leaving home, even to seek treatment. One way to expand availability of services to those in need is through home-based treatments such as those by Jannoun and colleagues (1980) described in Chapter 5. The further refinement of these outreach treatment procedures, along with making them available to persons in need, could markedly enhance the lives of thousands of persons who are homebound.

With the rapidly accumulating knowledge in these areas I do not believe that it is idle speculation or wishful thinking to expect that within the foreseeable future the vast majority of anxiety disorders will be treatable. Further, I would hope this increased knowledge will contribute to subsequent development of preventive strategies.

REFERENCES

Agras, W. S., Chapin, H. N., & Oliveau, D. C. (1972). The natural history of phobia. *Archives of General Psychiatry, 26,* 315-317.

Agras, W. S., Sylvester, D., & Oliveau, D. (1969). The epidemiology of common fears and phobia. *Comprehensive Psychiatry, 10,* 151-156.

Akhtar, S., Wig, N. N., Varma, V. K., Pershad, D., & Verma, S. K. (1975). A phenomenological analysis of symptoms in obsessive-compulsive neurosis. *British Journal of Psychiatry, 127,* 342-348.

American Psychiatric Association. (1980). *Diagnostic and Statistical Manual of Mental Disorders (DSM-III),* (3rd ed.). Washington DC: American Psychiatric Association.

Anderson, D. J., Noyes, R., & Crowe, R. R. (1984). A comparison of panic disorder and generalized anxiety disorder. *American Journal of Psychiatry, 141,* 572-575.

Andreassi, J. L. (1980). *Psychophysiology: Human behavior and physiological response.* New York: Oxford University Press.

Angelino, H., Dollins, J., & Mech, E. (1956). Trends in the "fears and worries" of school children as related to socio-economic status and age. *Journal of Genetic Psychology, 89,* 263-276.

Arrindell, W. A. (1980). Dimensional structure and psychopathology correlates of the Fear Survey Schedule (FSS-III) in a phobic population: A factorial definition of agoraphobia. *Behaviour Research and Therapy, 18,* 229-242.

Auerbach, S. M. (1973). Trait-state anxiety and adjustment to surgery. *Journal of Consulting and Clinical Psychology, 40,* 264-271.

Baker, B. L., Cohen, D. C., & Saunders, J. T. (1973). Self-directed desensitization for acrophobia. *Behaviour Research and Therapy, 11,* 79-89.

Bandura, A. (1969). *Principles of behavior modification.* New York: Holt.

Bandura, A. (1977a). Toward a unifying theory of behavioral change. *Psychological Review, 84,* 191-215.

Bandura, A. (1977b). *Social learning theory.* Englewood Cliffs, NJ: Prentice-Hall.

Bandura, A., Blanchard, E. B., & Ritter, B. (1969). Relative efficacy of desensitization and modeling approaches for inducing behavioral, affective, and attitudinal changes. *Journal of Personality and Social Psychology, 13,* 173-199.

Bandura, A., Jeffery, R. W., & Wright, C. L. (1974). Efficacy of participant modeling as a function of response induction aids. *Journal of Abnormal Psychology, 83,* 56-64.

Bandura, A., & Menlove, F. (1968). Factors determining vicarious extinction of avoidance behavior through symbolic modeling. *Journal of Personality and Social Psychology, 8,* 99-108.

Barlow, D. H., Cohen, A. S., Waddell, M. T., Vermilyea, B. B., Klosko, J. S., Blanchard, E. B., & Di Nardo, P. A. (1984). Panic and generalized anxiety disorders: Nature and treatment. *Behavior Therapy, 15,* 431-449.

Beck, A. T. (1976). *Cognitive therapy and the emotional disorders.* New York: International Universities Press.

Beecher, H. K. (1959). *Measurement of subjective responses: Quantitative effects of drugs.* New York: Oxford University Press.

Berecz, John M. (1968). Phobias of childhood: Etiology and treatment. *Psychological Bulletin, 70,* 694-720.

Bergin, A. E., & Lambert, M. J. (1978). The evaluation of therapeutic outcomes. In S. L. Garfield & A. E. Bergin (Eds.), *Handbook of Psychotherapy and Behavior Change* (2nd ed.). New York: Wiley.

Bernstein, D. A., & Allen, G. J. (1969). Fear Survey (II): Normative data and factor analysis based on a large college sample. *Behaviour Research and Therapy, 7,* 403-408.

Bernstein, D. A., & Borkovec, T. (1974). *Progressive relaxation training: A manual for the helping professions.* Champaign, IL: Research Press.

Bernstein, D. A., Kleinknecht, R. A., & Alexander, L. D. (1979). Antecedents of dental fear. *Journal of Public Health Dentistry, 39,* 113-124.

Bernstein, D. A., & Nietzel, M. T. (1974). Behavioral avoidance tests: The effects of demand characteristics and repeated measures on two types of subjects. *Behavior Therapy, 5,* 183-192.

Biran, M., Augusto, F., & Wilson, G. T. (1981). In vivo exposure vs. cognitive restructuring in the treatment of scriptophobia. *Behaviour Research & Therapy, 19,* 525-532.

Blackwell, B. (1973). Psychotropic drugs in use today: The role of diazepam in medical procedure. *Journal of the American Medical Association, 225,* 1637-1641.

Blom, B. E., & Craighead, W. E. (1974). The effects of situational and instructional demand on indices of speech anxiety. *Journal of Abnormal Psychology, 83,* 667-674.

Borkovec, T. D. (1984). Relaxation induced anxiety: Mechanisms and theoretical implications. *Behaviour Research and Therapy, 22,* 1-12.

Borkovec, T. D., & Craighead, W. E. (1971). The comparison of two methods of assessing fear and avoidance behavior. *Behaviour Research and Therapy, 9,* 285-291.

Bowers, K. S. (1968). Pain, anxiety and perceived control. *Journal of Consulting and Clinical Psychology, 32,* 596-602.

Brandon, R. K., & Kleinknecht, R. A. (1982). Fear assessment in a dental analogue setting. *Journal of Behavioral Assessment, 4,* 317-325.

Braun, P. R., & Reynolds, D. J. (1969). A factor analysis of a 100-item survey inventory. *Behaviour Research and Therapy, 7,* 399-402.

Bregman, E. (1934). An attempt to modify the attitudes of infants by the conditioned response technique. *Journal of Genetic Psychology, 45,* 169-196.

Broadhurst, P. L. (1960). Application of biometrical genetics to the inheritance of behaviour. In H. J. Eysenck (Ed.), *Experiments in personality,* (Vol. 1). London: Reutledge.

Bromberg, W. (1959). *The mind of man: A history of psychotherapy and psychoanalysis.* New York: Harper and Row.

Cammer, L. (1976). *Freedom from compulsion.* New York: Simon & Schuster.

Cannon, W. B. (1929). *Bodily changes in pain, hunger, fear and rage,* (2nd ed.). New York: Appleton-Century-Crofts.

Castaneda, A., McCandless, B. R., & Palermo, D. S. (1956). The children's form of the manifest anxiety scale. *Child Development, 27,* 317-326.

Cattell, R. B., & Scheier, I. H. (1961). *The meaning and measurement of neuroticism and anxiety.* New York: Ronald Press.

Chambless, D. L., Gallagher, R., & Bright, P. (1981). The measurement of fear in agoraphobics: The agoraphobic cognitions questionnaire and the body sensations questionnaire. Paper presented to Association for Advancement of Behavior Therapy.

Chauinard, G., Annable, L., Fontaine, R., & Solyom, L. (1982). Alprazolam in the treatment of generalized anxiety and panic disorders: A double-blind placebo-controlled study. *Psychopharmacology, 77,* 229-233.

Clum, G. A., Luscomb, R. L., & Scott, L. (1982). Relaxation training and cognitive redirection strategies in the treatment of acute pain. *Pain, 12,* 175-183.

Cohn, C. K., Kron, R. E., & Brady, J. P. (1976). Single case study: A case of blood-illness-injury phobia treated behaviorally. *The Journal of Nervous and Mental Disease, 162*(1), 65-68.

Connolly, J., Hallam, R. S., & Marks, I. M. (1976). Selective association of fainting with blood-injury-illness fear. *Behavior Therapy, 7,* 8–13.

Cooke, G. (1966). The efficacy of two desensitization procedures: An analogue study. *Behaviour Research and Therapy, 4.* 17-24.

Costello, C. G. (1982). Fears and phobias in women: A community study. *Journal of Abnormal Psychology, 91,* 280-286.

Crowe, R. R., Noyes, R., Pauls, D. L., & Slymen, D. (1983). A family study of panic disorder. *Archives of General Psychiatry, 40,* 1065-1069.

Crowe, R. R., Pauls, D. L., Slymen, D. J., & Noyes, R. (1980). A family study of anxiety neurosis. *Archives of General Psychiatry, 37,* 77-79.

Di Nardo, P. A., O'Brien, G. T., Barlow, D. H., Waddell, M. T., & Blanchard, E. B. (1983). Reliability of DSM-III anxiety disorder categories using a new structured interview. *Archives of General Psychiatry, 40,* 1070-1074.

Doctor, R. M. (1979). A large scale survey of agoraphobics. Unpublished manuscript, California State University, Northridge.

Donner, L., & Guerney, B. G. (1969). Automated group desensitization for test anxiety. *Behaviour Research and Therapy, 7,* 1-13.

Dworkin, S., & Chen, A. C. N. (1982). Pain in clinical and laboratory contexts. *Journal of Dental Research, 61,* 772-774.

Edelberg, R. (1972). The electro-dermal system. In N. S. Greenfield & R. A. Sternbach (Eds.), *Handbook of psychophysiology,* New York: Holt.

Ellis, A. (1962). *Reason and emotion in psychotherapy.* New York: Lyle Stuart.

Elmore, Jr., R. T., Wildman, II, R. W., & Westefeld, J. S. (1980). The use of systematic desensitization in the treatment of blood phobia. *Journal of Behaviour Therapy and Experimental Psychiatry 11,* 277-279.

Emmelkamp, P. M. G. (1982). *Phobic and obsessive-compulsive disorders.* New York: Plenum Press.

Emmelkamp, P. M. G., & Wessels, H. (1975). Flooding in imagination vs. flooding *in vivo:* A comparison with agoraphobics. *Behaviour Research and Therapy, 13,* 7-16.

English, H. B. (1929). Three cases of the conditioned fear response. *Journal of Abnormal and Social Psychology, 34,* 221-225.

Errera, P. (1962). Some historical aspects of the concept, phobia. *Psychiatric Quarterly, 36,* 325-336.

Evans, P. D., & Harmon, G. (1981). Children's self-initiated approach to spiders. *Behaviour Research & Therapy, 19,* 543-546.

Eysenck, H. J. (1952). The effects of psychotherapy: An evaluation. *Journal of Consulting Psychology, 16,* 319-324.

Eysenck, H. J. & Eysenck, S. B. G. (1963). *Eysenck Personality Inventory.* San Diego: Educational and Industrial Testing Services.

Eysenck, H. J. & Eysenck, S. B. G. (1969). *Personality structure and measurement.* London: Routledge & Kegan Paul.

Fazio, A. F. (1972). Implosive therapy with semiclinical phobias. *Journal of Abnormal Psychology, 80,* 183-188.

Foa, E. B., & Chambless, D. L. (1978). Habituation of subjective anxiety during flooding in imagery. *Behaviour Research and Therapy, 16,* 391-399.

Fordyce, W. (1976). *Behavioral methods for chronic pain and illness.* St. Louis: C. V. Mosby.

Fordyce, W., & Steger, J. (1979). Chronic pain. In O. F. Pomerleau & J. P. Brady (Eds.), *Behavioral medicine: Theory and practice.* Baltimore: Williams and Wilkens, pp. 125-154.

Frankel, V. E. (1963). *Man's search for meaning.* New York: Washington Square Press.

Freud, S. (1936). *The problem of anxiety.* New York: Norton.

Gallup, G. G., Jr., & Maser, J. D. (1977). Tonic immobility: Evolutionary underpinnings of human catalepsy and catatonia. In J. D. Maser & M. E. P. Seligman (Eds.), *Psychopathology: Experimental models.* San Francisco: W. C. Freeman, p. 335-357.

Garfield, Z. H., Darwin. P. L., Singer, B. A., & McBreaty, J. F. (1967). Effect of "in vivo" training on experimental desensitization of a phobia. *Psychological Reports, 20,* 515-519.

Geer, J. H. (1965). The development of a scale to measure fear. *Behaviour Research and Therapy, 3,* 45-53.

Geer, J. H., Davison, G. C., & Gatchel, R. I. (1970). Reduction of stress in humans through nonveridical perceived control of aversive stimulation. *Journal of Personality and Social Psychology, 16,* 731-738.

Girodo, M. (1974). Yoga meditation and flooding in treatment of anxiety neurosis. *Journal of Behavior Therapy and Experimental Psychiatry, 5,* 157-160.

Glasgow, R. E., & Rosen, G. M. (1978). Behavioral bibliotherapy: A review of self-help behavior therapy manuals. *Psychological Bulletin, 85,* 1-23.

Goldfried, M. R. (1971). Systematic desensitization as training in self-control. *Journal of Consulting and Clinical Psychology, 37,* 228-234.

Goldfried, M. R., & Davison, G. C. (1976). *Clinical Behavior Therapy,* New York: Holt.

Goldstein, A. J., & Chambless, D. L. (1978). A reanalysis of agoraphobia. *Behavior Therapy, 9,* 47-59.

Goodwin, D. W. (1983). *Phobia: The facts.* New York: Oxford University Press.

Gottesman, I. (1962). Genetic variance in adaptive personality traits. *Journal of Child Psychology and Psychiatry. 9,* 223-227.

Graziano, A. M., DeGiovanni, I. S., & Garcia, K. A. (1979). Behavioral treatment of children's fears: A review. *Psychological Bulletin,* 1-72.

Greenblatt, D. J., & Shader, R. I. (1972). *Benzodiazepines in clinical practice.* New York: Raven.

Gross, R. T., & Collins, F. L. (1981). On the relationship between anxiety and pain: A methodological confounding. *Clinical Psychology Review, 1,* 375-385.

Hackett, G., & Horan, J. J. (1980). Stress inoculation for pain: What's really going on? *Journal of Counseling Psychology, 27,* 107-116.

Hafner, J., & Marks, I. M. (1976). Exposure *in vivo* of agoraphobics: Contributions of diazepam, group exposure and anxiety evocation. *Psychological Medicine, 6,* 71-88.

Hallam, R. S., & Hafner, R. G. (1978). Fears of phobic patients: Factor analysis of self-report data. *Behaviour Research and Therapy, 16,* 1-6.

Hassett, J. (1978). *A primer of psychophysiology.* San Francisco: W. H. Freeman & Co.

Hathaway, S. R. (1948). Some considerations relative to non-directive counseling. *Journal of Clinical Psychology, 4,* 226-231.

Hebb, D. O. (1946). On the nature of fear. *Psychological Review, 53,* 259-276.

Hersen, M. (1973). Self-assessment of fear. *Behavior Therapy, 4,* 241-257.

Hogan, R. A., & Kirchner, J. H. (1967). A preliminary report of the extinction of learned fears via short term implosive therapy. *Journal of Abnormal Psychology, 72,* 106-111.

Holden, Jr., A. E., O'Brien, G. T., Barlow, D. H., Stetson, D., & Infantino, A. (1983). Self-help manual for agoraphobia: A preliminary report of effectiveness. *Behavior Therapy, 14,* 545-556.

Hugdahl, K. (1978). Electrodermal conditioning to potentially phobic stimuli: Effects of instructed extinction. *Behaviour Research and Therapy, 16,* 315-321.

Hugdahl, K., & Karker, A-C. (1981). Biological vs. experiential factors in phobic conditioning. *Behaviour Research and Therapy, 19,* 109-115.

Husek, T. R., & Alexander, S. (1963). The effectiveness of the anxiety differential in examination stress situations. *Educational and Psychological Measurement, 23,* 309-318.

Ihli, K. L., & Garlington, W. K. (1969). A comparison of group versus individual desensitization of test anxiety. *Behaviour Research and Therapy, 7,* 207-210.

International Association for the Study of Pain: Subcommittee on Taxonomy (1979). Pain terms: A list with definitions and notes on usage. *Pain, 6,* 249-252.

Jacobson, E. (1938). *Progressive relaxation.* Chicago: University of Chicago Press.

Janda, L. H., & O'Grady, K. E. (1980). Development of a sex anxiety inventory. *Journal of Consulting and Clinical Psychology, 48,* 169-175.

Jannoun, L., Munby, M., Catalan, J., & Gelder, M. (1980). A home-based treatment program for agoraphobia: Replication and controlled evaluation. *Behavior Therapy, 11,* 294-305.

Jersild, A. T., & Holmes, F. B. (1935). Children's fears. *Child Development Monographs,* No. 20, New York: Columbia University Press.

Johnson, J. E., & Dabbs, J. M., Jr. (1967). Enumeration of active sweat glands: A simple physiological indicator of psychological changes. *Nursing Research, 16,* 273-276.

Jones, E. (1961). *The life and works of Sigmund Freud.* Garden City, NY: Doubleday.

Jones, H. E., & Jones, M. C. (1928). Fear. *Childhood Education, 5,* 136-143.

Kagan, J. (1984). Inhibition and lack of inhibition in the young child. Paper presented to the 92nd Annual Convention of the American Psychological Association, Toronto, August.

Katkin, E. S., & Hoffman, L. S. (1976). Sex differences and self-report of fear: A psychophysiological assessment. *Journal of Abnormal Psychology, 85,* 607-610.

Kazdin, A. E. (1973). Covert modeling and the reduction of avoidance behavior. *Journal of Abnormal Psychology, 81,* 87-95.

Kazdin, A. E. (1974). The affect of model identity and fear-relevant similarity on covert modeling. *Behavior Therapy, 5,* 624-635.

Kelly, D. (1980). *Anxiety and emotions: Physiological basis and treatment.* Springfield, IL: Thomas.

Kimble, G. (1961). *Hilgard and Marquis' Conditioning and Learning.* (2nd ed.). New York: Appleton-Century-Crofts.

Kirkpatrick, D. R. (1984). Age, gender and patterns of common intense fears among adults. *Behaviour Research and Therapy, 22,* 141-150.

Klein, D. F., & Fink, M. (1962). Psychiatric reaction patterns to imipramine. *American Journal of Psychiatry, 119,* 432-438.

Klein, D. F., Gittelman, R., Quitkin, F., & Rifkin, A. (1980). *Diagnosis and drug treatment of psychiatric disorders: Adults and children* (2nd ed.). Baltimore: Williams & Wilkins.

Kleinknecht, R. A. (1982). The origin and remissions of fear in a group of tarantula enthusiasts. *Behaviour Research and Therapy. 20,* 437-443.

Kleinknecht, R. A., & Bernstein, D. A. (1978). Assessment of dental fear. *Behavior Therapy, 9*, 626-634.

Kleinknecht, R. A., & Bernstein, D. A. (1979). Short term treatment of dental avoidance. *Journal of Behavior Therapy and Experimental Psychiatry, 10*, 311-315.

Kleinknecht, R. A., & Boucher, J. (1981). Unpublished manuscript.

Kleinknecht, R. A., & Donaldson, D. (1975). A review of the effects of diazepam on cognitive and psychomotor performance. *Journal of Nervous and Mental Disease, 161*, 399-411.

Kleinknecht, R. A., Klepac, R. K., & Alexander, L. D. (1973). Origins and characteristics of fear of dentistry. *Journal of American Dental Association, 86*, 842-848.

Klepac, R. K., Dowling, J., & Hauge, C. (1982). Characteristics of clients seeking therapy for the reduction of dental avoidance: Reaction to pain. *Journal of Behavior Therapy and Experimental Psychiatry, 13*, 293-300.

Klepac, R. K., Hauge, G., Dowling, J., & McDonald, M. (1981). Direct and generalized effects of three components of stress inoculation for increased pain tolerance. *Behavior Therapy, 12*, 417-424.

Klepac, R. K., McDonald, M., Hauge, G., & Dowling, J. (1980). Reactions to pain among subjects high and low in dental fear. *Journal of Behavioral Medicine, 3*, 373-384.

Klorman, R., Weerts, T. C., Hastings, J. E., Melamed, B. G., & Lang, P. J., (1974). Psychometric description of some specific-fear questionnaires. *Behavior Therapy, 5*, 401-409.

Kopacz, F. M., II, & Smith, B. D. (1971). Sex differences in skin conductance measures as a function of shock threat. *Psychophysiology, 8*, 293-303.

Lacey, J. I., & Lacey, B. C. (1958). Verification and extension of the principle of autonomic response stereotyping. *American Journal of Psychology, 71*, 50-73.

Lacey, J. I., & Lacey, B. C. (1967). The Law of Initial Value in the longitudinal study of autonomic constitution. *Annals of the New York Academy of Sciences, 38*, 1257-1290.

Lader, M. H., & Wing, L. (1966). Physiological measures of sedative drugs and morbid anxiety. *Maudsley Monographs No. 14*. London: Oxford University Press.

Lang, P. J. (1968). Fear reduction and fear behavior: Problems in treating a construct. In J. M. Schlien (Ed.), *Research in psychotherapy* (Vol. 3). Washington, DC: American Psychological Association, pp. 90-102.

Lang, P. J., & Lazovik, A. D. (1963). The experimental desensitization of a phobia. *Journal of Abnormal and Social Psychology, 66,* 519-525.

Lang, P. J., Melamed, B. G., & Hart, I. (1970). A psychophysiological analysis of fear modification using an automated desensitization procedure. *Journal of Abnormal Psychology, 76,* 220-234.

Lapouse, R., & Monk, M. A. (1959). Fears and worries in a representative sample of children. *American Journal of Orthopsychiatry, 29,* 803-818.

Lazarus, A. A. (1961). Group therapy of phobic disorders by systematic desensitization. *Journal of Abnormal and Social Psychology, 63,* 504-510.

Lazarus, A. A. (1971). *Behavior Therapy and Beyond.* New York: McGraw-Hill.

Lazarus, R. S. (1966). *Psychological Stress and the Coping Process.* New York: McGraw-Hill.

Levitt, E. (1980). *The Psychology of Anxiety* (2nd ed.). Hillsdale, NJ: Lawrence Erlbaum Associates.

Lewis, M., & Brooks, J. (1974). Self, other and fear: Infants reactions to people. In M. Lewis and L. Rosenblum (Eds.), *The origins of fear.* New York: John Wiley & Sons, Inc.

Lick, J. R., & Katkin, E. S. (1976). Assessment of anxiety and fear. In M. Herson and A. Bellak (Eds.)., *Behavioral assessment: A practical handbook.* New York: Pergamon Press.

Licky, M. E., & Gordon, B. (1983). *Drugs for mental illness: A revolution in psychiatry.* New York: W. H. Freeman.

Liddell, A., Lyons, M. (1978). Thunderstorm phobias. *Behaviour Research and Therapy, 16,* 306-308.

MacFarlane, J. W., Allen, L., & Honzik, M. (1954). *A developmental study of the behavior problems of normal children between twenty-one months and fourteen years.* Berkeley, CA: University of California Press.

Marks, I. M. (1969). *Fears and phobias.* New York: Academic Press.

Marks, I. M. (1978). *Living with fear.* New York: McGraw-Hill.

Marks, I. M., & Gelder, M. G. (1966). Different onset ages in varieties of phobia. *American Journal of Psychiatry, 123,* 218-221.

Marks, I. M., Gray S., Cohen, D., Hill, R., Mawson, D., Ramm, E., & Stern, R. S. (1983). Impiramine and brief therapist-aided exposure in agoraphobics having self-exposure homework. *Archives of General Psychiatry, 40,* 153-162.

Marks, I. M., & Lader, M. (1973). Anxiety states (Anxiety Neurosis): A review. *The Journal of Nervous and Mental Disease, 156,* 3-18.

Matarazzo, J. D., & Wiens, A. N. (1972). *The Interview: Research on its anatomy and structure.* Chicago: Aldine.

Mathews, A., Teasdale, J., Munby, M., Johnston, D., & Shaw, P. (1977). A home based treatment program for agoraphobia. *Behavior Therapy, 8,* 915-924.

Maurer, A. (1965). What children fear. *The Journal of Genetic Psychology, 106,* 265-277.

May, R. (1969). *Love and will.* New York: Norton.

May, R. (1981). Value conflicts and anxiety. In I. L. Kutash & L. R. Schlesinger (Eds.), *Handbook on stress and anxiety.* San Francisco: Jossey-Bass.

McCandless, B. R., & Trotter, R. (1977). *Children: Behavior and development* (3rd ed.). New York: Holt, Rinehart and Winston.

Meichenbaum, D. H. (1971). Examination of model characteristics in reducing avoidance behavior. *Journal of Personality and Social Psychology, 17,* 298-307.

Meichenbaum, D. H. (1977). *Cognitive-behavior modification: An integrative approach.* New York: Plenum.

Melamed, B. G., Weinstein, D., Hawes, R., & Katin-Borland, M. (1975). Reduction of fear-related dental management problems with use of filmed modeling. *Journal of the American Dental Association, 90,* 822-826.

Melzack, R. (1975). The McGill pain questionnaire: Major properties and scoring methods. *Pain, 1,* 277-299.

Melzack, R., & Wall, P. (1982). *The challenge of pain.* New York: Basic Books.

Migler, B., & Wolpe, J. (1967). Automated desensitization: A case report. *Behaviour Research and Therapy, 5,* 133.

Miller, B., & Bernstein, D. (1972). Instructional demand in a behavioral avoidance test for claustrophobic fear. *Journal of Abnormal Psychology, 80,* 206-210.

Miller, H. R., & Nawas, M. M. (1970). Control of aversive stimulus termination in systematic desensitization. *Behaviour Research and Therapy, 8,* 57-61.

Miller, L. C., Barrett, C. L., Hampe, E., & Noble, H. (1972). Factor structure of childhood fears. *Journal of Consulting and Clinical Psychology, 39,* 266-268.

Miller, S. M. (1979). Controllability and human stress: Method, evidence and theory. *Behaviour Research and Therapy, 17,* 287-304.

Morris, R. J., & Kratochwill, T. R. (1983). *Treating children's fears and phobias: A behavioral approach.* New York: Pergamon Press.

Murphree, O. D., Dykman, R. A., & Peters, J. E. (1967). Genetically-determined abnormal behavior in dogs: Results of behavioral tests. *Conditional Reflex, 2,* 199-205.

Murray, E. J., & Foote, F. (1979). The origins of fear of snakes. *Behaviour Research and Therapy, 17,* 489-493.

Nesse, R. M., Curtis, G. C., Thyer, B. A., McCann, D. S., Huber-Smith, M. J., & Knopf, R. F. (March, 1984). Endocrine and cardiovascular responses during phobic anxiety. Paper presented to the American Psychosomatic Society.

Noyes, R., Jr., Anderson, D. J., Clancy, J., Crowe, R. R., Slyman, D. J., Ghonein, M. M., & Hinrichs, J. V. (1984). Diazepam and propranolol in panic disorder and agoraphobia. *Archives of General Psychiatry, 41,* 287-292.

Nunnally, J. C. (1970). *Introduction to psychological measurement.* New York: McGraw-Hill.

Ohman, A., Erixon, G., & Lofberg, I. (1975). Phobias and preparedness: Phobic versus neutral pictures as conditioned stimuli for human autonomic responses. *Journal of Abnormal Psychology, 84,* 41-45.

O'Leary, K. D., & Wilson, G. T. (1975). *Behavior Therapy: Application and outcome.* Englewood Cliffs, NJ: Prentice-Hall.

Orne, M. (1962). On the social psychology of the psychological experiment: With particular reference to demand characteristics and their implications. *American Psychologist, 17,* 776-783.

Osgood, C. E., Suci, G. J., & Tannenbaum, P. H. (1957). *Measurement of meaning,* Urbana: University of Illinois Press.

Öst, L.-G. (1978). Behavioral treatment of thunder and lightning phobias. *Behaviour Research and Therapy, 16,* 197-207.

Öst, L.-G., & Hugdahl, K. (1981). Acquisition of phobias and anxiety response patterns in clinical patients. *Behaviour Research and Therapy, 19,* 439-447.

Öst, L.-G., Johansson, J., & Jerremalm, A. (1982). Individual response patterns and the effects of different behavioral methods in the treatment of claustrophobia. *Behaviour Research and Therapy, 20,* 445-460.

Öst, L.-G., Sterner, U., Lindahl, L. I., (1984). Physiological responses in blood phobics. *Behaviour Research and Therapy, 22,* 109-117.

Paul, G. (1966). *Insight vs. desensitization in psychotherapy: An experiment in anxiety reduction.* Stanford: Stanford University Press.

Paul, G., & Shannon, D. T. (1966). Treatment of anxiety through systematic desensitization in therapy groups. *Journal of Abnormal Psychology, 71,* 124-135.

Price, R. H. (1978). *Abnormal behavior: Perspectives in conflict* (2nd ed.). New York: Holt, Rinehart & Winston.

Prochaska, J. O. (1971). Symptom and dynamic cues in implosive treatment of test anxiety. *Journal of Abnormal Psychology, 77,* 133-142.

Prokasy, W. F. (Ed.). (1965). *Classical conditioning.* New York: Appleton-Century-Crofts.

Rachman, S. J. (1966). Studies in desensitization II: Flooding. *Behaviour Research and Therapy, 4,* 1-6.

Rachman, S. J. (1977). The conditioning theory of fear acquisition: A critical examination. *Behaviour Research and Therapy, 15,* 375-388.

Rachman, S. J. (1978). *Fear and courage.* San Francisco: W. C. Freeman.

Rachman, S. J., & Hodgson, R. J. (1980) *Obsessions and compulsions.* Englewood Cliffs, NJ: Prentice-Hall.

Rachman, S. J., & Wilson, G. T. (1980). *The effects of psychological therapy* (2nd ed.). Oxford: Pergamon Press.

Richardson, F. C., & Suinn, R. M. (1973). A comparison of traditional systematic desensitization, accelerated massed desensitization, and anxiety management training in the treatment of mathematics anxiety. *Behavior Therapy, 4,* 212-218.

Richardson, F. C., & Tasto, D. L. (1976). Development and factor analysis of a social anxiety inventory. *Behavior Therapy, 7,* 453-462.

Richardson, S., & Kleinknecht, R. A. (1984). Expectancy effects on anxiety and self-generated cognitive strategies in high and low dental-anxious females. *Journal of Behavior Therapy and Experimental Psychiatry, 15,* 241-247.

Rickels, K., Downing, R. W., & Winoker, A. (1978). Antianxiety drugs: Clinical use in psychiatry. In L. L. Iverson, S. D. Iverson, & S. H. Snyder (Eds.), *Handbook of psychopharmacology: Vol. 13, Biology of mood and antianxiety drugs.* New York: Plenum, pp. 395-430.

Rimm, D. C., Janda, L. H., Lancaster, D. W., Nahl, M., & Dittmar, K.

(1977). An exploratory investigation of the origin and maintenance of phobias. *Behaviour Research and Therapy, 15,* 231-238.

Rimm, D. C., & Masters, J. C. (1979). *Behavior Therapy: Techniques and empirical findings.* New York: Academic Press.

Robertson, J., Wendiggensen, P., & Kaplan, I. (1983). Towards a comprehensive treatment for obsessional thoughts. *Behaviour Research and Therapy, 21,* 347-356.

Robins, L. N., Helzer, J. E., Weissman, M. M., Orvaschel, H., Gruenberg, E., Burke, J. D., & Regier, D. A. (1984). Lifetime prevalence of specific psychiatric disorders in three sites. *Archives of General Psychiatry, 41,* 949-958.

Rosenhan, D. L., & Seligman, M. E. P. (1984). *Abnormal psychology.* New York, W. W. Norton.

Sackett, G. P., (1966). Monkeys reared in isolation with pictures as visual input: Evidence for an innate releasing mechanism. *Science, 154,* 1468-1473.

Sarason, I. G. (1957). Test anxiety, general anxiety and intellectual performance. *Journal of Consulting Psychology, 21,* 485-490.

Scarr, S. (1965). The inheritance of sociability. Paper presented to the American Psychological Association Meetings, Chicago, September.

Scarr, S., & Salapatek, P. (1970). Patterns of fear development in infancy. *Merrill Palmar Quarterly, 16,* 53-90.

Schneirla, T. C. (1965). Aspects of stimulation and organization in approach/withdrawal processes underlying vertebrate behavioral development. In D. S. Lehrman, R. A. Hinde, & E. Shaw (Eds.). *Advances in the study of behavior,* (Vol. 1). New York: Academic Press.

Schubot, E. D. (1966). The influence of hypnotic and muscular relaxation in systematic desensitization of phobic behavior. Unpublished doctoral dissertation. Stanford University.

Seligman, M. E. P. (1972). Phobias and preparedness. In M. E. P. Seligman & J. L. Hager (Eds.), *Biological boundaries of learning.* New York: Appleton-Century-Crofts, pp. 451-462.

Seligman, M. E. P. (1975). *Helplessness: On depression, development, and death.* San Francisco: W. C. Freeman.

Seligman, M. E. P., & Hager, J. L. (1972). *Biological boundaries of learning.* New York: Appleton-Century-Crofts.

Shader, R. I., Goodman, M., & Gever, J. (1982). Panic disorders: Current perspectives. *Journal of Clinical Psychopharmacology, 2,* (Supplement) 2S-26S.

Shapiro, S., Skinner, E. A., Kessler, L. G., von Korff, M., Gesman, P. S., Tischler, G. L., Leaf, P. J., Benham, L., Cattler, L., & Regier, D. A. (1984). Utilization of health and mental health services: Three epidemiologic catchment area sites. *Archives of General Psychiatry, 41*, 971-978.

Sheehan, D. V., Ballenger, J., & Jacobsen, G. (1980). Treatment of endogenous anxiety with phobic, hysterical and hypochondriacal symptoms. *Archives of General Psychiatry, 37*, 51-59.

Shields, J. (1962). *Monozygotic twins brought up apart and brought up together.* London: Oxford University Press.

Speltz, M. L., & Bernstein, D. A. (1976). Sex differences in fearfulness: Verbal report, overt avoidance and demand characteristics. *Journal of Behavior Therapy and Experimental Psychiatry, 7*, 117-122.

Spielberger, C. D., Edwards, C. D., Lushene, R. E., Montuori, J., & Platzek, D. (1973). *State-trait anxiety inventory for children.* Palo Alto: Consulting Psychologists Press.

Spielberger, C. D., Gorsuch, R., & Lushene, R. (1970). *The State-Trait Anxiety Inventory (STAI).* Riverside, CA: Consulting Psychologists Press.

Stampfl, T. G., & Levis, D. J. (1967). Essentials of implosive therapy: A learning-theory-based psychodynamic behavioral therapy. *Journal of Abnormal Psychology, 72*, 496-503.

Stern, R. (1983). Antidepressant drugs in the treatment of obsessive-compulsive disorders. *Journal of Behavior Therapy and Experimental Psychiatry, 14*, 19-23.

Stern, R., & Marks, I. M. (1973). Brief and prolonged flooding: A comparison in agoraphobic patients. *Archives of General Psychiatry, 28*, 270-276.

Sternbach, R. (1965). *Principles of psychophysiology.* New York: Academic Press.

Sternbach, R. (1968). *Pain: A psychophysiological analysis.* New York: Academic Press.

Sue, D. (1975). The effect of duration of exposure on systematic desensitization and extinction. *Behaviour Research and Therapy, 13*, 55-60.

Sundberg, N. D., Taplin, J. R., & Tyler, L. E. (1983). *Introduction to clinical psychology.* Englewood Cliffs, NJ: Prentice-Hall.

Taylor, J. A. (1951). The relationship of anxiety to the conditioned eyelid response. *Journal of Experimental Psychology, 41*, 81-92.

Taylor, J. A. (1953). A personality scale of manifest anxiety. *The Journal of Abnormal and Social Psychology, 48*, 285-290.

Templer, D. I. (1970). The construction and validation of a death anxiety scale. *The Journal of General Psychology, 82,* 165-177.

Thomas, A., Chess, S., & Birch, H. (1970). The origin of personality. *Scientific American, 223,* 102-109.

Thompson, S. C. (1981). Will it hurt less if I can control it? A complex answer to a simple question. *Psychological Bulletin, 90,* 89-101.

Tryer, P. (1976). *The role of bodily feelings in anxiety.* London: Oxford University Press.

Turk, D. C., Meichenbaum, D., & Genest, M. (1982). *Pain and behavioral medicine: A cognitive-behavioral perspective.* New York: The Guilford Press.

Uhlenhuth, E. H., Balter, M. B., Mellinger, G. D., Cisin, I. H., & Clinthorne, J. (1983). Symptom checklist syndromes in the general population: Correlations with psychotherapeutic drug use. *Archives of General Psychiatry, 40,* 1167-1173.

Valentine, C. W. (1930). The innate basis of fear. *Journal of Genetic Psychology, 37,* 394-419.

Venables, P. H., & Martin, I. (1967). The relation of palmar sweat gland activity to level of skin potential and conductance. *Psychophysiology, 3,* 302-311.

Vingerhoets, A. J. J. M. (1984). Biochemical changes in two subjects succumbing to syncope. *Psychosomatic Medicine, 46,* 95-103.

Walk, R. D. (1956). Self-ratings of fear in a fear invoking situation. *Journal of Abnormal and Social Psychology, 52,* 171-178.

Watson, J. B., & Raynor, R. (1920). Conditioned emotional reactions. *Journal of Experimental Psychology, 3,* 1-14.

Weiner, C. (1982). *Psychopathology from infancy through adolescence.* New York: Random House.

Welner, A., Reich, T., Robins, E., Fishman, R., & Van Doren, T. (1976). Obsessive-compulsive neurosis: Record, follow-up and family studies. I. Inpatient record study. *Comprehensive Psychiatry, 17,* 527-539.

Williams, L. S., & Rappoport, A. (1983). Cognitive treatment in the natural environment for agoraphobics. *Behavior Therapy, 14,* 299-313.

Wolpe, J. (1958). *Psychotherapy by reciprocal inhibition.* Stanford, CA: Stanford University Press.

Wolpe, J. (1973). *The practice of behavior therapy.* Oxford: Pergamon.

Wolpe, J. (1981). The dichotomy between classical conditioned and cognitively learned anxiety. *Journal of Behavior Therapy and Experimental Psychiatry, 12,* 35-42.

Wolpe, J. (1982). *The practice of behavior therapy* (3rd ed.). New York: Pergamon.

Wolpe, J., & Lang, P. J. (1965). A fear survey schedule for use in behavior therapy. *Behaviour Research and Therapy, 2,* 27-30.

Wolpe, J., & Lazarus, A. (1966). *Behavior therapy techniques: A guide to treatment of the neuroses.* Oxford: Pergamon Press.

Wooley, C. F. (1976). Where are the diseases of yesteryear? DaCosta's syndrome, soldier's heart, the effort syndrome, neurocirculatory asthesia and mitral valve prolapse syndrome. *Circulation, 53,* 749-751.

Young, J. P. R., Fenton, G. W., & Lader, M. H. (1971). The inheritance of neurotic traits: A twin study of the Middlesex Hospital Questionnaire. *British Journal of Psychiatry, 119,* 393-398.

Yule, W., & Fernando, P. (1980). Blood phobia—beware. *Behaviour Research and Therapy, 18,* 587-590.

Zimbardo, P. G. (1977). *Shyness: What it is and what to do about it.* Reading, MA: Addison-Wesley Publishing Co.

Zitrin, C. M. (1983). Differential treatment of phobias: Use of imipramine for panic attacks. *Journal of Behavior Therapy and Experimental Psychiatry, 14,* 11-18.

INDEX

DATE DUE